REVIEWERS' COMMENTS ON THIS BOOK

"Exploring Jupiter *excels in practical usefulness, writing style, and motivational thrust. Arroyo brings out the meaning and hidden facts of all aspects of Jupiter. . . , ultimately arriving at what must be regarded as the finest sourcebook on Jupiter anywhere.*

"*Arroyo's profound understanding of astrological principles and his gift for clear, well-organized, and thoughtful writing make* Exploring Jupiter *a literary jewel. Arroyo is among a handful of modern writers on the leading edge of psychological astrology. . . . And, like Jupiter, Arroyo is creating a sense of direction for astrology through his inspirational descriptions and metaphysical insights.*"
—Chris Lorenz, Horoscope *Magazine*

"*. . . a book that is timely indeed, and this one doesn't disappoint. It's intelligent, psychologically sound, and should be a welcome addition to any astrologer's library. . . . this book offers a broad overview of the existing literature on Jupiter, along with some deep psychological insights.*

"*An additional plus for this book is the layout. Not only is* Exploring Jupiter *well-written, it's inviting to use. . . . It will probably become another classic and is an excellent reference . . . .*"
—Donna Van Toen, The Mountain Astrologer *Magazine*

STEPHEN ARROYO is the author of numerous best-selling books on astrology, all of which have presented a type of astrology that is modern, innovative, and directed toward self-understanding. He is internationally renowned as a pioneer of in-depth astrology, which his writings express with remarkable clarity. His work is extremely popular around the world, with translations now appearing in ten languages. He has also been awarded the Astrology Prize by the British Astrological Association, the Regulus Award by the United Astrology Conference, and the International Sun Award by the Fraternity of Canadian Astrologers. Mr. Arroyo holds a M.A. degree in psychology and for many years maintained a busy counseling practice. In addition, he taught some of the first credit classes in astrology in American colleges.

BARBARA McENERNEY holds a B.A. from the University of California (Davis) and has been an editor and consultant for CRCS Publications for the past twenty years. She has been involved with the field of astrology since 1972, and she has edited books by Stephen Arroyo, Tracy Marks, Donna Cunningham, Joanne Wickenburg, and others. In addition to researching a wide range of material for this book, she also made many creative suggestions and did much of the biographical research on well-known people, as well as writing numerous mini-biographies that are included in this book.

EXPLORING JUPITER

The Astrological Key to Progress, Prosperity & Potential

STEPHEN ARROYO

Edited by Barbara McEnerney

CRCS Publications
Post Office Box 1460
Sebastopol, California 95473

Library of Congress Cataloging-in-Publication Data
Arroyo, Stephen.
    Exploring Jupiter: the astrological key to progress, prosperity
& potential/Stephen Arroyo.
        p. cm.
    Includes bibliographical references.
    ISBN 0-916360-58-x (pbk.)
    1. Astrology. 2. Jupiter (Planet)—Miscellanea. I. Title.
    BF1724.J87A77 1995
    133.5'3—dc20   95-40869
                                                    CIP

INTERNATIONAL STANDARD BOOK NUMBER: 0-916360-58-X

Published simultaneously in the United States and Canada by
CRCS Publications
Distributed in the United States and internationally by
CRCS Publications
(Write for current list of worldwide distributors.)

Acknowledgments

I am indebted to many people for helping this book to be born and for providing encouragement, suggestions, and inspiration that kept me going when my own Jupiter seemed to have deserted me. Special thanks go to Kathe McDonald for inputting my inscrutable manuscript; long-time colleague Jerilyn Marshall for proofreading most of the final work with her usual grace and patience; and Paul Wright, who generously allowed me to quote from his unpublished manuscript on Jupiter and whose superb books provided me with numerous quotations, insights, and examples.

Special mention must also go to that power we call Jupiter; to the spiritual masters who have given me some distant glimpse of what nobility and generosity really mean; and to Cathy Corzine Williams, who not only sparked the idea for this book while I was having strong Jupiter transits but who also did the calligraphy and all the charts for this volume.

I would also like to thank various Jupiterians I know who invariably keep life interesting, hopeful, upbeat, and—thankfully—quite often fun: Including Sagittarius rising artist Tony White, who did the cartoons for this book; Pisces Sun cover artist Rebecca Wilson; and Pisces Sun/Sagittarius Moon colleague and friend Jim Feil, who helped facilitate two expansive trips to Spain (a Sagittarius country) during the period of writing this book. Thanks also to Basilio Tucci and Dolores Sabido for making the Spain speaking tour possible, as well as to other organizers and translators in various Spanish cities. Appreciation also to Laura Takahashi for her hospitality in Barcelona.

I also must mention Gail Ford, for helpful feedback on some of the biographies, and Aina Kemanis, Don Ryan, Lisa Fitzpatrick, and Susan Erkel Ryan for their contributions toward the final production of this book.

And lastly, but crucially, I am once again humbled by the dedication and Virgoan thoroughness of my editor, Barbara McEnerney, whose work on this book has included far more extensive research than in any other book we have worked on over the past two decades. This book would be much poorer in content and clarity if she had not used her Jupiter on the Ascendant to augment and improve so much of what I wrote.

—S.A.

Other Books by the Author

Contents

Charts, Biographies & Illustrations

Prologue

This book had its rather sudden origin when a friend reminded me that Pluto would soon be going into Sagittarius, and therefore a much more powerful surge of Sagittarian (and Jupiter's) energies would soon be apparent worldwide and within each individual. I could not at first pinpoint why I responded to this idea so positively, especially since a new writing project would necessarily interrupt a book I was already working on. And yet, whenever I mentioned this idea to a person who was familiar with astrology, I found myself getting more enthused about the prospect of doing a book on Jupiter. I was especially motivated since this largest of all the planets, and one which has traditionally been known as the "greater benefic," nevertheless gets rather brief and often simplistic treatment in the astrological literature.

After dwelling on the project for a few days, I finally realized that my own astrological cycles were reflecting a strong and increasing Jupiterian tone. Not surprisingly, some, if not all, of my previous books bore strong features of the essential energies and cycles I had been going through when they were created. So, although I tried in some ways to dismiss the idea as impractical or just a diversion from my other carefully formulated plans, I found myself daily making notes for such a book. Evidently, I was Jupiterian enough myself not to see what was right in front of me. When I finally checked all my planetary cycles, I was reminded that not only was I having a Jupiter return, an every-twelve-years renewal of one's innate Jupiter energies and urges, but also transiting Jupiter was going to conjoin my chart's ruling planet three times during the year when I would be writing such a book.

Then, when I looked into my progressions, I noticed that my progressed Sun and Moon were both about to enter Sagittarius and that, in fact, there would be a progressed New Moon in the first degree of Sagittarius right in the middle of the time allotted to this project. As students of Dane Rudhyar's work, especially his *Lunation Cycle*, will recall, the progressed New Moon was regarded by Rudhyar as one of the most important cyclic occurrences in one's life, one which happens only about every 29½ years, and which marks the beginning of an entirely new cycle of growth and personal unfolding. Therefore, resigned to my evidently-more-Jupiterian fate, I had to concede that it would not be wise to cross thunderbolts with Jupiter, and so this project got underway.

Then, in gathering up the references and notes I would need for the book, I stumbled upon still more evidence that I hadn't been seeing clearly that was right in front of me. It turned out that, in the last book I had published (*Stephen Arroyo's Chart Interpretation Handbook*), I had written an extensive footnote about Jupiter that included the following:

> *The importance of Jupiter in the birth chart is underesti-mated in interpretation and tradition. It actually guides us into the future and motivates future growth and development, espe-cially along idealistic lines. Jupiter's deeper meanings are neglected...In some ways, Jupiter is too simple a principle for a complex age, and it is too philosophical for a relativistic, materialistic age.* (p.77)

In fact, Jupiter is usually taken for granted by students of astrology, just as people so often take for granted the talents and special qualities which Jupiter's position in their charts indicates.

Finally, it should be stated that this book is more of an *explora-tion* of Jupiter's abundant and limitless dimensions than a system-atic analysis that purports to define the last word about Jupiter's meaning in astrology. Jupiter is, in fact, a far more *dynamic* planet than it is given credit for. It is always moving and expanding, always seeking, always exploring new horizons. Never content with the *status quo*, Jupiter invariably wants to climb the next mountain, to grow and develop freely toward a fuller expression of potential. As the brilliant astrologer Charles Carter wrote in perhaps his most profound book, *Essays on the Foundations of Astrology*, "Jupiter rules the future and movement towards progressive change." By "progressive," I believe he means the word literally, as in *progress* and *improvement*, for Jupiter is always seeking to augment what is, to improve or increase, and to go beyond current limits. Thus, in accord with the nature of this book's subject, although this material is only a small part of a long journey, perhaps it can at least aid the reader to go beyond his or her current level of understanding in astrology and toward a significant improvement in one's own life.

NOTE ON EXAMPLE CHARTS

The complete birth charts illustrated in this book are from the most accurate data available. The bibliography lists the specific sources used, most of the charts being derived from the Gauquelin chart collection and from the excellent reference books compiled by Lois Rodden. Since both Gauquelin and Rodden use the Placidus house system, and since that system still seems to be by far the most widely used, I have retained it in the reference charts.

However, the charts are drawn in the style most commonly used in Europe, a style which I have in fact always preferred myself. It emphasizes the zodiac signs far more than the houses and makes aspect patterns extremely easy to detect and understand. It simultaneously de-emphasizes the intermediate house cusps (2nd, 3rd, 5th, 6th, 8th, 9th, 11th and 12th) which vary significantly, depending on which house system is being employed. The profound significance of the remaining four angles of the chart (the Ascendant, Descendant, M.C. & I.C.) seems to be widely agreed upon, and in fact the Gauquelin statistical studies confirm their importance. Hence, those four angles remain emphasized in the chart style used in this book. The intermediate cusps are drawn in at the correct degree for the Placidus house system; they are merely visually de-emphasized. This also is appropriate for my approach to the houses, which views the cusps not as the exact beginning of a house but rather as a powerful peak of that house's energy continuum.

One final word regarding the style of the charts is necessary. In order to keep the example charts uncluttered and easily accessible, even to relative novices in astrology, all positions of both planets and house cusps have been rounded up to the full degree. This approach was decided upon since so many astrologers and students refer often to the *Sabian Symbols*, Rudhyar's *Astrological Mandala*, or other symbolic systems which assign an image to each *whole degree* of the zodiac.

We shall not cease from exploration
And the end of all our exploring
Will be to arrive where we started
And know the place for the first time.
                              —T.S. Eliot

(Perhaps the most philosophical modern poet, born September 26, 1888, with Jupiter in Sagittarius, closely sextile his Sun & exactly opposite his Neptune; Mars was also in Sagittarius.)

Introduction

*It will readily be perceived that a deep and wide
significance attaches to the position of Jupiter in the
horoscope. Without its help, we are necessarily destined to end, materially and intellectually, where we
began.* —Charles Carter, *Some Principles of
Horoscopic Delineation*

Many of the most positive expressions of Jupiter are out of
fashion in this era, for Jupiter's concerns are in many ways the
opposite of Mercury's rationalistic, analytical interests and detailed
approach to life. (This is further illuminated by the zodiacal polarity
of Sagittarius and Gemini, as I will explain in Chapter 1.) Such
subjects and qualities as ethics, nobility, forthrightness, altruism,
and high-mindedness have in fact almost a quaint, old-fashioned
ring to them today, so thoroughly has the media, along with the
educational establishment, buried such lofty concerns in scorn and
derided them as irrelevant to our "scientific," individualistic (i.e.,
egocentric) age.*

However, there is no avoiding Jupiter's intimate association
with the urge to align one's life with a greater ideal or with a revealed
truth, or at the minimum to merge one's energies into something
"larger than life." This alignment or merger tunes one into a greater
understanding and an enlarged view of life (i.e., a more *comprehensive* perspective), or gives one a sense of exhilaration at participating
in a vaster reality than merely the individual personality. Everyone,
of course, has a Jupiterian urge and Jupiterian needs within himself,
but in this "scientific" age, we tend to rationalize everything! But in
doing so, by trying to sterilize life's greater concerns and by trying to
deny the ethical and moral dimensions of life, we not only overlook

---

*Many of Jupiter's most negative manifestations, however, are emphasized, idealized
and even promoted in the world today: self-righteous, intolerant religious beliefs;
greed and "lifestyles of the rich and famous"; the cult of celebrity as a treasured goal
in itself; an over-extended, wasteful lifestyle that constantly pulls one away from
one's center and from one's duties toward such trivialities as children; excessive
growth and development, at the expense of the living atmosphere, the architectural
heritage, and the environment, etc. One might even say that the negative expression
of Jupiter is exemplified in Western society today. As my editor suggested to me,
perhaps by living out the negative side of Jupiter so grandiosely, Jupiter's positive
side has become "the shadow" side in our lives today.

or crush many of the more noble aspects of human potential, but we also often wind up wandering through life with no sense of direction and no deeper feeling for life's meaningfulness.

As I heard a spiritually-oriented doctor once say in a lecture, "If one does not mold one's life to an ideal, one will mold one's ideals to one's life." I think this quotation encapsulates an essential function of Jupiter in each of our lives. Jupiter, by instilling us with an ideal, by inspiring us with a long-term goal, by making us aspire to become something better than we are, gives a sense of meaning and direction in life. Charles Carter even suggests that Jupiter has a connection with one's "life purpose." Jupiter can provide this sense of meaning through an attraction to a particular religion or philosophy of life, or it can do so simply through a dedication to achieving a long-term future goal. (Note how Jupiter-ruled Sagittarius has always been associated with philosophy and religion, and its archer must have a *target* for its arrows—a goal, a direction.) In short, Jupiter gives *meaning* to life.

By no means does the connotation of Jupiter with religion and philosophy imply that strongly Jupiterian people always are or should be "believers" in some particular school of thought. Many of us have seen, for example, dozens of people with strong Sagittarian or Piscean (the other sign traditionally "ruled by" Jupiter) influence in their charts exemplify a "philosophical optimism" or a strong sense of morality that has no apparent link to adherence to a particular belief system. However, in many cases these people simply have never verbalized or felt the need to consciously formulate and acknowledge their deeply held attitudes toward life. In fact, the broad-minded acceptance of others and the cheerful tolerance for the variety of human nature and behavior that one sometimes sees in such people is one of the better and more uplifting expressions of Jupiter that we can observe—certainly a more truly "religious" acceptance of life than we often witness in cases of self-righteously "religious" people precipitating all sorts of heinous acts on others out of sheer bigotry and intolerance.

Religion and philosophy are reputed to be within Jupiter's domain because they are (or can be) examples of *inspired mind*, acting toward a goal of universality of consciousness and comprehensive acceptance of truth. Many types of higher mental activity can provide an individual with a broader perspective on life. As Charles Carter writes:

Religion, too, is placed correctly under Jupiter, or at least it lies for the most part in his province. For religious thought offers scope for the widest sweeps into the mysteries of space and time, and beyond into the Eternal and Infinite. Metaphysics and philosophy come under Jupiter, for similar reasons. Then, again, must not the planet of the future, of progress, look beyond the grave? (Essays, page 31)

Carter further points out that "Faith, too, is under Jupiter, for faith is opposed to the hard facts of Saturn; faith is, in a sense, taking a chance." Carter is in fact one of the few authors to point out Jupiter's connection with taking a chance, with running a risk, a feature of Jupiter that will help us interpret it in birth charts. But for the moment, let us just acknowledge Jupiter's connection with that transformative experience in life called "the leap of faith." It can happen in many areas of life, and it can happen a number of times, but Jupiter always wants to move from the petty to the great, from the details to the whole.

Actually, this faith in something beyond oneself is not just a delusion, as the cynics and skeptics of our day would have us believe. This open-minded faith is actually *a mode of learning.* Once again, we see the Jupiter connection with *exploration.* Just as exploring a new territory on earth is the surest way to know it, so energetically exploring the possibilities of life and giving space for perhaps undreamed-of potentials to surface is another *way of knowing* on other levels of life. This faith-related method of discovery reminds me of the quotation from the philosopher Pascal, which I have referred to in earlier books:

Earthly things must be known to be loved;
Divine things must be loved to be known.

Jupiter, in short, is just as valid a mode of learning as is Mercury, which so dominates the modern mind and the way our mind is trained in educational institutions. And seeing Jupiter as a method or path of learning should be kept in mind whenever one is trying to understand Jupiter's significance in a particular chart. Jupiter at best can be supportive and *uplifting;* it gives a person buoyancy and the capacity to bounce back vigorously from adversity. This uplifting quality also extends to Jupiter's urging us to rise above petty problems and trivial human differences and to gain the vaster, more comprehensive overview that is far more satisfying to a Jupiterian person. Strongly Jupiterian people cannot stand the *petty,* and in fact, they regularly overlook the details which are right in front of them and which are quite obvious to everyone else.

This tendency reminds me of the Sherlock Holmes sentiment that "My life was spent in one long effort to escape the commonplaces of existence." One could also make a case for this statement's being an expression of Neptunian escape urges as well as Jupiter's aspirations. So what do we find in the birth chart of Arthur Conan Doyle, the author of the Sherlock Holmes stories? Simply Jupiter in his Sun Sign Gemini and in the first house, widely conjunct Mars as well. In addition, Jupiter is closely square to Neptune, and the Moon is in the 9th (Jupiterian) house! The reader may find it of interest to know that, after achieving the status of the highest-paid author of his time and after having created a character of very prominent Geminian

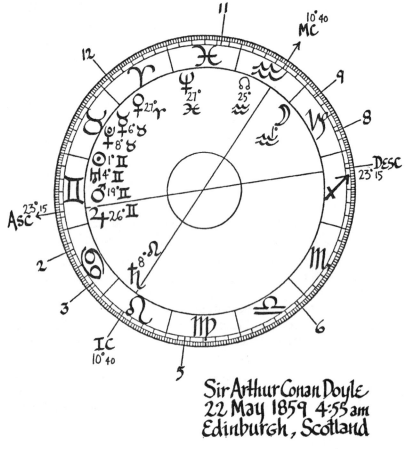

Sir Arthur Conan Doyle
22 May 1859 4:55 am
Edinburgh, Scotland

features ("Cold logic and analysis, Watson!"), Conan Doyle spent the later years of his life and much of his fortune investigating, experimenting with, and lecturing internationally about, spiritualism and various other topics related to immortality! We might, in fact, conclude that his tremendous urge to *communicate* (Sun, Mars and Jupiter in Gemini) was expanded through the Jupiter influence to include even greater realms of life, including spirit communication (Jupiter square to *Neptune*).

In the sense that astrology itself is a higher mental study, a mode of exploring and learning that encompasses vast dimensions of life, then in that way astrology is also a part of Jupiter's world. Astrology, for thousands of people worldwide, provides a sense of meaning in life far more satisfying than these people ever found elsewhere. For many people, astrology is virtually a philosophy of life, and—I dare say—it is for some a religion, although not all of them would agree with that statement. Certainly, astrology connects us to an enlarged perspective on life and gives us a wholistic, comprehensive, open-ended system through which much of life can be better understood and appreciated.

Further evidence of a Jupiterian imprint on astrology is the fact that Jupiter has always been associated with prophecy, and astrology of course has often been used as an attempt to predict the future. This has been an attraction to astrology for the masses, as well as in some cases astrology's virtual undoing by lending itself to ready denigration and easy criticism for perhaps too fervent a claim to prophetic powers. As Jeff Mayo wrote,

> *Astrology as a subject has survived thousands of years. Today it is emerging from a "dark period" of several centuries, during which its truths were scorned as mere superstitions as man's increasing scientific knowledge developed parallel with an increasing materialistic evaluation of life. During this period the charlatans and fortune-tellers debased and misinterpreted a great truth.* (The Planets & Human Behavior)

In addition, Jupiter has often been associated with the priesthoods of various religions, and such a role has evidently been quite comfortable for a good number of astrologers, although many of their colleagues have felt extremely ill at ease in a "priestly" role that encourages the public to project prophetic and omniscient expectations upon them. Fortunately, there does seem to be a significant

*Jupiter as a monk, by Andrea Pisano, from
the Campanile in Florence, Italy.*

number of astrology practitioners in recent years who elicit professional respect by keeping their claims and promises to a scope that
they can realistically fulfill. *Astrology* may be as expansive and
unlimited as Jupiter, but each *astrologer* does have certain limits
and areas of inexperience as well as areas of expertise.

> *"She believed that astrology without a spiritual connection was
> hollow. You had to love the person you were reading a chart for. She
> felt the astrological chart was like a road map that people could use,
> but it was necessary to see the spiritual principles that were underly-
> ing it. She once stated that during a conversation that if you kept
> looking down at the chart and not into the person's eyes, you were
> probably not a good astrologer. It was necessary to operate from a
> caring and loving space in order to be effective when dealing with
> peoples' lives."* (Said of pioneering astrologer Isabel Hickey, from the
> book *From Chains to Wings* by Joey Crinita.)

If in fact, as is often accurately claimed by its practitioners,
astrology can help reveal an individual's *potential for growth* and
what he or she may *become* as well as what he or she now is, then it
follows that Jupiter should be emphasized in the practice of astrology far more than it is today. *Growth* and *becoming* implicate the
future, and probably nothing else in the birth chart is so closely
related to future direction, aspirations, and plans as Jupiter. Its
natal sign, house, and aspects help us pinpoint areas of growth, rapid

development, probable success, meaningful improvement, and expanded understanding. It therefore follows that any practitioner of astrology would do well to make sure that some focus on Jupiter has its place in every birth chart studied and in every consultation, for surely all clients can benefit from the broadened perspective that Jupiter provides. And the therapeutic effect of placing a major emphasis on such a positive, optimistic energy as Jupiter represents will go a long way to offset the fears, anxieties, and fixation on the past that those who consult astrologers have unfortunately so often felt as the principal lingering result of contacting an astrologer.

I feel that Jupiter has also been underemphasized in astrology's literature, perhaps because its infinite potential for growth is so completely unpredictable! Jupiter's role in life is either undervalued and too narrowly understood, probably because we try to comprehend Jupiter through simplistic Mercurian analysis; or it is overestimated in purely materialistic chart interpretations as the key to wealth, luck, and worldly success. I am not denying that it has a role to play in worldly prosperity, but it certainly short-changes Jupiter's wealth of meanings and its relationship to many other dimensions of life to restrict the interpretation to so narrow a scope. Sometimes I am reminded of various Christian fundamentalist preachers, who I suppose must be obsessed with Jupiter in some way; they seem to be saying, "Have faith, ask for money from God; He will provide you with wealth, and then please remember to send some of it to me!" The widely-publicized salesmen (and women) of success and prosperity self-help techniques are likewise Jupiterian to a major extent; and they are certainly onto something. But I keep having a lingering doubt that all they really have to sell is faith and promises. We should not forget that Jupiter also needs Saturn as a balance.

In examining the importance of Jupiter as a principle, we can look to characteristics of the planet itself in the solar system. It is not only by far the largest planet in the solar system, but also it may be a small star. Dr. Robert Widey of the U.S. Geological Survey's Center of Astrogeology was quoted in that institution's survey as saying that Jupiter seems to be radiating 2.5 times as much energy into space as it gets from the Sun. Some scientists have speculated that Jupiter still contains ongoing nuclear processes like our sun has that could account for this release of energy. When we follow Jupiter's urge to move beyond our current way of being, we can then "radiate" from our expanded capacities and bring these gifts out into the world.

Jupiter, at the center of the zodiac.
2nd Century; Villa Albani, Rome.

CHAPTER 1

A Framework for Understanding Jupiter

> *To believe in something not yet proved and to underwrite it with our lives is the only way we can leave the future open....To find the point where hypothesis and fact meet; the delicate equilibrium between dream and reality; the place where fantasy and earthly things are metamorphosed into a work of art; the hour when faith in the future becomes knowledge of the past...this is what man's journey is about....*
> —Lillian Smith (A Sagittarian Sun writer, from her work entitled *The Journey.)*

The largest planet in our solar system, Jupiter conveniently stays in each zodiacal sign for approximately one year, since its complete revolution around the Sun takes eleven years and 315 days. Historically, Jupiter has been associated with the king, the patriarch, and the chief god in various pantheons. It has also been associated with the principle of divine preservation and bountiful increase, being known as the "greater fortune" or the "greater benefic" planet, as distinguished from the "lesser benefic" Venus. It has long been regarded as the patron of philosophers, theologians, moral leaders and crusaders, and speculative thinkers of all kinds.

The grandeur of ancient people's vision of Jupiter is hard for us to imagine today, and it is probably impossible for us to feel the awe with which such a cosmic force (or deity) was experienced. After all, as Theodore Roszak writes in *Why Astrology Endures*, "The main task of modern astronomy since Newton has been to demystify the heavens." Therefore, what Roszak calls the "organic sense of nature that mingled cosmology and psychology" has disappeared from the consciousness of modern, scientifically educated people. The ancient perception of unity between the human soul (the microcosm) and the vast world soul of the cosmos (the macrocosm) has become impossible for most people today, and the ancient formulation "As above, so below," has been relegated to the junk heap of "outdated superstitions." And yet, what Roszak refers to as the "spiritual communion between the human and the heavenly" seems to be eternal, arising again and again like the phoenix from the ashes of bygone concepts and beliefs, taking on yet again another form to enable human beings to explore transcendent truths. In recent years, there has arisen some evidence in the "new physics" that the macrocosm-microcosm dictum of the ancients will again be revitalized and more widely accepted. Another expression of the perennial human dialogue with the whole of nature is the following observation by astronomer Antony Aveni from his book *Conversing with the Planets*:

> *Turn out the lights and watch the real ones in heaven—those our ancestors' imaginative minds used to mold a wonderful poetic imagery about themselves and their relation to the universe. For long ago the fingertips of humankind touched earth and sky more sensitively, and from those sensations there came a self-awareness that we could never be separate from nature. Our predecessors expressed their conscious presence in a living universe through a vivid and imaginative dialogue with its many aspects—with mountain, water, moon, and sun. They explained what the real world meant to them through their art, architecture, and the written and spoken word, and they passed their revealed truths down to succeeding generations, who accepted some eternal verities and altered others.*

In contemplating the profound qualities and aspirations that Jupiter represents in astrology, I cannot help but feel that Jupiter's *bigness* and broad vision is inextricably linked to the perennial human search for a larger truth and for an experience of oneness with the universe. In perhaps no other planet (and in no other sign than Jupiter-ruled Sagittarius) do we find such a natural, spontaneous, and obvious intermixing of the physical and the non-physical; the material aspiration to improve one's situation is combined with a redemptive preoccupation with uplifting dreams, ideals, inspirations, and ethical causes. Witness, for example the symbol for Sagittarius: the centaur. This unique creature is still grounded on the earth with an animal body, but that does not stop him from using his human half to carefully aim his arrow at a specific goal on the distant horizon. It should be said here that large numbers of people worldwide have found in astrology an effective method of refocusing

and experiencing today the age-old sense of unity with the cosmos. In that sense, astrology, when properly used and appreciated, represents a Jupiterian link with the vaster universe, and it provides a helpful method of encouraging growth and self-knowledge. Once again, to quote Theodore Roszak,

> *For a growing number of people, the rich imagery of these old traditions has become a more inspirational way of talking about emotions, values, motivations, and goals than conventional psychiatry. The astrological universe is, after all, the universe of Greco-Roman myth, of Dante, Chaucer, Shakespeare, Milton, Blake. It has poetry and philosophy built into it. Where, for example, Freud offers a colorless psychic menagerie of ids, egos, superegos, cathexes and complexes, astrology unfolds the evocative symbols of the zodiac, the great archetypal images of the sun and moon, the mythological resonance of the planets. To speak of our masculine and feminine impulses with reference to Mars and Venus immediately brings myth and poetry back into psychology.*

In view of the power of the ancient traditions and myths of Jupiter, therefore, it seems important to touch upon these multicultural images before going more deeply into the astrological details of Jupiter. As Jeff Mayo points out, the deities identified with Jupiter were variously known as gods of thunder and storms, learning, wisdom, justice, and prophetic vision. I am indebted to Jeff

Mayo for the following details of such Jupiter-related deities, as set forth in his book *The Planets and Human Behavior*.

BUSSUMARUS: A Celtic god, later identified by the Romans with their Jupiter.

Manjusri, Buddhist God of Wisdom.

DONAR: Thunder-god of the heathen Germans, predecessor of Thor. The day sacred to Jupiter, Thursday, was dedicated to the German thunder-god, Donnerstag.

INDRA: The Hindu thunder-god as well as sun-god. Attributed with many of Thor's characteristics and considered to be Thor's counterpart.

JUPITER: The mighty Roman deity, the most powerful and the highest among the gods. Originally an elemental divinity, his name signifying the father or lord of the heaven. Thus he was worshipped as the god of storms, thunder, lightning and rain. The Romans believed that he determined the source of all human affairs. He presided over the great Roman games. He was the seer who foresaw the future, and was the god invoked at the beginning of every undertaking. He was the guardian of law, protector of justice and virtue. As the lord of heaven and the prince of light, the white colour was sacred to him, and white animals were sacrificed to him. Identified with Zeus of the Greeks.

MARDUK (Merodach of the Bible): Babylonian (Euphratean) god which the planet Jupiter was said to be an aspect of. Robert Eisler in The Royal Art of Astrology says that the god was "a personification of the spring sun drying the soil after the inundations, restoring order from

Jupiter (Roman) or Zeus (Greek). Chief God, ruling Heaven and Law, Thunder and Lightning.

chaos, the slayer of the dragon, the builder of the celestial house and organizer of the world. He produces storms as his weapons in the fight against the primeval monster." At a later period the name Marduk came to be applied to the Sun.

THOR: The mighty Scandinavian thunder-god, whose cult had a long life in Western Europe. His symbol was a hammer. In his association with the natural world he was both destroyer and protector. His equation with the Roman Hercules suggests that many of his attributes were akin to those of the personification of Mars. He was called upon to hallow and protect the many aspects of men's lives in the community. Identified with the Roman Jupiter and the Greek Zeus.

Nordic-Germanic Expression of Jupiter. Thor or Thunar, God of Thunder and War.

THUNOR: Old Anglo-Saxon thunder-god identified with the Roman Jupiter. He was the protector of the world against giants and had power over the weather, especially storms. When the Roman calendar was accepted in Britain after A.D. 300 the Britains named the fifth day of the week Thunresdaeg (Thursday).

TINIA: The chief Etruscan god, corresponding to the Greek Zeus and the Roman Jupiter.

ZEUS: The greatest of the Olympian gods, identified with Jupiter by the Romans. Zeus presided over the heavens and the upper regions of the world. He is called the father of gods and of men, the most high and powerful among the immortals, whom all other deities obey. The supreme ruler who manages everything; the founder of law and order. Even fate itself was subordinate to him. He is armed with thunder and lightning. Jupiter was clearly the "star of Zeus."

An especially important feature of Jupiter's nature in mythology, as well as in the interpretation of Jupiter in astrology, is the link between Jupiter and what was often traditionally called "higher mind." This aspect of mind can also be called "nobler mind" or "divine mind," and this superconscious mind's connection with Jupiter will be explored further later in this chapter when we discuss the Jupiter-Neptune pair. Just contemplating the idea of a "higher mind" can, however, be a humbling and, in fact, somewhat depressing experience, once one realizes that the very idea of "higher mind," which only a few decades ago would need no explanation to anyone over seven years old, seems out of place and alien today. One rarely hears of its existence, and the concept may seem to many people to be rather obsolete. But studying Jupiter can help to reinvigorate this important dimension of each human being. Jupiter's "higher mind" is not irrational; it is a form of reason, but inspired reason. In recent decades, a particularly narrow notion of rationality and learning has been oversold in the Western world, with disastrous results. We will continue to explore Jupiter as a broader mode of thought and learning later in this chapter, but before leaving this subject, let me quote from one of the great classics of astrology, first published in 1911, Isabelle Pagan's *Signs of the Zodiac Analysed* (first published as *From Pioneer to Poet*).

> *Jupiter is thus the ruling representative of the 'Divine Mind' in the mythology of classic times, and is consequently hailed as 'Optimus Maximus.' His Greek counterpart is spoken of with equal reverence; for the Zeus of Homer is the Greatest and the Best, and the most to be revered of all the deities; the God of Light, of Justice, and of Truth; the Father of Gods and of men. He dominates all the planes, because his thought comprehends all things. One vibration of his mighty will makes the whole universe tremble. One movement of his eyebrow shakes high Olympus, and the very gods upon their thrones. Princes and rulers are appointed by his divine decree, according to the deserts of the nations; and when he has bowed his head, his decision is irrevocable and cannot be altered. Above all things he is beneficent, benevolent and kindly—ever ready to hear the prayers of his children, and to grant their requests. The ancient Greek hymns addressed to him, besides acknowledging his goodness and greatness, begged of him such boons as rain after drought, healthful breezes, and favourable weather generally.*

The mountain peaks are his sacred places, and in his sterner aspect he is the God of lightning, of tempest, and of cloud. He holds the thunderbolt as well as the sceptre, and beside his golden throne stand two brimming cups, from which he pours out, according to his divine will, good and evil for the sons of men. It is he who appoints the judges of the infernal regions, and the condemned criminal was regarded as a suitable sacrifice upon his altar. The Divine Mind is intimately connected with every part of the Universe, and gives rise to innumerable forms of activity.

♃ Jupiter's Symbol

The symbol (or glyph) commonly used for Jupiter has been said by many authors to represent this theme of higher mind, expanding its scope beyond the limits of the material world. Most authorities state that the half-circle and a cross make up the Jupiter symbol.

$$\supset + \dagger = ♃$$

The half-circle is said to represent soul or mind, and the cross symbolizes matter. The half circle in Jupiter's glyph is *above* the horizontal (or horizon) of the cross, unlike in Saturn's symbol, where it is below (and thus symbolically subservient to nature and matter). [In fact, Saturn's symbol is essentially that of Jupiter upside down.] Jeff Mayo says that this denotes that "the human soul and mind must expand and develop new awareness and a higher consciousness beyond, yet out of, physical experience and the earthly environment." Hence, once again we find this intermixing of the spiritual and material that I mentioned earlier. In fact, Mayo nicely summarizes the meaning of Jupiter's symbol to mean *ideally* something similar to what Jung calls the "individuation process," the constant growth toward more inclusive wholeness, which Mayo says—in the case of Jupiter—involves learning "through deep and wise participation in and understanding of mundane experiences" while *simultaneously* preserving "his natural right to develop his own unique nature." (*The Planets and Human Behavior*)

Jupiter, Learning & The Rulers Of
The Mutable Signs

In order to understand deeply the type of mind and mode of learning that Jupiter represents, we have to contrast it with Mercury and, to some extent, Neptune, the other ruling planets of mutable signs. In fact, we have to explore as well the *signs* of the "mental cross," as it is often called (it is referred to also as the "mutable quadruplicity" since there are four signs involved). All the signs of the mental cross and their ruling planets have to do with *learning*.

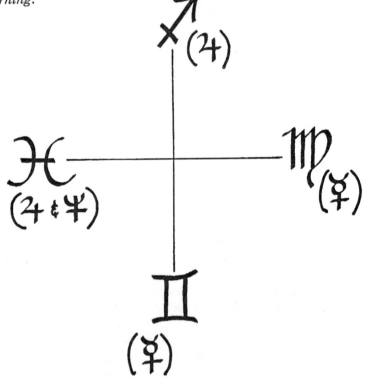

And a comprehensive understanding of all their principles will allow us to appreciate the various modes of learning. Each takes a different approach and achieves a different perspective, and each actually complements the others in filling in part of the whole picture of knowing and understanding life. It has been unfortunate that the Mercurian approach of separation and detailed analysis (through both Geminian and Virgoan modes) has dominated Western society and education for well over a century.

A well-reasoned and powerful indictment of the profoundly negative and troubling consequences of this domination of the data-obsessed analytical mind upon Western educational institutions can be found in *Killing the Spirit: Higher Education in America* by Page Smith, an experienced educator and historian. He points out that, by declaring so many religious, philosophical, and not-politically-correct subjects out of bounds for study in our schools, it constitutes a profound impoverishment and a shrinkage of the scope of human experience that students are able to explore. He points out that the exclusive focus on "research," a respectable name for endless gathering of data, most of which yield no insight or useful improvement, leads to a "barrenness of intellect beyond calculating."

The argument that will be made here can be simply stated. It is that the vast majority of the so-called research turned out in the modern university is essentially worthless. It does not result in any measurable benefit to anything or anybody. It does not push back those omnipresent "frontiers of knowledge" so confidently evoked; it does not in the main result in greater health or happiness among the general populace or any particular segment of it. It is busywork on a vast, almost incomprehensible scale. It is dispiriting; it depresses the whole scholarly enterprise.

Professor Smith's book shows clearly how "the spiritual aridity of the American university is the most depressing aspect of all," which results from the Jupiter principle and method of learning and growing being so tragically neglected in the Western world during the last century.

By 1900 the university had cast out every area of investigation and every subject that could not be subsumed under the heading "scientific" and had made all those that remained (like literature and philosophy) at least profess to be scientific. Excluded were such ancient and classic human concerns as love, faith, hope, courage, passion and compassion, spirituality, religion, fidelity—indeed, one is tempted to say, anything that might be somewhat encouraging to young people eager to receive some direction, or, in the words of a student survey form, develop "a philosophy of life."

In a classic explanation of the conflict between what I am calling
the Mercurian and Jupiterian approaches to learning, he quotes the
following statement by Robert Lichtman regarding the academic
world:

> *"Quality, uniqueness, creativity, and the moral dimension
> of existence fall before a reductive insistence upon measure-
> ment, qualification and restrictive processes of infinitely te-
> dious and irrelevant observation. The view of man which*

The Jupiter Sign As A Mode Of Learning

Educator David Hamblin, M.A. has published some extremely
interesting and original findings in *The Astrological Journal*,
published by the British Astrological Association in Summer, 1978
and Summer, 1981. He kept track of the Jupiter signs of students
in various classes that he led, which was quite easy because they
tended to bunch into one or two signs each year, since Jupiter stays
in one sign for about one year. Each Jupiter sign group, he
concluded, responded to a learning exercise in the manner of its
Jupiter sign, and "seemed to behave in the classroom in the manner
of their dominant Jupiter sign." He points out that these findings
have important implications for teachers, enabling them to predict
in advance the behavior of particular groups and thus to design
their teaching plans accordingly.

Although he had not finished evaluating all Jupiter signs when
he published his first two articles, the following quoted excerpts
from his articles give a clear idea of what he discovered and enable
astrologers further to determine with confidence specific characteristics of people with certain Jupiter placements.

*The Jupiter-in-Gemini group responded to it very well, with
very free and lively discussion and exploration of ideas; the
Jupiter-in-Cancer group responded poorly because they preferred
a more authoritarian style of teaching which would have given
them more protection and less exposure; and the Jupiter-in-Leo
group responded well, but in a much more flamboyant and
"theatrical" style than the other two groups.*

*The Jupiter-in-Libra group coped only moderately well with
the exercise. What was very noticeable, however, was that they were
much less interested in the content of the exercise than in their own*

emerges is ahistorical, atomistic, mechanical, disjunctive, and, again, ostensibly neutral."

In other words, the resulting views of human nature and human life completely lack the *wholistic* perspective which Jupiter could contribute. Sir Richard Livingstone, former Vice-Chancellor of Oxford University is also quoted at length, and this quotation is superbly insightful into the problems of the modern era as they relate to the "Mercury-Jupiter" conflict that I have mentioned.

interpersonal relationships within the group: their aim was to achieve group harmony for its own sake (rather than for the sake of improving their performance at the task, which did not greatly interest them).

The Jupiter-in-Scorpio group did better than predicted. Most of this class applied themselves to the task with a great deal of determination and enthusiasm. There were however two sub-groups which went through the task in an extremely somnolent state, displaying neither commitment nor hostility but only apathy. Thus the tendency of Scorpio to veer between extreme involvement and extreme apathy was confirmed.

The Jupiter-in-Sagittarius group did less well than predicted. They were an extremely effervescent and "bubbly" group, and their problem with the exercise was that it did not sufficiently tie them down: they were always going off at irrelevant tangents or "goofing around", and the problem of absenteeism was greater than with any other group. However, their inter-group presentations were riotously funny, and were better than those of any other group except Jupiter-in-Leo.

I have had some experience with a mixture of Jupiter in Capricorn and in Aquarius but they seem in fact to show mainly Capricornian characteristics. They work hard, and their written work is mostly very good; also they seem to enjoy discussion (perhaps because of the Aquarian element); but their attitude to work is extremely instrumental, showing an obsession with marks and grades, and they have caused more trouble to the lecturers with seemingly petty complaints about the "system" than any other group since Jupiter in Virgo.

Quotes from *Jupiter in the Classroom.*

Mercury represents *means*, Jupiter *ends;* and Livingstone calls our time

> *"The civilization of means without ends; rich in means beyond any other epoch, and almost beyond human needs; squandering and misusing them, because it has no over-ruling ideal; an ample body with a meagre soul...The break-up of the philosophy of the West is the great problem of our time,"* he added, *"on which all its lesser problems depend: for in the last resort the conduct of men is governed by their beliefs." Those beliefs are no longer readily identifiable.*

It should be clear that we need a balance of Mercury and Jupiter to function well in many areas of life, but the imbalance from over-emphasizing Mercury needs to be offset in some way. After all, it is in the Jupiter mode that we are especially open to *new* experience, especially keen to explore unknown areas of life; and so the Jupiterian way of learning must be utilized to enable us actually to *let in* the new facts and observations that Mercury will later analyze. Jupiter's openness and faith will allow new discoveries to happen; Jupiter's theories at their best and most alive tend to be open-ended, which is important since, as Albert Einstein said, "It is theory that decides what we can observe." Perhaps the passage of Pluto through Sagittarius will bring to the surface once again the expansive, hopeful, open-ended, life-enhancing modes of learning that Jupiter always represents.

$$ 2\!\!\!+ / \; \female $$

We can approach our exploration of the mutable signs and their rulers from many angles, but let's continue with the contrast between Jupiter and Mercury. Charles Carter succinctly expresses this contrast in his book *Some Principles of Horoscopic Delineation*:

> *Jupiter is a constructive and progressive Mercury. The latter is concerned with things as they are; it examines, it does not speculate or plan ahead. Jupiter seems to be the type of the explorer and experimenter, always ready to sweep its gaze towards wider horizons whether mental or physical. It is always known as the planet of growth. This is not merely growth in the sense of a thing becoming enlarged; it is a perpetual unfoldment into fresh combinations and variations. The whole of Nature is*

an exemplification of this aspect of Jupiter—evolution is a typical Jovian manifestation and one of the most important. In the human being it is Jupiter which unfolds our possibilities and brings that which is latent into full expression; indeed, if self-expression is the purpose of life, then Jupiter, significantly the largest body in the solar system after the Sun itself, is the symbol of that purpose, the three prior planets (Mercury, Venus, Mars) representing principles which are prerequisites to this purpose.

Paul Wright, in a lecture on Jupiter, pointed out the contrast between the Mercurian and Jupiterian methods of reasoning. At best, Jupiter can of course be inspired reason, but, Wright points out, Jupiter is more commonly *unreasonable*.

Jupiter argues from principle, with opinions born of conviction or faith, impervious to argument. Jupiterian truth is absolute and unconditional and not open to debate. Reason in the sense of logical justification, or reasonableness, that is, being open to an alternative point of view, is a Mercurial trait.

At best, Jupiter is very broad-minded and tolerant of many points of view; Jupiterians in fact very often love debate for its own sake, but, as Wright stated above, Jupiter is very rarely easily influenced by others and their ideas, unlike Mercury, which is easily swayed. In chart interpretation, too, Jupiter holds its own and is not much influenced by other factors, whereas Mercury is always easily influenced and colored by anything that touches it. Like mercury in a thermometer, the astrological Mercury constantly reacts to outside changes.

Before the discovery of Neptune, Jupiter was regarded as the *sole* ruling planet of Pisces, and hence, at that time, Mercury and Jupiter had all four of the mutable (or "mental") signs under their dominion. We will soon explore how Neptune fits into this mental cross today, but it is significant that the Jupiter-ruled signs Sagittarius and Pisces oppose the Mercury-ruled signs Gemini and Virgo. One way of expressing their contrast is, again to quote Carter, "Jupiter manifests on a far broader canvas than Mercury." He goes on to write:

The vision of Gemini is normal, that of Virgo microscopic; but Jupiter is telescopic, scanning distant horizons. Mercury studies local maps; he is usually an authority on tubes and bus routes. But Jupiter asks for atlases and maps of continents.

Exactly the same qualities appear in the intellectual life. Jupiter seeks general principles and universal ideas, whilst Mercury is a critic and commentator, an annotator of margins. (Essays)

Another of the fathers of modern astrology, Dane Rudhyar, has further insights into the difference between Mercury and Jupiter, as expressed in his breakthrough book *An Astrological Study of Psychological Complexes*:

Jupiter is the symbol of health and sanity, of inner integration and successful living. It makes the life whole and counterbalances the over-individualistic and separative trend of the ego and its tool, the analytical mind (Mercury).

Rudhyar goes on to point out what has rarely been discussed in astrological literature or conferences: namely, that Mercury and Jupiter must be in *balance* for psychological and physical health, as well as for ease of communication and social relationships. An overemphasis on Mercury results in the mind being over-worked by an infinite number of details that essentially have no meaning or organization, but which are over-burdening the nervous system and the mind with data, trivia, endless unrelated "facts," etc. This sort of person may seem to know everything but understand nothing. This imbalance may also manifest as nervous difficulties, difficulty gaining weight, being thrown off balance mentally and emotionally by every minor experience, and having difficulty determining a personal sense of direction. An over-emphasis on Jupiter, on the other hand, may be expressed as a mind full of big ideals and fervently-held beliefs, but with little knowledge to support them. The mind may be undernourished by a lack of practical facts and concrete details, and there may be a tendency to gain and keep too much weight on the body, with a resultant loss of flexibility and dynamic energy.

In her innovative book *The Astrology of Self-Discovery*, Tracy Marks identifies various Gemini/Sagittarius issues which we can likewise apply to illuminate this Mercury/Jupiter comparison:

knowledge vs. understanding
logic vs. intuition

concrete vs. abstract
means vs. ends
diversity vs. unity
the present vs. the future
the here-and-now vs. the faraway

In the same section of the book, she also lists some keywords that describe the integration of Mercury and Jupiter principles, as well as balancing of the signs Gemini and Sagittarius:

practical wisdom	*meaningful diversity*
the expanded present	*the dissemination of wisdom*
inspired reasoning	*purposeful interaction*

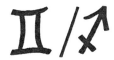

The Gemini/Sagittarius Polarity

My business is to teach my aspirations to conform themselves to fact, not to try and make facts harmonize with my aspirations. —Thomas Huxley

Many a time I have wanted to stop talking and find out what I really believed. —Walter Lippman

Let's now extend our exploration into the Gemini/Sagittarius sign polarity, the mental tension of which is beautifully illustrated by the above two quotations, which were selected by Tracy Marks and printed in her book *The Astrology of Self-Discovery*. Although both signs do indeed have a lot in common, and in fact people with those "opposite emphases" often get along quite well and find each other very stimulating, their differences are also illuminating. For example, Charles Carter writes:

Sagittarius contrasts with Gemini in its profuseness and carelessness, both fire characteristics. Gemini is a teacher of facts and figures, exact and precise; Sagittarius is a teacher of ideas and theories. It seeks to get beyond the already ascertained, which satisfies Gemini, into the unknown and unexplored. Physically it is not by any means always the great traveller that tradition describes, but mentally it is a perpetual

*voyager into uncharted seas. Hard facts are confining things,
and the sign hates confinement. (Essays)*

NOTE: I am quoting Charles Carter so often not only because of
how succinctly and incisively he expresses striking observations,
but also because much of his best work is completely out of print and
hence unavailable to upcoming generations of astrology students
unless it is at least referred to extensively in newer publications.
Even his remaining in-print books are almost never found in
bookstores.

Before referring to more contrasts and differences between
Gemini and Sagittarius, for the sake of newer students of astrology
to whom these signs' *similarities* may not be obvious, I should briefly
explain their parallel qualities. Like all opposite signs in the zodiac,
they have a great deal in common, and are complementary in many
ways, while being virtually opposite in other ways. These two signs
are the two "positive" or active, outgoing mental (or mutable) signs,
one air and one fire. They are both very inquisitive, unusually open
and friendly, and constantly in need of new mental stimulation.
They are both so involved with communication and interaction with
others that it is no wonder that, in my experience, they are two of the
most commonly found emphases in the charts of successful salespeople, who have to enjoy the give-and-take with others to be
successful in such a field. They both like reaching out to others and
into the world for new ideas and experiences; and the freedom to do
so is extremely important to both signs. They both need stimulation
to such an extent that, once a particular person or experience no
longer is energizing, boredom rapidly sets in, and each has great
difficulty with maintaining constancy, consistency, and commitments thereafter.

Quite a revealing comparison of Gemini to Sagittarius is found
in Paul Wright's superb book *The Literary Zodiac*:

*Sagittarius...tends to look beyond the real object to find
significance in an underlying and...spiritual stratum of existence. Gemini, on the other hand, is a sign which tends to
demystify...Just as Gemini represents the real over the abstract,
it also stands for other variations on this polarity: the parts over
the whole, the particular over the general, facts over principle*

and so on. In the same vein Gemini is humanist rather than deist, or at least vaunts natural and pragmatic religion over the supernatural variety. It is objective, empirical and rational rather than subjective and intuitive.

As a matter of fact, I have often found Geminis (as well as Virgos, the other Mercury-ruled sign) taking delight in finding the one exception to a rule or belief or guiding principle that a Jupiterian person might find completely satisfying and inspiring.

The complementary natures of these two signs are further explained, as well as illustrated physiologically, by Marcia Moore and Mark Douglas in their vast and extraordinarily comprehensive textbook *Astrology, the Divine Science.* They point out that, whereas Gemini *connects*, Sagittarius *coordinates*: "Gemini links the separate parts of a system while Sagittarius directs the organism as a whole." Traditionally, Gemini rules the arms, shoulders, and hands, whereas Sagittarius is said to rule the hips and thighs. The authors of the above book aptly point out a physiological fact that also has a broader application in the understanding of these two signs: "The Geminian arms and hands move a great deal without going anywhere, while the Sagittarian hips and thighs carry the body purposefully toward a goal." The hands, of course, are useful for finer skills.

Students of Polarity Therapy, as well as of Somatics (another energy-balancing system), learn of the complementary and compensating energy flows of the arms/shoulders with the legs; and in fact anyone can easily experience this by walking in slow motion while paying attention to how the opposite sides of the body work together fluidly and effortlessly. Gemini traditionally also rules the lungs and smaller nerves, whereas Sagittarius rules the lower spine (and its nerves), the longest nerve in the body—the sciatic nerve—and the liver, the largest interior organ. Moore and Douglas explain the important relationship of other physical processes with these extremely mental signs:

The link between the breath, nerves, and thinking processes accounts for the calming effect of deep breathing exercises. Breath control has been featured in various spiritual disciplines as a device for focusing thought and expanding consciousness. Stretching motions are Jupiterian since they involve reaching beyond oneself, and their tranquilizing effects are especially beneficial for nervous, fidgety, or flighty Geminians.

Sagittarians, with their love of sports, instinctively realize that exercise strengthens the lungs and induces the body to burn the oxygen required to produce both mental and physical well-being. Geminian inspiration is literally the act of inhaling, while Sagittarian inspiration elevates the mind, and these two are closely connected.

♐ / ♍

Sagittarius/Virgo Contrasts

Since Virgo is also a Mercury-ruled sign, many of the Jupiter-Mercury contrasts discussed above apply here as well. In addition, Virgo also tends to want to *demystify* life, as Paul Wright wrote about Gemini. After all, Virgo is opposite Pisces, as well as square Sagittarius; and Pisces is rightly regarded as the sign most inclined to mysticism and to mystifying all aspects of life. Actually, Virgo is more incompatible with Sagittarius and more different from it than is Gemini. As I said earlier, the *opposite* signs invariably do have a lot of similarities, but Virgo has few similarities to Sagittarius other than, perhaps, a tendency to be sharp-tongued, cynical, and sometimes inclined to pointed statements that are focused on puncturing the listener's point of view or pretenses.

One could fill pages with the contrasts between Sagittarius and Virgo, but at least I should mention a few observations. First, Virgo is usually notably more humble than Sagittarius; and Virgo usually prefers a simpler, more specific mode of thought as well as a more conventional and restrained mode of life. Sagittarius has trouble accepting a simple fact or idea, preferring endless debate for its own sake—possibly for the sheer enjoyment of it. Virgo often prefers to be genuinely helpful to others in whatever way they truly need, although it must be admitted that—all too often—the Virgo critical faculty is applied to others in ways that they neither need nor have asked for! Sagittarius can also be helpful, primarily through its generosity and capacity for inspiration and encouragement; but—like Virgo—Sagittarius can also express its "helpfulness" in ways that are not appreciated by the recipient. For example, the ultimate preacher/proselytizer of his own viewpoint often wants to help others on his or her *own* terms, to improve others who are not

Paul Wright's *The Literary Zodiac* has this to say regarding the large number of Sagittarians who are noted as social critics, either expressing their observations through humor (Mark Twain and Woody Allen), poetry (William Blake), controversial dialogues or columns (William F. Buckley, Jr.), or other means:

The second important variation of the ideal-reality theme is expressed through those Sagittarians who are noted as social critics. Many writers of all signs tend to lament the shortcomings of society but there is often a unique mocking quality about Sagittarius. But what more essentially characterizes the sign is that the criticism often centers upon a divorce between the real and ideal. And this can take two distinct forms: pointing out too much "ideal," or too little. Sagittarian writers are often intent on deflating dreams, on cutting through the romance and delusion with which men tend to shroud themselves and their world.

Another Sagittarian, Jonathan Swift, the author of *Gulliver's Travels*, also punctured the pretenses of human nature in an entertaining way. For example, he revealed the foolish and self-destructive tendencies we so often see in human society when he reflects this in the Lilliputians going to war over the correct way to break an egg!

interested in being improved and thus are not receptive to the Sagittarian suggestions. Since Virgo's focus is microscopic and Sagittarius' is telescopic, they have very different and sharply contrasting perspectives on life, but neither is especially sensitive to the immediate sensitivities and emotions of other people around them. In fact, people who have *both* of these signs emphasized in their charts are always extremely mental creatures, and there is a sharpness to their tongue and their reactions to others which can manifest as an argumentative and often insensitive disposition.

When the energies of these two signs work together well, we see such complementary skills and talents as: Virgo keeping track of the details while Sagittarius retains a perspective on the whole picture; Virgo helps to apply and give form to Sagittarius' inspirations; and likewise, since Virgo is disinclined to take risks until all the details are checked out and confirmed, Virgo can temper the Sagittarian's tendency to take a leap of faith prematurely, being caught up completely in vast possibilities but usually overlooking the practical facts. Actually, both Virgo and Sagittarius are concerned with *improvement;* Virgo simply takes a more immediate and narrow focus.

The obviously noble intentions of Sagittarians seem at times to go to their heads, leading to a certain form of ego-inflation that, admittedly, is commonly found in all of the fire signs. On the other hand, Virgo usually has such a well-developed fault-finding mechanism in their natures, which does not spare anyone, including himself/herself, that ego-inflation is not usually a major problem for them. And neither is susceptibility to flattery, which Sagittarius is somewhat prone to (however, the Sagittarian, though perhaps liking flattery almost as much as childlike Leo, doesn't let its delight show so obviously!).

In a similar vein, Sagittarius cannot take criticism nearly so well as Virgo, who is always looking for more! (Virgos often seem to relish the number of defects they can find in themselves—and in others.) This contrast in personalities is probably most obvious if one examines the Virgo and Sagittarius Moon signs, since the Moon symbolizes an instinctive reaction mode that happens so spontaneously that it is difficult to hide or change. Whereas Virgo Moon people, as one of them said to me, have "a well-developed sense of guilt" that leaves them open to assuming that any criticism may indeed be valid, the instinctive reaction of Moon in Sagittarius people is to want to rise above petty details and to avoid looking at facts whenever possible. Thus, harsh facts often stimulate them to turn on their flame-thrower tongues, evidently to try to burn up the critic. In other words, like all Fire sign Moons, they tend to get immediately and aggressively defensive, sometimes later regretting their behavior. This rejection of criticism, however, does keep them from getting emotionally depressed and helps maintain their buoyancy.

♃/♆

Jupiter & Neptune

The only true happiness comes from squandering ourselves for a purpose. —John Mason Brown

The above quotation, I expect, will ring true with both strongly Jupiterian people and those with a powerful attunement to Neptune. One of the most fascinating and somewhat surprising things my research for this book has shown me is how much Jupiter and Neptune really do have in common. Shortly after Neptune was discovered, astrologers began to speak of Neptune as the "higher octave" ruler of Pisces. I would have to agree with that designation, but—unlike most modern astrologers—I would not give over the entire rulership of Pisces to Neptune. Jupiter is still extremely powerful for all people who have prominent Pisces factors in their natal charts. Those who are familiar with my work on what I call "subtones" (see my *New Insights in Modern Astrology*) will know that I consider the *sign position* of Jupiter to be an especially strong energy attunement and personality tone of *anyone* who has the Sun, Moon, Ascendant, or a major stellium in Pisces. This is, of course, also true for those with these major factors in Sagittarius.

First of all, both Jupiter and Neptune represent functions of personal growth and transformation toward another, higher level of consciousness. They both, in their own ways, represent *superconscious* needs of a human being. They both represent higher mental yearnings toward an ideal. They both can *inspire* an individual with a transcendent meaning to his or her life, infusing this lifetime with significance through helping the individual to merge his or her purpose and dreams with a larger power, force, or truth. Both planets tend toward a religious, metaphysical or philosophical interpretation of life, although obviously Pisces is generally more mystical and Sagittarius more orthodoxly religious within established traditions and institutions. Both planets need to give of themselves and are known for their generosity. Both yearn to feel and to believe in some sort of unity of and with all humankind. They both look beyond petty details and human beings' personal faults, and they both prompt a person to shoot for a far-off goal that can only be imagined but not yet grasped or logically proven.

In addition, one can say that both Jupiter and Neptune represent a yearning for freedom. And, oddly enough, both often seek to experience that freedom through obedience to a higher law. It is well known that Neptunian people easily give of themselves in a submissive mode, seeking to lose the isolation of the self through merger in another person, group, service, or being. As Paul Wright points out in his book *Astrology in Action*, Jupiter shares a somewhat similar inclination and might open our eyes to a new sense of what "freedom" can mean that is quite different from the "do-your-thing" individualistic trend so widely promoted by Western media.

> *[Jupiter] stands for universalism, particularly the creation of one law or one belief system. Jupiter symbolizes faith in the broad sense, and religion as a collective phenomenon. The Jupiter principle does not, as is commonly supposed, relate to freedom, but to obedience and subservience to what is perceived as a higher authority—some religious, political or moral principle. However, it can be argued that this surrender in itself represents a type of freedom, albeit different from the contemporary Western concept of freedom. In the same way, it can be argued that the Western (Mercurial) concept of freedom, of thought and speech, the freedom to be different, is itself illusory and irrelevant.*   (Astrology in Action)

The poet Robert Frost describes this attainment of freedom through obedience like so: "You have freedom when you're easy in your harness."

Perhaps the most surprising thing to me about Jupiter that has surfaced while researching it is that, the more I look into Jupiter, the more elusive it becomes! Jupiter, like Neptune, will not be and cannot be compressed within the narrow definitions and "logic" of the analytical mind that wants to write a neatly-organized book! Actually, all the rulers of the mutable (i.e., *changeable*) signs are quite elusive; even Mercury will impress you with its elusiveness if you ever try to capture quicksilver! It endlessly divides and jumps all over the place. In short, Jupiter is not nearly so simple as I had imagined, and is far more dynamic than I had known.

In order to contrast the natures of Jupiter and Neptune, we will do best by focusing on Sagittarius and Pisces, which will help bring out the similarities as well as some of the differences between these two planets. The main thing I should still, however, make clear is that Neptune is a more refined mode of perception and knowledge than Jupiter; Neptune is more unknowable and ineffable, and its perceptions, if expressable at all, can only be expressed through music or art or poetry or devotional utterances. Jupiter, on the other hand, although difficult to summarize and impossible to constrain within logical parameters, does deal with somewhat conceptualizable knowledge within the domain of philosophy and higher mental/theoretical pursuits.

Both planets can lead to ego inflation, delusion and/or illusion, misuse of idealism, and a fondness for empty show and glamour. However, the tendency is for Jupiter to encourage growth and

Jupiter and Neptune have much in common,
although Jupiter is far more confident and forceful.

expansion of the ego and personality, whereas Neptune often encourages a dissolving of the ego and personality, or at least a refining of it so that a subtler reality may flow through it. Jupiter has an extroverted momentum, towards expansion into and expression toward the outer world, acting out one's faith in outer activities. Neptune has an inward pulling direction in many people, toward subtler dimensions of life and levels of consciousness. In other words, whereas both planets have a connection with idealism, Jupiter is more likely to put those ideals into worldly actions that have a noticeable impact on society. Even when Neptune does put ideals into action through service to others in the world, it tends to be more self-sacrificing and to stay more in the background than does Jupiter.

Sagittarius/Pisces Similarities & Contrasts

Often in the old books on astrology, one comes across statements like: "Jupiter is active in Sagittarius and passive in Pisces." There is a certain amount of truth to this, but we can take that comparison further with revealing results. The Jupiterian quality expresses itself mentally in both signs, but with far more emotion, compassion, and sympathy in Pisces. Sagittarius gets tired of listening to other people's troubles eventually, but Pisces rarely does. Both signs indulge in considerable intellectual speculation and argument. When first studying astrology while in college, I was surprised how many aspiring academics were Pisces Sun-signs. In a way, much of the work done in the world of academia is like a fantasyland, with its own rules, laws, realities, and language; and I cannot help but wonder if that is one of the attractions for Piscean types of people. Perhaps they feel safe in that separate, "ivory tower" world. (Remember that the early universities evolved out of monasteries, institutions with which Pisces traditionally has great affinity.)

Grant Lewi, the extremely talented Gemini Sun author of such best-sellers as *Astrology for the Millions* and *Heaven Knows What,* makes an important observation about Sagittarius in his lesser-known book *Your Greatest Strength*:

> *...the greatest of Sagittarian weaknesses [is] an inability to recognize a motive less lofty than his own; a wishful thinking that turns to sugary optimism, and a blind faith in all men; a tendency to be gullible and to believe what he wants to believe, about himself and others.*

Now if the reader will simply substitute the word Pisces for Sagittarius and re-read the above quote, I think it will be found equally accurate. In fact, in my book *Astrology, Karma & Transformation*, I specifically related the planet Neptune to the tendency to "believe what you want to believe," often leading to self-deception. I think we can accurately summarize as follows: anyone who has a strong Neptune or Jupiter, Sagittarius or Pisces emphasis in the birth chart may well have a proclivity toward this form of gullibility. One might even say it results from too much faith!

So often I have seen those with lots of Sagittarius or Pisces emphasis (or people with an especially prominent Jupiter or Neptune, *even if there are no planets in Sagittarius or Pisces)* fall victim to this tendency. They seem to project their own virtues onto others and have faith in the nobility and high-mindedness of others. They assume that others are moral and will keep their word. Those with either of the two Jupiter signs *rising* seem perhaps to win the prize for gullibility. Just last week, for example, I received a letter from a friend who has Sagittarius rising (thus, he is "ruled by Jupiter"). It seems he has finally gotten to the bottom of some of his perpetual financial problems. The accountant on whom he has relied for many years to keep his company solvent and to give him proper advice not only was giving him useless and wasteful advice, but in addition was embezzling funds!

Another Sagittarius rising person over a period of decades enthusiastically launched over two dozen business partnerships without checking the qualifications or references of his "partners." And in almost every case he would end up having to go to court as a result of these entanglements. He either had to sue them, or they sued him, or some third party sued him because of the criminal actions of the business associates in whom he had so much faith. At least three of them were in fact convicted of felonies, and probably quite a few others should have been! It did not help matters, of course, that this man had Pluto, the planet of the underworld, in his seventh house.

Paul Wright points out in *Astrology in Action* that both Sagittarius and Pisces often demonstrate breadth of thought or vision, although both are poor at discrimination (Mercury). In fact, his section comparing the two signs is so good that this chapter would be incomplete if I did not quote it in full:

Sagittarius particularly can be uncompromising and inflexible. Jupiter and its signs are intuitive in that they can see the potential in an idea before it has unfolded, and have faith enough to bring it to reality. Though equally, people with these influences accented are full of impractical big ideas and grandiose schemes.

Both signs are given to mood swings, and Pisces in particular has a tendency to emotional extreme. Pisces can be self-deprecating, self-pitying, or a self-denying martyr. But it is also compassionate, with an instinctive empathy with outcasts and underdogs. It is a sign that invariably forgives. There can be a shy, passive, retiring nature. It values solitude more than any other sign. There can be torpor, lethargy, sometimes a sort of paralysis of the will.

Sagittarius is probably the most forthright influence of the zodiac, and the most dogmatic and didactic. It can be moralistic and self-righteous. There is a very upright, high-minded side to the sign, and a striving to be above baseness and to live according to the dictates of a conscience. In both signs there is a need for something other than the mundane working world, something more exciting, elevated, heroic, adventurous, glamorous, or refined, and so an attraction to those spheres that embody these things (or, more generally, to where the boundary between reality and fantasy is blurred).

The escapist tendency is strong in Pisces. It will often look ahead to a brighter future and condition life by the hope of this. Jupiter and both its signs stand for optimism, or equally just wishful thinking. Deception is one facet of the Jupiter principle and it is more evident in Pisces. There is the tendency and capacity to confuse and dissemble. Sagittarius is an essentially honest influence although the tendency here is to self-deception and delusions of grandeur. There can be a tendency to inflate the ego and imagine oneself greater or more glamorous than one really is.

Jupiter and its signs have a flair for language. They are stimulated by travel and foreign places, although this aspect has been somewhat over-stated in the past. A strong Jupiter influence usually imparts spirit or enthusiasm in manner, or what is sometimes called a passionate nature. There can be a jovial, buoyant side. Sagittarius makes for a good raconteur, knowing what to keep as fact and what to exaggerate and embroider. Extravagance can be marked in both signs, with a tendency to live beyond the means. Both can be generous and philanthropic. There can be a tendency to take on too much, and not be aware of limitations.

We should once again remind ourselves that all the mutable signs are signs of *learning*, and constant change and movement are necessary to encounter the vast array of life experiences that these signs need in order to learn more. As Charles Carter said (quoted earlier), Sagittarius is a "perpetual voyager into uncharted seas;" and I think that phrase is equally apt for the water sign Pisces. Carter further quotes the widely-traveled author Robert Louis Stevenson, creator of *Treasure Island* and many other popular books: "to travel hopefully is a better thing than to arrive." Surely this is a Jupiterian sentiment! (Stevenson, by the way, has the following in his chart: Jupiter trine the Ascendant, Neptune and the Moon in the first house in Pisces, and the Sun and Mars in the ninth house!) Carter then goes on to say that *incompletion* is characteristic of Jupiter's signs and that, since Jupiter is the symbol of cosmic progress, this is as it should be. He goes on to conclude, quite poetically,

Air and Earth can see their tasks completed in perfection, witness the triumphs of Greek statuary, but Water must ebb and flow, even when it has reached the ocean of Pisces, and in Sagittarius there is the unending flare and flicker of the upward tending flames. (Essays)

CHAPTER 2

Jupiter in the Birth Chart: Key Concepts & Interpretive Guidelines

Survey the circling stars, as though yourself were in midcourse with them. Often picture the changing and rechanging dance of the elements. Visions of this kind purge away the dross of our earth-bound life. —*Marcus Aurelius's* Meditations*

Apart from the fact that *Meditations* by the Roman Emperor Marcus Aurelius provides a good example of a Jupiterian philosophy that has a practical, Saturnian anchor, this particular quote to me is especially reminiscent of the uplifting, inspirational dimensions of Jupiter's best "influence" on our lives. (Astrologers can also use this quote as ammunition to further exemplify another benefit of studying astrology!)

However, before we discuss specifics about Jupiter's position and possible manifestations in the birth chart, a few general comments are needed. First, one thing not sufficiently emphasized by astrology practitioners or astrology books is the overriding fact that virtually all astrological theories about what will or will not manifest strongly in a birth chart are secondary to various other non-astrological factors. Astrology's reliable applicability can only be focused correctly if astrology is seen in perspective, as a fundamental—but not the *only* fundamental—factor contributing to human personality, consciousness, behavior, and motivation. Astrological theories should be used as working hypotheses when applying them to specific human beings' lives, and they should be viewed only as rough guidelines toward understanding; they constitute a starting place

---

* Marcus Aurelius' chart has Jupiter in Scorpio opposite Mercury in Taurus, an apt symbol for "visions purging away the dross of our earth-bound life"!

for detailed inquiry and interpretation, but they are not the end of the journey toward deep understanding.

For example, no matter where your Jupiter is or what its aspects are, the society, environment, and—especially—the parents' influence as you grew up invariably change, color, suppress, or encourage how that Jupiter potential will be expressed. When outer factors reinforce the inborn tendencies, they will be supported and their expression speeded up, amplified, and developed. When outer factors discourage or suppress the inborn tendencies, they may be almost completely thwarted or perhaps forced into other channels of expression, channels that may be too narrow for expansive Jupiter. Especially if the birth charts of one's parents interact harmoniously with your Jupiter, those abilities and tendencies shown by Jupiter will then be more easily expressed—most likely quite early in life. If the opposite is true and there is friction, disapproval, or excessive criticism of one's Jupiter qualities and mode of expression, that essential energy may either be substantially blocked or, more often, pushed into other, more acceptable or more secret channels.

♃/♄

Balancing Jupiter with Saturn

Ideally, as the famous psychic Edgar Cayce said so often in his "Life Readings," Jupiter is an *ennobling* influence.

In Jupiter, we find the great ennobling influences—the broad-mindedness, the ability to consider others, the Universal consciousnesses that are a part of the entity's unfoldment.

Cayce also repeatedly referred to Jupiter as a "benevolent" and beneficent influence in the soul life of most people. However, in order to bring these beneficial and ennobling vibrations of Jupiter into concrete manifestation, both within oneself and to influence and uplift others, the individual needs a balance of Jupiter's enthusiastic approach to life with Saturn's more prudent, cautious perspective. In other words, it is extremely important *consciously* to balance one's visions of infinite possibilities with what experience shows is likely to be possible. Along the same lines, it is important to sustain and test one's personal potential (and one's faith in one's own potential) with proven accomplishment. Everyone knows how tiresome it is to listen to a blowhard braggart who endlessly recounts his or her grand schemes and multifarious talents, but who never has anything to show for it.

The importance of Saturn as a balance for Jupiter is a significant theme in the writings of many of the 20th century's greatest astrologers. For example, Dane Rudhyar wrote in *An Astrological Study of Psychological Complexes:*

> *The passion for self-aggrandizement is a typical expression of an over-active Jupiter function. It can be a compensation for a weak Saturn...it can also reveal a lack of balance....*

Grant Lewi describes a common problem for Jupiterians, which especially fits many young people who have strong Jupiter or prominent Sagittarius or Pisces emphases in their charts. Again, one notes the results of a lack of the groundedness of Saturn when he writes that such a person...

> *...can feel himself to be "only a sort of thing in a dream"—an inhabitant not of the real world, but of some compound of ideals and fancies, of high aspirations and expansive philosophies*

that prevent him from ever getting his feet moving in a consistent direction on the solid crust of the earth.

(Your Greatest Strength)

In addition, Lewi, in describing a particular political leader, writes of a common inherent weakness in those with a strong Jupiterian tendency unbalanced by Saturn:

> *In his faith in God, he failed to be realistic about the forces that were closing around him; he failed to recognize that he needed to take practical steps to implement his faith.*

Charles Carter repeatedly emphasizes the need for a Saturnian balance to Jupiter's tendencies in many places in his writings. In *Essays on the Foundations of Astrology*, he writes that the Jupiter type of person is...

> *...neither patient nor painstaking and is apt to lose interest when a topic or scheme has been, to his mind, exhausted. Thus we constantly find that Jupiter, without the co-operation of his opposite Saturn, is ineffective, brilliant but undependable, here one day and gone tomorrow.*

Furthermore, in the same book, Carter gives a succinct example of Jupiter's *need* for Saturn for everybody's ultimate welfare:

> *Jupiter rules horses and motor-cars; the former needs the rein; and to drive a car without brakes is an operation fraught with danger to driver and public alike.*

In fact, Carter points out in *Some Principles of Horoscopic Delineation* that Jupiter is meant to function *within* the domain of Saturn, for Jupiter's cycle is within Saturn's orbit. Jupiter needs the *discipline* of Saturn, much as it often dislikes it or neglects it. Jupiter is infinite potential; Saturn is finite limitation. But the need for balance works both ways. While Jupiter represents the unfoldment of life, Saturn, if carried to an extreme, says Carter, can become "the veritable enemy of life" by prematurely truncating possibilities for growth.

A perfect example of the Jupiter/Saturn ideal balance is found throughout the classic works of Chinese philosophy, such as the *I Ching* and the *Tao Teh King*. The complementary qualities of the polarized creative powers of the universe are everywhere evident in these great writings, often characterized as *yin* and *yang*. For example, from the *Tao Teh King* edition translated by Archie J. Bahm, we find this advice from Lao Tsu:

> *Going to extremes is never best...The way to success is this: having achieved your goal, be satisfied not to go further. For this is the way Nature operates.* (Published by Ungar Publishing Company, New York, 1986)

Another way of characterizing the complementary principles represented by Jupiter and Saturn is to contrast Saturn's *gravity* with Jupiter's *levity*. Saturn is invariably heavy, serious, and ponderous. It anchors us, brings us down to earth, and makes us focus on the here-and-now reality. Jupiter, on the other hand, is light, playful, and buoyant. It lifts us up, helps us to "rise above it all," and gives us a perspective that only can be achieved from the high mountaintop of idealism or humor.

The fact that Jupiter is within the orbit of Saturn prompts Carter also to make the pointed observation that, while fond of change, Jupiter is "yet strangely conventional." He may explore widely and go after difficult and large goals, but he is still hampered by conventional limitations. "Jupiter is growth," Carter writes, "but it is always growth to a pattern set and approved."* There is thus a tremendous difference between the pioneering and creative activities of Jupiter and those of Uranus. Uranus is far more original and does not tend to rely on social conventions. In fact, Uranus is more likely to want to overthrow social rules and traditions! Jupiter is more prone to expand and improve what already exists, whereas the Uranus energy is most clearly seen in radical departures from all previous mental patterns and social traditions.

Jupiter, Gambling & "Pushing Your Luck"

When a sufficiently strong Saturn is not present in a person's nature to lend a bit of caution to his or her approach to life, there is often a tendency to rely on luck. I have, over the years, come to use the phrase "tempting fate" to describe the behavior of many such people I have known. No matter how good their luck has been, no matter how generous God or fate has been with them, they want to gamble once again and even risk all they've gained, evidently in an addiction to compulsive expansionism! Never is enough enough. Lao Tsu's wisdom quoted earlier is completely absent. Donna Cunningham has a section on gambling in the Jupiter chapter of her excellent book *An Astrological Guide to Self-Awareness*, in which she refers to "pushing your luck" as a manifestation of negative Jupiter—"a kind of stupid optimism or over-confidence."

Similarly, Charles Carter refers to the type of overly-Jupiterian person who relies more on "luck" or "fate" than on effort and diligence when he describes the typical sort of gambler who is always assuming that his "luck will turn," although it has not been too good so far. In fact, in his basic astrology textbook *The Principles of Astrology*, Carter finds Jupiter's connection with "luck" sufficiently important to devote quite a long paragraph to it, even in an introductory book for beginning students of astrology:

> *Indeed, Jupiter, unless badly afflicted, is the planet of luck, i.e., of good fortune not clearly attributable to merit, and those with the planet angular and in a congenial sign are usually fortunate beyond the average, especially if they possess common sense and a sense of moderation; otherwise they tempt their fortunes too far. In some respects it resembles the Sun and Mars, though more mental, and under affliction it runs, like these bodies, to excess of energy, optimism, and self-indulgence. The*

---

* Cf. Carter's *Some Principles of Horoscopic Delineation.*

faith becomes an unbounded belief in luck and a reckless disregard of consequences, so that, although seldom anyone's enemy but his own, the Jovian often ruins himself by pushing his luck too far, taking unreasonable hazards, gambling, and wasting time, money, and energy.

In summary, in any comprehensive evaluation of a birth chart, one should consider the relative strength of both Saturn and Jupiter in the overall chart. I am not saying something simplistic like: "Look at Jupiter-Saturn aspects," although such aspects are always important. But more broadly, it is advisable to consider comprehensively how well attuned the individual is to both Jupiter and Saturn principles, for effectiveness in the world depends upon the individual having a significant attunement to both. For example, it is no accident that many people with Jupiter/Saturn conjunctions are extraordinarily successful and prosperous in business. But a similar degree of worldly success may be found in a wide variety of people who do not have such a conjunction but who have virtually an infinite number of chart combinations, featuring perhaps Saturn aspecting the Moon closely while Jupiter aspects the Sun or Mars, or, for another example, a prominent Jupiter complemented by strong, but

Jupiter's boundless enthusiasm appalls Saturn and leaves him incredulous at such a perpetually positive attitude.

not debilitating, aspects between Saturn and the Ascendant or Midheaven or Mars, or the Moon. The combinations are endless, and the practitioner of astrology should remain open to discovering the truth of the person's life whose chart is being examined, rather than giving in to the tendency to impose a preordained and often rigid theory upon the person's God-given potential. Astrology should lend itself to the development of peace of mind, not instilling defeatism or nervous anxiety or baseless fears.

For success in finance and investing, likewise, there needs to be a balance of Jupiterian optimism with prudent, practical realism. As noted investor and author Al Frank has written, for investment success one needs *faith* in the future of the companies invested in, along with *patience* (Saturn). The factors tempering Jupiter's tendency toward extravagance are not limited to Saturnian influences alone. Many other chart factors can combine with Jupiter's energies in order to support and encourage overall prosperity. The shrewdness of Scorpio, for example, or even some cheapness (coming from Cancer or Taurus perhaps) could counter the Jupiterian urge toward wastefulness and excessive risk-taking. The prudence and realism of Virgo and Capricorn could also complement Jupiter's expansiveness.

A good example of a Jupiterian individual whose expansiveness is prudently tempered by other factors is John Templeton, the founder of Templeton Mutual Funds. Born November 29, 1912 in Tennessee, Templeton has Mercury conjunct Jupiter in his Sun sign Sagittarius—certainly the perfect keynote of a positive thinker! His Moon in Leo adds to his inveterate optimism, and in fact, to many admirers he is one of the most upbeat and enthusiastic people in the business world. His optimism is not untempered by practicality, however, for his Venus is in Capricorn (a "money" planet in a very conservative sign) and Saturn is opposite both his Sun and his Scorpio Mars.

Best known for being a pioneer in *international* investing, he is also an extremely religious man who has contributed millions of dollars to charitable causes. For him, religious principles and his investment philosophy go hand in hand. As *Forbes* magazine wrote of him,

> *If all human beings are fundamentally brothers, why shouldn't Japan or Latin America be as good a place to invest as the U.S.? This sense of ultimate humanity made Templeton a pioneer in*

allocating assets around the world....Templeton early on devel-
oped an ability to see the world as a whole, not as a collection of
pieces.

Templeton freely speaks of his unified view of life, in which the
spiritual and the material are not mutually exclusive:

A person is more likely to be successful managing money if he
uses spiritual principles, and the more you practice spirituality,
the more you learn. I think all careers are more successful and
satisfying if you use spiritual principles. I can't think of a single
exception.

In his philanthropic work, he does not favor any single religion, but
he is also skeptical of organized religion since "No religion ever set its
heart on progress. Their interests are in looking backwards." In fact,
Templeton is the ultimate optimist and believes in "progress," both
material and religious, although he is troubled by the fact that material
progress is far outrunning worldwide spiritual development. This is
one reason that he has contributed so heavily to religious causes—over
$10 million given in 1994 alone. His projects also include the Templeton
Prize in Religion and prizes for teenagers who write essays on spiritual
experiences that help them live their lives.

What can we learn from a person like John Templeton? In the
newsletter *Bottom Line,* there appeared an article in the September,
1994 issue in which Templeton outlined his "Secrets of Leading a
Fulfilling Life." It is worth quoting at length, since it constitutes a
virtual essay on "How to think, live, and succeed in a Jupiterian way."
Keep in mind that Templeton has *Mercury completely attuned to*
Jupiter since they are conjunct and also in Jupiter's sign Sagittarius.

Success is not a set of circumstances—it is a set of attitudes....Energy
and enthusiasm...are essential to reach goals and overcome minor setbacks. My strategies are:

- **Be grateful for what you have.** All of us have things for which we
  should be thankful. But we often overlook accomplishments such as a
  solid job or good health because we are obsessed with trying to achieve
  what we don't yet possess.

  Working hard to reach a goal is important, but it can cause problems
  for those who focus on that goal and nothing else. Without stopping to
  appreciate what you have already achieved—and realizing that it can all
  disappear overnight due to some quirk of fate—you leave yourself
  unprepared for inevitable setbacks.

- **Be enthusiastic about everything you do.** Enthusiasm—that state of exuberance in which all things seem possible—is what drives each of us to pursue something we love.

    The individual who takes up an activity as a positive adventure can inspire the same attitude in others. The employee who looks for ways to enjoy his/her work—and to be enthusiastic about it—sets the stage for others to follow his example.

    It takes practice to do anything well. Instead of dwelling on your dissatisfaction, focus on your happiness and watch it expand. A smile is contagious...and while no one can be sunny all the time, if you take up your task with enthusiasm, it is likely that those around you will catch your spirit. Conversely, negative behavior can destroy that spirit.

    It's also important to evaluate your level of enthusiasm. *Questions to ask yourself...*

    When I am asked to do a job, do I accept it enthusiastically and give it my all?

    Do I avoid cutting corners and give as much effort as promised or even more?

    Do I accept each assignment as a fresh challenge and a chance to grow as both a professional and a person?

    If the answer to any of these questions is *no*, you must assess why your enthusiasm has diminished.

    By developing a happy, positive acceptance of the good things that you have right now, you can be sure that you will know how to enjoy the surprises that come your way in the future.

- **Make sure your job is your career.** A job can sustain your interest while you make enough money to support yourself in a comfortable lifestyle.

    But a career is more than that—it is a *vocation*. The word *vocation* comes from the Latin root *to call*. Therefore, your vocation is a *calling* and, in a very deep sense, finding your vocation is finding yourself. When you have found your calling, you can give love through your work.

    In fact, love is the key to successfully mastering your vocation. It directs you to those special talents you can give the world and shows you how to share them with others. It can return rewards far greater than the accumulation of wealth.

- **Realize that success is a journey, not a destination.** Successful people do not stop working hard once they've reached their goals. Instead, they set new goals.

- **Learn as much as possible from those around you.** You possess an inner wisdom that enables you to determine who your teachers are and what they have to teach you.

    To find your teachers, look at the people closest to you—your family, your friends and your co-workers. The people with whom you spend the most time can tell you much about yourself.

To find teachers who will help you to become successful, carefully study the behavior and actions of those you admire a great deal. Look for someone with honesty, integrity and compassion, since these are the basic ingredients of a truly successful person.

And by becoming this kind of person, you will attract others of similar virtue. Your inner success will automatically create your outer success.

- **Perseverance is the difference between success and defeat.** Reaching a goal may require repeated attempts. Each attempt brings you closer to achieving the objective and in the process helps you set other goals as well. Among these may be personal redirection or the achievement of a greater good that you had not initially planned.

Perseverance is the voice within, urging you that *if at first you don't succeed, try, try, again.* To persevere is to remain constant to a purpose, idea or task in the face of obstacles and discouragement.

In order to persevere, you must have positive and loving thoughts. That's because they spark a whole range of feelings that lift your spirits. If, on the other hand, you concentrate on negative thoughts and fearful emotions, you'll conjure up an even greater negativity. You'll also be more likely to abandon the goal you are trying to achieve.

♃ / ♀
Jupiter/Venus Contrasts

Jupiter is enhancing and furthering, extending and enriching energy. Being much slower than Mercury, it works with a different level of issues: power in society, self-esteem and belief in ourselves, and progress and bounty in nature. Jupiter, when waxing strong, urges us to cross the great water, make steps forward, reach out and externalize ourselves. It stimulates activity, bravado, confidence and intensity of social energy.
—Palden Jenkins in *Living in Time*

"Intensity of social energy" I find a particularly apt phrase for Jupiter, and we cannot explore Jupiter's nature thoroughly without mentioning the intriguing similarities and differences between Venus's social activity and that of Jupiter. Obviously, Jupiter is far more impersonal than Venus *at the level of the archetypal symbol;*

Jupiter is universal whereas Venus focuses on other people in a more immediate setting and in a personal way. When one compares Venus in any sign with Jupiter in the same sign, some very interesting comparisons emerge which give us a new perspective on both Venus and Jupiter. Such an exercise demonstrates how Jupiter operates in a larger arena than does Venus, which is probably why Jupiter has been called the "greater benefic" and Venus the "lesser benefic."

Venus, on one hand, weighs everything and is very self-oriented, pleasure-loving and limited to a relatively narrow field of action. It is often possessive; witness, for example, Venus in Taurus [a Venus sign] and its keyword "I have." Jupiter is usually more generous and supportive of freedom of behavior in others. Jupiter is, at best, more tolerant, less exclusive, less judgmental, more accepting, and more trusting than Venus. Venus is far more *demanding* in human relationships than is Jupiter, because it tends to focus on exclusively personal needs and tastes. In fact, it is instructive that, when Venus is in the two Jupiter signs (Pisces and Sagittarius), it more often than not exemplifies Venus' more generous and noble qualities.

Perhaps the most surprising thing I have come across in my research into Jupiter for this book is how consistently many of astrology's most gifted writers have referred to a Venus/Jupiter link, even though I had not consciously noticed it to be prominent, except for the age-old joint reference to Venus and Jupiter as the two "benefics" which traditionally smooth the road of life and success, providing wealth, pleasure, and prosperity. However, their interrelationship goes much deeper than that and pervades our entire outlook on life and social relations.

Charles Carter once again holds up some interesting observations for us to consider:

> *Jupiter is pre-eminently the planet of fresh contacts and new acquaintance. Venus is social, but it has a certain static element and does not seek fresh experiences*; this is the province of Jupiter, and it is generally found that, if this body be strong, the native has many happy and fruitful associations with others, which are none the less profitable because the Jovian*

---

* This is an important, extremely accurate, and rarely-mentioned aspect of Venus. Witness Venus in its own signs, Taurus and Libra, where it is especially strong, and you will find a remarkable passivity in all types of human relations, and a notable disinclination toward dynamic action.

does not hold himself tied by them and constantly shuffles his friendships and his interests.

Landis Knight Green, in *The Astrologer's Manual*, also explores Jupiter's involvement with love and romance:

> *Jupiter tends to idealize love and to create romantic enthusiasm. An exaggeration of this would be seen in the tendency to worship the lover by putting him or her on a pedestal: Don Quixote rides in this direction. Jupiter can also describe a more spiritual or intellectual form of love. In a general sense, it expands whatever it comes in contact with; in contrast, Saturn has a subduing effect. Jupiter's effect in one's love life may be more important than has been previously supposed. There may be a sense of excitement and adventure associated with this planet, especially during the period of adolescence (fourteenth to twenty-first years). Its transits through the Zodiac and the aspects it forms to the natal planets have a strong effect on a person's love life.*

Likewise, Green states, "The beauty of Jupiter can be Venusian beauty magnified or amplified many times" and adds that Jupiter always "gives something out, extending itself." Venus, on the other hand, is more magnetic—drawing to itself.

In *Astrology, the Divine Science*, Moore and Douglas likewise connect Venus and Jupiter, as well as the Moon:

> *The glyph for Jupiter shows the crescent Moon turned outward and surmounting an arm of the cross. It is reminiscent of Venus but with the Moon rather than the Sun raised aloft. This elevated Moon suggests the spiritualizing of Matter through the orderly process of evolution. Jupiter, the planet of wisdom and planned expansion, is related to the Moon and Venus because the unfoldment of man's higher abstract mind is a natural outgrowth of his gradually developing psychic mechanism of personal feelings and social responses.*

> *Together, the Moon, Venus, and Jupiter represent successive stages in the evolution of consciousness through the creation of family, social, and civic relationships. Jupiter lives up to its name of the greater benefic by bestowing the abundance for which the Moon provides the raw materials and Venus the artistic inspiration. It stimulates the mind to look beyond the*

names and forms of things in order to encompass their deeper purposes and philosophical implications.

Even the psychic readings of Edgar Cayce, whose brand of astrology was not at all traditional nor derived from old-fashioned textbooks, repeatedly interweave Venus and Jupiter, as in the following two excerpts from Life Readings for two different individuals:

> *In Venus with Jupiter, we see the ability to appreciate those things and experiences which are from the realm of the Universal Consciousness—as indicated in the song of the bird, the music of the stream, the beauty of nature. Yet, with Jupiter these become Universal forces, or activities in the material plane which will have to do with groups and masses, rather than with individuals—though the application may be individual. (2869-1)*

> *As we find...those influences in the astrological aspects show Jupiter as the ruling force (entered from Jupiter). Hence...the entity's activities must have to do with the many...Those influences in Venus make for an open, frank, loving disposition; making for friends in almost every walk of life. (1442-1)*

Note that, in the second quote, both planets have a *social* role to play.

Ellen McCaffery, a talented historian of astrology as well as the author of an excellent basic textbook of astrology, expresses beautifully and concisely Jupiter's contribution to the life of the affections and the human capacity for giving of one's self:

> *The emotions can become beautiful under Jupiter, but they are always expanded in scope. The moon and Venus may express tenderness to one, but Jupiter may express benevolence, kindness and generosity to everyone...Under its ray, the moral qualities within man begin to develop. Largeness of outlook is cultivated. There is nothing petty or small about Jupiter. It stands for soul growth, expansion and magnanimity.*
>
> *(Graphic Astrology)*

Jupiter & "Success"

> *Only the money earned by meritorious actions can lead to happiness, peace, patience and contentment. Money earned otherwise leads to ever increasing greed and covetousness. A rich man without contentment is a beggar and very poor, for the hunger*

*of such a man would not be satisfied even if he got all
the good things of the world, as none can be satisfied
without contentment.*
                    —From *Philosophy of the Masters*

I mentioned earlier in this chapter that both Venus and Jupiter are traditionally regarded as the two "benefics" which make life easier, more pleasurable, and which contribute toward wealth and prosperity. (There is no doubt about this correlation, although once again I must pour cold water on the fantasies of lazy people by reminding them that Saturn's effort and discipline must always be employed as well.) Before leaving the subject, we should briefly explore why Jupiter is so intimately connected with worldly success of many sorts.

In essence, Jupiter might be regarded as living proof of the power of positive thinking. If one radiates open-minded, tolerant, high-spirited joy in living, it does tend to attract positive responses in return. In addition, a generous, broadly-inclusive approach toward all sorts of people, wherein one authentically respects the humanness of all other individuals, cannot help but engender a certain loyalty and admiration in the minds of others. Grant Lewi put it this way when writing about Sagittarian types of people:

*...success is something that will accrue when the life is
active, alert, eager, whole-souled, warm-hearted, joyous, linked
to realities greater than those of the mere workaday world.*
                    (Your Greatest Strength)

On another, more esoteric level, one might hypothesize that Jupiter's gift of success is actually good karma, something one has earned in past lives through effort, generosity, and cultivating the nobler dimensions of self. A mind that is born with an elevated point of view and an inherent faith in a greater beneficent power is more likely to be free of fear and thus is naturally open to life's opportunities on all levels.

Edgar Cayce characterizes Jupiter as often having a connection with "great amounts of this world's goods," a description which coincides with the *abundance* and bounty Jupiter often seems to represent. Cayce, importantly, cautions one parent of a strongly Jupiterian person that the child should be trained throughout his youth "as to the use of wealth—as its being *lent from Creative Forces and energies*, and not for self-indulgence..." (Life Reading #1206-3).

Dale Carnegie

In a book about Jupiter, we cannot pass by the most famous exponent of "the power of positive thinking" in the 20th century, Dale Carnegie. Born in poverty on November 24, 1888, he developed expertise in public speaking, both teaching it and doing it extensively himself on lecture tours. In 1936, his book *How to Win Friends and Influence People* was published; it went on to sell over 5 million copies by the time he died in 1955. It was brimming with optimism and such homilies as "Believe that you will succeed and you will."

His birth data, not surprisingly, exhibits numerous cosmic imprints for an optimistic, visionary—and yet practical—view of life. Both his Sun and his Jupiter were in Sagittarius, and his Jupiter is also trine Saturn (he always directed his advice mostly to business people) and sextile Uranus. In addition, his Sun was opposite the Neptune/Pluto conjunction in Gemini, another indication of visionary creativity. Perhaps his philosophy is best summed up in the title of another best-seller that he published in 1948: *How to Stop Worrying and Start Living*. —S. A.

This is an important distinction to keep in mind, for Jupiter can indeed be great and bountiful; and this vastness of spirit and abundance of energy is really too enormous to be contained within one human being. When individuals try to contain it or to own it or claim it as their personal achievement, there ensues a massive ego-inflation which—if allowed to grow unchecked—can often lead not only to self-indulgence, but to various forms of self-destruction.

As we will see later in this chapter, *waste* is often the worst trait of Jupiterians. I believe this is what Cayce was referring to in the above quotation when he warned that such people need training in the proper use of wealth. Ideally, Jupiterians *share* their abundance freely and happily, grateful that they have been given the opportunity to help God or life or nature dispense the abundance that they are channels for. And, when Cayce said that wealth should be regarded as being "lent from the Creative Forces and energies," he is setting forth an example of the proper attitude that anyone should have who is blessed with not only especially great wealth, but also anyone with a great talent or personality or love. If one can see those creative energies as *flowing through* himself or herself, and see such abundance as a *gift,* the positive influence of these special abilities will grow continually, for the benefit of many people far beyond the individual's immediate circle.

Andrew Carnegie & Paul Mellon: Jupiterian Philanthropists

Although Andrew Carnegie is better known than Paul Mellon, there are certain similarities astrologically, and certainly both men's humanitarian activities are remarkable. Since Andrew Carnegie is the more controversial of the two, let us first discuss the chart of this Sagittarian steel magnate, born in Scotland November 25, 1835.

Carnegie grew up in poverty and received little more than a primary school education. In 1848 he emigrated to the United States with his family and settled in what is now the Pittsburgh area. Convinced by his experience with the Pennsylvania railroad of the coming importance of iron and steel, he formed his own company; eventually his organizational abilities and business acumen led to his developing the most dominant steel company in the industry. He eventually made a huge fortune, partly with the help of extraordinarily talented associates whom he was able to recognize and retain, and in 1889 he consolidated all his holdings into the Carnegie Steel Company. That same year, he published an article entitled *Wealth* that became extremely popular and which was widely reprinted and discussed during that era when America was rapidly growing fantastically wealthy. In that article, Carnegie outlined his view that it was the duty of the rich to see that their surplus wealth was distributed for the betterment of civilization.

Before discussing how he attempted to live up to this *credo,* I should mention some of the key factors in his birth chart. Although his exact birth time is unknown, we do know that his Sun, Mars and Venus were all in Sagittarius, with his Sagittarian Venus exactly quincunx Jupiter (exalted) in Cancer. (His Venus was thus doubly colored by Jupiter's hue.) How much he patriotically gave to the U.S.A. and its people (Cancer Jupiter) will be shown below, but the intensity of this exact aspect between the two benefics should not be underestimated. (It is yet another example of how *all* aspects which are multiples of 30° should be considered strong, especially in a natal chart.) His humanitarian proclivities are also clearly seen in his Aquarian Moon, augmented by Uranus and Neptune also being in Aquarius! Pluto in Aries trine Mars also reflects an excellent image of the steel industry!

All the while he worked dynamically for business success, he closely followed national and international developments as the 20th Century dawned, particularly the quest for world peace—a perfect manifestation of the idealistic humanitarianism of a Sagittarius/Aquarius combination. He expressed his views in many writings and before legislative committees. During his leisure time, he traveled, wrote, and expanded his artistic tastes. He was always conscious of the disparities of wealth between social classes; and—even though he was at times criticized for being too tough on labor in the steel industry—the fact is that early in his career he had written of the right of labor to organize (a radical idea at that time!). Also, he had introduced the idea of a sliding scale based on how the business was doing, an early precursor of the profit-sharing plans now pervasive in U.S.A. industries. In addition, the contrast he saw between American egalitarianism and the unequal class structures in Britain and other European societies drove him to the conclusion that access to education (Jupiter and Sagittarius) was the key to American democracy's stability and industrial accomplishments—a view which motivated him to initiate many of his philanthropic projects.

It is estimated that Carnegie gave at least $350 million to various humanitarian causes and foundations, an amount—if translated into today's dollars—which would exceed two billion dollars! And the value of these cultural resources today is virtually incalculable. For example, in addition to supporting a great many colleges, he endowed approximately 3,000 "free public libraries" throughout the English-speaking world, most of which are in the United States. He financed the Carnegie Institute of Pittsburgh, housing an art gallery, a natural history museum which also supported archeological expeditions, a hall for musical performance, and the Carnegie Institute of Technology, today the basis for Carnegie-Mellon University. In addition, The Carnegie Institution of Washington was set up to encourage pure research in the natural and physical sciences, and The Foundation for the Advancement of Teaching was created to provide pensions for university professors. Throughout Andrew Carnegie's life, from impoverished beginnings to a preoccupation with international affairs and education to his ultimate unprecedented level of philanthropy, we see the Jupiterian principles of faith, improvement, and generosity constantly expressed.

Although perhaps less well known than his father Andrew Mellon, a successful banker as well as Secretary of the U.S. Treasury in the 1920's, Paul Mellon is—like Carnegie—another Pittsburgh-based person who has Jupiter in Cancer. Unlike Carnegie, whose family was extremely poor, Mellon was born into great wealth and culture on June 11, 1907. As *Current Biography Yearbook* says, "Paul Mellon has distinguished himself as a philanthropist, a conservationist, an art collector, and a benefactor of the humanities. Concerned less with directing the financial empire created by his father...than in using the family fortune to benefit mankind, he has worked through several foundations to sponsor projects in education, the arts, archeology, and medicine." (This seems a natural expression of his stellium of Jupiter, Neptune, and Mercury in Cancer opposite a wide Uranus/Mars Conjunction in Capricorn.)

Most people who have been to Washington, D.C. have visited the National Gallery of Art, of which Mellon was President for years. He was broadly educated and knowledgeable in art, history, and the classics, and he had a special appreciation for French and British paintings. All of this is nicely symbolized by his Mercury (especially strong since his Sun is in Gemini) at 8° Cancer being conjunct Neptune at 11° Cancer and Jupiter at 14° Cancer. His Cancerian attunement (augmented by Jupiter in that sign) is shown in the many ways he cultivated an appreciation of varied cultural heritages, particularly specific artistic traditions; and in fact, museums are specifically Cancerian in that they are repositories of artifacts and memories of the past. The fact that he was also an especially active *collector* of great art also points to the prominence of the Cancer Jupiter in his chart. (Additionally, he was always an avid horseman—an expression of a strong Jupiter opposite Mars and Uranus.)

Although it would require many pages to detail all the contributions Mellon made personally and through trusts he was involved in, he was far ahead of his time (Jupiter) in supporting activities, research, services, and publishing related to public health, conservation, mental health, and psychology. In fact, the visionary qualities of his Mercury/Jupiter/Neptune stellium were most evident in his establishing the Bollingen Foundation, named after C.G. Jung's retreat at Bollingen, Switzerland and dedicated to a wide variety of scholarship in the humanities, including poetry, archeology, mythology, and the history of religion. Perhaps most importantly, this foundation financed the publication of C.G. Jung's collected works in excellent translations and at quite low prices due to the subsidy of the Foundation. This enabled Jung's work to reach a much broader range of individuals and libraries than would have otherwise been possible.

Mellon was, in fact, Chairman of the Bollingen Foundation and was described by a college president as an ideal person to run such a foundation, always "alert to ideas, objective in judgment, unafraid of controversy, but not given to charging after trouble for its own sake." Perhaps when the cultural history of this century's renewed interest in astrology, mythology, and the psychology of religion is written many years from now, Mellon will be recognized as a major pioneer in his promotion of new thinking who, while respecting traditions in every field, also smashed open the doors to new and intellectually revolutionary visions of humanity's potential—an expression of natal Jupiter (conjunct Mercury and Neptune) opposite both revolutionary Uranus and courageous Mars.
—S.A.*

Donna Cunningham shows how people can in many situations make their own luck, and she illuminates the connection between luck and worldly success in the following paragraphs from *An Astrological Guide to Self Awareness.*

Openness and gregariousness are also Jupiter traits, and they play a part in success too. One executive has analyzed the circumstances that led to the big job offers in successful executives' lives. He found that, in the majority of cases, they arose through a chain of acquaintances. He found that lucky people were gregarious and took an interest in people. In turn, their

---

* The birth charts are not printed here because they would be based on speculative birth times and thus probably misleading. Nevertheless, the data included in the above analysis is reliable.

openness also made it easy for other people to approach them in a friendly manner.

Apparently, then, that old saying about "It's who you know that counts," is true, but you make your own luck by making positive connections with people—not that this should be our purpose in making friends or being helpful, but it can be an outgrowth of it.

Optimism and enthusiasm are also associated with Jupiter, and their relationship to good luck is very significant. Enthusiasm is contagious and makes others more receptive to you and your ideas. Out of two equally qualified people, who is more likely to be hired, the depressed, apathetic person or the enthusiastic ball of fire? Thus, enthusiastic persons often have more "luck" coming their way—they land the job, they make the sale, they meet their loves.

Jupiter's influence does not *guarantee* luck or worldly success, but certainly one increases the odds of such positive outcomes if one can express the better possibilities of Jupiter's potential.

Jupiter & Emotions? A Secret About Jupiter

It may seem strange to some readers to speak of Jupiter in relation to "emotions" or to hear authors quoted regarding how "the emotions can become beautiful" under Jupiter, as Ellen McCaffery wrote. After all, no one has ever described a Sagittarian Sun sign person as "emotional" and certainly not "sensitive." Actually, "emotional" and "sensitive" are quite different things, although these terms are usually used almost interchangeably these days. Although no fire sign could be described accurately as "sensitive," certainly they all dramatically *e-mote!* (From the Latin, *to move out,* to release energy outwardly!) When one defines emotion literally like that, then of course Leo and Sagittarius become two of the most "emotional" signs!

However, the link between Jupiter and sensitivity is important because those who have a strong attunement to Jupiter need not only Saturn but also human sensitivity to bring their largeness of vision and grand schemes down to realizable human dimensions. Sensitivity is needed for Jupiterians to avoid the excesses that they are so prone to. Sensitivity to others and their feelings enables the Jupiter person to harness that expansive, encouraging power to nurture and sustain human beings and their aspirations.

This necessary link between Jupiter and sensitivity is perfectly symbolized by the traditional "exaltation" of Jupiter in Cancer. In stark contrast to a Jupiterian's tendency never to see what is right in front of them and to always focus on the large and distant, Cancer's focus is always on the *immediate* circle of family, friends, tribe, community. Cancerians pay attention to how others *react* emotionally to what they do and say. And it must be said that, if there is one fault of strongly Jupiterian types, it may be that they don't really notice the emotional reactions of others to what they do and say. In fact, they are known for being "tactless," feeling propelled to express their grand beliefs and "truths" regardless of others' reactions. In this light, Jupiter's co-rulership of Pisces becomes more important; for Pisces combines the idealism of Jupiter with sensitivity to people's emotions, something Sagittarius often fails to achieve.

When I first started studying astrology in the mid-1960's, one of my earliest observations was how well Cancer and Sagittarius energies combined in individuals I met at that time. I especially liked their outspokenness and enthusiasm, but tempered by the sensitivity of Cancer. And the Sagittarius influence seems to eliminate the worst Cancerian traits, such as fearfulness, paranoia, and, in general, hiding from life.

It seemed that the qualities of those two signs complemented each other perfectly. It was only later that I discovered the concept of "exaltation" and learned that even the Greeks over 2,000 years ago considered Jupiter to be exalted in Cancer. The idea that exaltations symbolize the *ideal* expression of a planet's function for spiritual growth and the optimum use of that planet's energy for creative purposes makes a lot of sense to me. And Jupiter's exaltation in Cancer shows that Jupiter is expressed best if combined with empathy and consideration for others. Jupiterian people need to cultivate "down-home" abilities to communicate with others on an emotional level.

Charles Carter writes:

> *[Jupiter] is exalted in Cancer, in which sign it gains kindliness and gentleness, and expands the sympathies of the sign beyond the home-circle to which they are apt to be limited.*
> *(The Principles of Astrology)*

Similarly, Isabel Hickey writes in *Astrology, A Cosmic Science:*

> *In the sympathetic, mothering sign of Cancer it is a powerful position.... It expands the feelings, and expansive, optimistic feelings are the secret of living fully.*

Jupiter's Positive & Negative Expression

Since we will be going into detailed explorations of Jupiter in each sign and house later in this book, at this point it is necessary only to mention some general guidelines and overall principles to be aware of. Interpreting Jupiter does present some unique problems, partially because it is such an abstract principle, and partly because, when functioning within an actual birth chart, Jupiter expands and amplifies whatever it touches. By itself, it mainly shows *potential*, a certain *orientation* depending on its house position, and a specific *energy* attunement based on its sign position. But just because Jupiter is a "benefic" planet in essence, there are still definite positive *and negative* manifestations that are not dependent solely upon the ease or discord of its aspects, as rigid-minded astrologers have often maintained. I have mentioned some of these manifestations earlier in this book, but certain others must also be explored to give the reader a full picture of this planet's operation in our lives. And, even though Jupiter at best is supremely positive in its action, we should not emulate the wild-eyed Jupiterian optimist who habitually neglects to see the not-so-positive facets right in front of him/ her. As Dane Rudhyar wrote in *An Astrological Study of Psychological Complexes,*

> *Jupiter, worshipped by medieval astrologers as the Great Benefic, [can] also...become a power for evil. It can of itself be a force of self-destruction, if the function of self-preservation and self-sustainment turns into an uncontrolled desire for self-aggrandizement at any cost.*

In its *positive* expression, Jupiter is generous, forward thinking, and perennially hopeful. As Moore and Douglas wrote, "the real magnitude of Jupiter lies in its *"power of vision"* (my italics).

> *Physically, Jupiter is a large planet with the largesse it promises. It is also extremely light, being composed of rarefied gases, and conveys a corresponding psychological quality of buoyancy. However, the real magnitude of Jupiter lies in its*

*power of vision. The spiritually evolved Jupiterian has the gift
of prophecy and is imbued with an optimistic faith in nature's
abundance. As a result of this capacity for positive thinking, he
is often favored with the personal prestige and general prosperity he assumes to be his due.   (Astrology, The Divine Science)*

Paul Wright wrote, as I quoted in Chapter 1, that the Jupiterian
person sees the future potential before others do. In fact, Jupiter is
obsessed with the future; to such a person, the grass is always
greener in the future and beyond the distant horizon. As Charles
Carter wrote in *Essays on the Foundations of Astrology,*

> *But it is natural that he should desire to know as much as
> he can, and hence arises the interest in prediction and prophecy
> that are Jovian traits, as well as the simple fact that it is largely
> in the future that the Jovian lives mentally: he is interested in
> it for its own sake. Jupiter seeks new experiences, and it is only
> in the future as regards time and in the unknown distances as
> regards space that he can find them.*

It seems to me that no other type of person needs a truth to live
by so profoundly as a Jupiterian person. In fact, nothing is so pitiful
as a Jupiter type of person who does not believe in anything. The
search for truth in itself gives such people some sense of direction,
even if in many cases they seem to specialize in never finding it!
Jupiter's positive and negative potentials are vividly described by
Landis Knight Green:

> *A positive Jupiter placement denotes a search for truth,
> frankness, optimism, good judgment, joviality, gregariousness,
> and an ability to reach for new or greater goals of a more
> universal nature. If it is poorly placed, Jupiter can contribute to
> pretension, exaggeration, excessive evangelism, rashness, gull-
> ibility, boasting, undirected wanderlust, and wasteful specula-
> tion (gambling). In a spiritual sense Jupiter represents revela-
> tion and the imparting of wisdom and knowledge...At the root
> of his deeds is the earnest need to seek and demonstrate (teach)
> truth and to encourage others. The weaker Jupiterian tends to
> romanticize his existence, and he is usually characterized by
> restlessness and an arrogant and unfruitful self-righteousness.*
> *(The Astrologer's Manual)*

You will note that Green mentions the words "boasting" and "arrogant." Those with strong Jupiter attunement want to be *bigger than life*; they want to express, and often want to be *seen* as expressing generosity, idealism, and high-mindedness. If such a tendency degenerates or is expressed negatively, however, then arrogance and obnoxiously self-righteous behavior can result. More than in any other sign, we see in Sagittarius quite frequent expressions of *indignation*. In other words, their substantial pride and dignity have been offended. And this is also a fairly common reaction in those with a strong Jupiterian attunement.

Jupiter's Positive Expression	Jupiter's Negative Expression
Faith; reliance on higher power or greater plan; openness to grace; optimism; openness to self's need for improvement	*Over-confidence; laziness; scattering energy; leaving the work to others; irresponsibility; over-extending self or promising too much*

Jupiterians can be great preachers (i.e., promoters of "truth") or salespeople (i.e., promoters of products), and they can inspire trust and encourage others toward greater aspirations; but they can also exhibit pomposity, bigotry, and cynicism. The writer "Raphael" nearly a century ago wrote that Jupiter can produce judges and archbishops, but also that Jupiter is responsible for quacks, cheats, and drunkards. One of the negative manifestations of Jupiter most often noted in astrological literature is hypocrisy; and it is often pointed out that politicians and priests are often guilty of this: posing as noble and upstanding, publicly saying one high-minded thing but doing another in their own lives. It is a fine line that people walk when they hold themselves out to others as leaders, idealists, and trustworthy sources of inspiration, and once again we can find a good explanation of this phenomenon in Charles Carter's writings.

In *Essays* (page 140) Carter points out that those who are truly qualified to offer good advice to others in most fields are necessarily few. Carter states that the "Jovian proclivity towards hypocrisy" stems from giving in to the temptation to pretend to possess "inside information"; and he mentions stock brokers, race horse tipsters, and the like as common examples of Jupiterians gone to excess in their claims to be able to impart special knowledge. If he had seen

Jupiter is given to long-winded and sometimes pompous preaching of personal beliefs.

1990's cable TV, he no doubt would have added to this list of charlatans the promoters of many get-rich-quick schemes and some of the self-help gurus who claim that overnight success in solving one's deepest problems should be expected. Carter also points out the parallel of proponents of "various cults that represent themselves as having the secret of some short-cut way to esoteric powers and knowledge." He also says that "giving good advice is strong in both Jovian signs" and that, since doing so is extremely flattering to many grateful people, it is extremely appealing to one's vanity when these people shower their thanks and admiration upon the advisor.

Paul Wright mentions some of the people who were considered by many to be great teachers or gurus, but who have been accused by others as promising more than they could deliver:

Bhagwan Rajneesh was a Sagittarian Sun who promised much and at the end of the day generated much disappointment and disillusion. Billy Graham has a Sag Moon; L. Ron Hubbard, the founding force of Scientology had a Sagittarian ascendant. Krishnamurti had a Sag Moon; he was the great hope for the theosophists, hailed as a Buddha incarnate. But in the end he rejected the title and their claims. Werner Erhard, the founder of EST in California in 1971 is a Sag Moon. Some of those figures held up in the 1960's as spiritual mentors were often strong in Sag: Alan Watts (Sagittarian ascendant), for example, wrote a number of books that became essential reading for spiritual seekers.

Some astrological writers have maintained that Jupiter is incapable of evil, but merely exemplifies an excess of expansionism and optimism at times. However, as we've shown, Jupiter's nature and energy can have many adverse manifestations. If pride was the cause of the "fall of man" in the Garden of Eden, then certainly Jupiterians have a capacity for making mistakes based on pride! Some writers have also noted, with considerable justification, that "the sins of Jupiter are sins of omission, not commission." In other words, they often promise the ultimate but quite often fail to deliver! And Carter states that, however one defines evil, surely Jupiter is capable of substantial negative behavior because of its tendency to be *reckless*. And then Carter mentions the details of a couple of major criminals who have, among other significant chart factors, major Jupiter aspects!

I trust that, at this point, readers will not be tempted to view Jupiter through rose-colored glasses. Undoubtedly, its most positive expressions are noble and admirable, but we should not ignore the other side of the coin. In *Your Greatest Strength*, Grant Lewi concisely summarizes some of the more problematical sides of Jupiter's range of expression in his section on Sagittarius. I am quoting this here because I think one would lose no accuracy by substituting "Jupiterian" for "Sagittarian" throughout the quotation.

Lack of purpose, fickleness of aim, shallowness, lack of direction, and lack of ability to concentrate are Sagittarius' worst faults. The negative Sagittarians are endlessly active, endlessly doing things with no apparent purpose, ceaselessly on the go, and likely to be chatterboxes. To those who value solitude, or some hiatus in the sound and fury of life, Sagittarius, in its negative polarities, can be pretty wearing. They are all outgoing, all for talk and going places and doing things, all for activity as such which, when it lacks a purpose or a direction, can simply wear out others—seldom the Sagittarian who, positive or negative, seems to draw on an endless supply of vitality.

Waste is the sin of the negative Sagittarius—waste of personal powers, when the universality of outlook scatters itself and becomes mere wandering of mind and attention; waste of money and material things, when the rising-above money becomes extravagance and lack of respect for property.

Lest I conclude this section on too negative a note for such a positive planet, I should emphasize that, in many people, Jupiter's gifts, positive qualities, and highly developed abilities are, more often than not, *taken for granted* by the individual himself or herself! Such abilities and modes of personal expression come so easily and naturally to many people that they are relatively unconscious. This is another reason for studying Jupiter in one's chart: not only to discover potential, but also to become not proud, but *realistic* about the more developed and positive forms of expression and talents that one is already attuned to.

General Guidelines for Interpreting Jupiter

*Wherever Jupiter appears in the horoscope there
is an area of potential improvement and expansion,
an opportunity to test or demonstrate one's higher
ideals and philosophy of life.*
(*The Astrologer's Manual* by Landis Knight Green)

In the following section, I want to list very concisely a number of guidelines which I have found especially useful for understanding Jupiter in specific charts. Referring to these guidelines can be a particularly fruitful exercise, whether one is exploring one's own chart's potential or engaging in a dialogue of discovery with a client. The reader will have to *apply* these guidelines to each specific chart, but it should be emphasized that they can pertain to Jupiter's sign position, house position, and/or aspects. It should also be stressed that any chart factor involving Jupiter is *especially important* if one has Pisces or Sagittarius emphasized in the birth chart.

NOTE: Whenever I mention a "strong Jupiter" or similar phrase, the statement will usually also apply to those with major placements in Sagittarius or Pisces.

---

a) Jupiter expands the flow of energy indicated by the element where it is placed in the birth chart; often, one has to simply tap into that source consciously to realize it and to use it.

b) A strong Jupiter usually manifests as a hopeful, buoyant, upbeat personality—often quite humorous. Jupiter's sign often gives a clue to the type of humor.

c) Jupiter's placement can give an indication of a sense of meaning and direction in life that can guide the person, and points to the quest for a truth to live by.

d) Wherever Jupiter is in the birth chart is where you want to constantly explore new horizons. This is easier to do in some signs and houses than others, depending on social conventions, moral upbringing, etc. In any case, one wants to continually *improve* whatever area of life is indicated by Jupiter in the chart.

e) Jupiter's placement often shows, upon deeper inquiry and especially with older people, where the individual is working on developing a system of values and deep, wide-ranging understanding through study and/or experience.

f) Jupiter's position indicates an area of enthusiasm and optimism, where the individual can readily put one's confidence into action. In this area, the person expects benefit and looks for opportunities to grow, as well as opportunities *to give of one's own inner abundance*. (This is an important point since Jupiter—an extraordinarily generous planet—indicates not only taking from life by grabbing hold of opportunities, but giving back to life, often in a universally beneficent way.)

g) Jupiter's placement shows where one invites experience (Marc E. Jones) and where one has the capacity to make use of opportunities (Grant Lewi).

h) Jupiter's position reveals where an individual feels a release from pressure and fear and experiences the room to breathe, expand, grow, and express oneself. Its placement (especially its sign) shows what sorts of things and activities can restore your faith when you're down and can help you bounce back. (Rebecca Wilson)

i) Jupiter lends a sense of moral conviction to anything it touches, giving meaning and motivation to the person for promoting certain ideas, ideals, goals, etc., as well as encouraging others toward those goals. There is a strong urge toward honesty and openness in the area of life Jupiter is focused on.

j) Jupiter represents an urge toward a larger order or to connect the self with something greater than one's self, and this urge is most strongly felt in the areas symbolized by Jupiter's sign, house, and closest aspects.

k) Jupiter's placement indicates where one should take risks, for taking chances is absolutely necessary to attain progress in any sphere of life. The door of opportunity may be there, but one must have the courage to walk through it.

l) Jupiter's position shows where probable success, prosperity, and rapid development are likely, for it is there that bountiful energy can be experienced and that one has enhanced abilities to express oneself and share with society at large.

m) Jupiter's placement reveals where one can develop confidence and self-esteem through actively taking chances, based on trust in one's own potential. This can develop only through tapping into the source of abundance within oneself and allowing this energy or talent or higher mind the room to operate in one's life.

CHAPTER 3

Exploring the
Jupiterian Personality

The size of a man can be measured by the
size of the thing that makes him angry.
—J. Kentfield Morley

In order to explore the Jupiter archetype in more detail than I have already mentioned, it will be necessary to describe various types of personalities and behaviors which naturally will bring to mind typical Sun in Sagittarius characteristics. In other cases, I may describe what sounds more like a Pisces expression of Jupiter's range of manifestation. And naturally, since so much more has been written in the astrological literature about Sun Sign characteristics than about planets' positions or aspects, I will necessarily be quoting often from various authors' observations about those with Sun in Sagittarius. However, it is important to clarify from the outset that I am using such commentaries to describe broadly those who have what we might call a "prominent Jupiter theme" in their birth charts. Such prominence can derive not only from the Ascendant or various planets being placed in Sagittarius or Pisces, but also from house placement (perhaps Jupiter in the first house or an energized ninth house) or close aspects or aspect structures (such as Jupiter square the Sun or conjunct the Moon or trine the Ascendant).

I should also mention that, although Jupiter does not usually hide its talents or make a secret of its dreams (one often wishes, in fact, that Jupiterians would be more modest or moderate!), invariably one must take into account the entire chart under consideration. A very Jupiterian person may at times veil his or her benevolence, for example, if the rest of the chart shows considerable humility. Another person who has, for example, many planets in water signs may feel too shy to express dramatically his or her higher abilities or expanded talents in a public way. And yet another person who has a prominence of Capricorn or Virgo in the birth chart may feel skeptical or even at times embarrassed about his or her own more expansive urges and natural ways of self-expression, and thus hold them back somewhat; but they will still manifest periodically, in which case there may be a bit of dual-personality syndrome that will puzzle many acquaintances. So, with that cautionary advice in mind, we can then explore the Jupiter archetype in the abstract, unmodified by the complicating factors always found in a real person and horoscope.

One accurate keyword for Jupiterians is *aspiration*. Such people are very goal-oriented, even if at times they scatter their energy on too many goals at once, or are not even fully conscious of what their goal is. As a Sagittarius-rising friend of mine once said, "I shoot lots of arrows in all sorts of directions; one is bound to hit the target!" Much the same idea is expressed in *Astrology, the Divine Science* by Moore and Douglas when they write of Sagittarians: "As soon as they spy a new vision, they shoot forth a volley of enthusiastic words in order to attract attention to their discovery." Their wide-ranging enthusiasm and boundless optimism lead to a proneness toward "doing things in a big way," or making a grand gesture or promise (much like the sign Leo in some cases) without stopping to think whether it is practical or even possible.

But in any case, those with Jupiter prominent always need at least one far-off goal to instill excitement and significance into their everyday lives. Simply having a distant dream is far more important than whatever the specific ideal or envisioned goal currently is. Some people, in fact, quickly replace one goal with another or one dream with another with lightning speed, especially those whose charts also have emphasis on Uranus, Aquarius, or Aries. Such people essentially find the humdrum of daily life to be tedious and intolerable if it is not infused with significance and enthusiasm by a great goal or vision.

The word *enthusiasm* is repeatedly encountered in the astrological literature regarding Jupiter and Sagittarius. As Grant Lewi writes of Sagittarius, "To live enthusiastically is as natural to him as to breathe" (*Your Greatest Strength*). Enthusiasm is indeed a great gift, and its importance should not be underestimated. Those who have lots of it tend to take it for granted, and those who almost totally lack it cannot imagine living in such a state of excitement! That state of exuberance in which all things seem possible is the very stuff of inspiration and creative motivation—the essential energy that drives us to pursue the distant goal, no matter how seemingly impractical or difficult the journey may be. This enthusiasm is contagious and accounts for a considerable portion of the leadership and inspirational abilities that Jupiterians exhibit. It does seem a special power—even a divine gift—to be endowed with such an energy and attitude; and in fact, the Greek root word *entheos* means "possessed by a god or other superhuman power"! Hence, in one sense, we can't blame Jupiterian people for being a bit excessive in many areas of life, and their overconfidence and extravagance is oftentimes harmless. However, if one lets oneself be caught up in this powerful, bigger-than-life energy and allows excessive ego-inflation and/or too vast an array of over-extended plans to take over one's life, this divine power can become over-amplified and all-consuming to the point that one can be destroyed or thoroughly exhausted in the process.

In addition, those around the Jupiterian may also be injured, inadvertent though this harmful result may be. It simply occurs naturally that, during those times that one feels the scope of one's personal power, energy, and influence to be expanding, promising ever greater results and realization of one's goals, one increasingly neglects the here-and-now details of everyday life and the emotional needs of those closest to him or her. Such concerns seem petty, if in fact they are noticed at all. And therefore, as has so often been said of the sign Sagittarius, the Jupiterian's sins are more often those of omission than commission; rarely do they *intend* to neglect others and their feelings. They simply do it because they have begun to feel "above it all," and often there results an impersonal insensitivity to human feelings. This naturally can make others feel small, even as the Jupiter personality increasingly feels large!

If the ego-inflation stage develops excessively, the worst traits of Jupiter sometimes begin to surface; along with the self-righteousness so often discussed can come an overbearing demeanor and a condescending way of speaking to or treating "underlings." Such a negatively manifesting Jupiter can be hurtfully demeaning to others, even though the Jupiterian may not notice the disdain in his or her attitude, but others cannot fail to experience it. Jupiter is considered exalted in Cancer for a good reason: such a placement

Jupiter is sometimes so inflated with self-importance that he's often insensitive to those around him.

symbolizes the sensitivity to others' feelings and the care for the immediate group that a Jupiterian ideally needs to have, as a balance to the more impersonal and far-reaching tendencies of this planet.

The difficulty for Jupiter types of people with dealing with the inconvenient necessities of human emotions is expressed well by Tracy Marks in her book *The Astrology of Self-Discovery*. When discussing the Moon in Sagittarius, she writes:

> *If we have a Sagittarian Moon, we need to be free to expand our boundaries—to discover and actualize new possibilities, to travel, and/or to develop our understanding. We have a generous heart and seek to give from our own bounty; we also seek to rise above our difficulties through humor and enjoyable companionship.*

> *When our real needs are not met or when we come into contact with feelings or needs which threaten us, we may express our Sagittarian nature in a defensive or distorted manner—procrastinating or avoiding immediate issues by focusing upon the future, abstract realms or escapist activities; becoming preoccupied with ideals or goals rather than current tasks; intellectualizing or philosophizing incessantly; joking inappropriately; or moving restlessly from activity to activity or person to person on an endless quest both to escape from responsibility and to fulfill our inner emptiness.*

She then goes on to explain how one's upbringing may have taught the person to be fearful of emotional closeness and to take refuge in distant realms rather than attending to one's real needs and feelings. I feel this tendency may be present in those who have a prominent Jupiter in the birth chart, not only those with Sagittarius emphasis. (Pisces is usually far more emotionally sensitive and responsive.)

The sense of superiority which people with a strong Jupiter sometimes develop can lead to rather obnoxious modes of expression, and the sense of fighting a dignified battle in a righteous and moral cause can degenerate into a hypocritical and uncompromising self-righteousness that attempts to justify virtually any heinous attitude by hiding under the veil of being morally superior. As the great psychologist and investigator of the human condition Eric Fromm wrote:

> There is perhaps no phenomenon which contains so much destructive feeling as "moral indignation," which permits envy or hate to be acted out under the guise of virtue.

This view of life dominated by a "morally superior" belief system is further explained by Paul Wright in *The Literary Zodiac*:

> Sagittarius and Jupiter, then, symbolise such things as the theocracy, or any sort of society where life is dominated by ideology, and where the prime reality is considered something over and above the world of appearances. They equate very closely to what Sorokin calls the 'ideational' culture. Sagittarius symbolises powerful and irrational belief in some entity greater than the individual, be this a religious being or a political idea. Such belief is deep rooted and impervious to argument. Convictions are not instilled by rational means and so there is no reason to assume that rational means [will] remove or modify them. Uncompromising is a word applied to Sagittarius more than to any other sign. And it is generally not enough for the Sagittarian simply to believe. His or her security seems to rest with others sharing the belief, and with expressing it. There can be a very forthright and self-righteous side to Sagittarius. In literature, a recurrent criticism leveled almost exclusively at the writers of this sign is the habit of preaching. There can be a tendency to trammel work in doctrinaire, to

burden it with a moral or political message.

Charles Carter likewise brings up the negative possibilities of the Jupiterian's love of preaching his or her inspired truth:

> *Sagittarius is certainly a vital sign in every sense and it does not keep its talents buried. It is restless, mentally and physically. What it has, it loves to impart. Hence it is not only generous or even prodigal with money, but it is also the general mentor, the preacher, the adviser. Herein lie two dangers. First of all, a preacher should be certain that he really has something useful to say and has the right to say it. Otherwise he is a mere windbag, proffering counsel to those who are as wise and virtuous as himself, or more so.*
>
> *(Essays on the Foundations of Astrology)*

These negative expressions of Jupiter are actually perversions of one of the greatest talents that this robust planet so often confers: that of the archetypal teacher of higher wisdom. As Moore and Douglas write in *Astrology, the Divine Science,*

The archetypal teacher of wisdom. (16th century France)

> *Sagittarius is both teacher and preacher. As a teacher, he tries to raise his students' sights to higher verities; as a preacher he realizes that men must be motivated to follow the paths of righteousness.*

In the most positive sense, the Jupiterian teacher *inspires* his or her students to search uncompromisingly for their own goals and truths. Such a teacher brings out the *meaning* of facts and traditions and points the student toward the possible and the potential. They can preach a philosophy of learning that is open-ended and hopeful, and which gives the student a confidence in the future and an appreciation for gaining comprehensive understanding by unflinchingly exploring endless possibilities. In a similar way, there is certainly a great need for the kind of preacher who is neither heavy-handed nor rigidly judgmental. This kind of preaching is an uplifting variety of teaching, and it fulfills the true definition of the word *education:* i.e., *to lead out* (of darkness). It is also interesting to note how many skillful teachers use that most Jupiterian of methods to draw out their students' thoughts: debate

> *If his nature is well balanced, and his environment helpful and congenial, he not only makes very rapid progress in evolution himself, but is a great centre of helpfulness and illumination for others; for he comes readily into touch with his fellow men, takes an eager interest in their true welfare, and especially in their education. He is sometimes a very successful teacher of the Socratic type, going straight to the goal and awakening the minds of his students, teaching them to observe and reason and think for themselves.* —Isabelle Pagan on Sagittarius, from *Signs of the Zodiac Analysed*, first published in 1911.

and argumentation. This kind of verbal dueling, rather similar to scoring points like an archer would when trying to hit his target, is an ancient and today much-neglected method of teaching which Jupiterians often find especially enjoyable and effective.

A primary cause of the disintegration of educational quality in the Western world, I feel, stems from the erosion of the student-teacher role because of cultural, financial, and other reasons. This has occurred at all levels of education, and the crowding of classrooms, along with the decline in authority and esteem in which the teacher is held by students and parents alike have accelerated this propensity. And now, with the increasing introduction of computer-based and TV-based instruction, this trend will no doubt continue to grow. However, if we could take advantage of the efficiencies which electronic instruction can indeed provide in certain areas of learning, and thus free up the time of teachers so they can function more as guides and counselors, monitoring the student's progress personally and academically, perhaps we could reinvigorate the teacher archetype today. As Page Smith wrote in *Killing the Spirit,*

> *There is no decent, adequate, respectable education, in the proper sense of that much-abused word, without personal involvement by a teacher with the needs and concerns, academic and personal, of his / her students. All the rest is "instruction" or "information transferral," "communication technique," or some other impersonal and antiseptic phrase, but* it is not teaching

and the student is not truly learning.

Jupiter's relationship to the teacher archetype is not confined in Western astrology. Indeed, in Hindu (or "Vedic") astrology, Jupiter is in fact called by the name *Guru* and is associated with the divine teacher who showers wisdom upon humanity, giving nobility and elevating the character spiritually and morally. This is yet another clue that indicates not only how important Jupiter is in this regard and in the science of astrology, but also how tragic it would be if we individually and as a society continue to neglect this crucial dimension of life.

A perfect example of a Jupiterian personality is Winston Churchill, born November 30, 1874, with Jupiter conjunct Mars, sextile Venus, and with both the Sun and Venus in Sagittarius. In addition to his vast writings (of *large* books), he was of course known for his oratorical skills (note the third house placements). In fact, you could say he was a preacher extraordinaire at a time when the entire Western world needed inspiration and optimism. Even his ruling planet (Venus) was in Sagittarius. Throughout World War II, he consistently assumed a higher moral plane in his speeches, which put Fascist aggression in clearer perspective. His references to "sunlit uplands," and similar visions of a brighter future, could not be more specifically Jupiterian. For example, the following quote from a speech given December 8, 1941, the day after the Pearl Harbor bombing by Japan, is especially appropriate for a fire sign leader:

> *In the past we have had a light which flickered, in the present we have a light which flames, and in the future there will be a light which shines all over the land and sea.* *

The following quote from Grant Lewi's *Your Greatest Strength* on Sagittarius reads as if it were particularly describing Churchill's role during World War II:

> *The positive Sagittarian has...the inner conviction that he has it in him to give much. If others are less fortunate than he, it is his privilege to give to them out of his abundance. He gives not so much material things as the gifts of the spirit—leadership, moral courage, self-respect, sparks for flagging faith and waning energies, a lift to the whole world that comes from*

---

* See Jupiter in Libra section of Chapter 6 for more details of Churchill's chart.

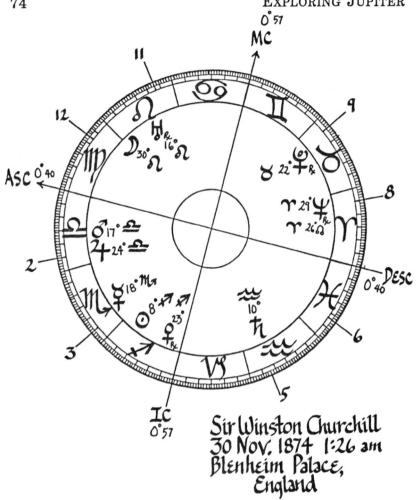

Sir Winston Churchill
30 Nov. 1874 1:26 am
Blenheim Palace,
England

contact however fleeting with the warmth, and the verve, and
the dash, and the directness, of the Sagittarian.

Lewi's reference to giving a "lift to the whole world" reiterates the *uplifting* quality that describes Jupiter types at their best.

It should also be pointed out that Churchill was remarkably prophetic as well, being years ahead of his time in his warnings about Naziism's menace, even though he was laughed at quite openly in Parliament and considered a pest and a nuisance by those in power in England. Again, he was prophetic regarding the "Iron Curtain" (a term he coined) that the U.S.S.R. would establish throughout Eastern Europe. His risk-taking, adventurous personality is legendary. His fearlessness, exemplified by his standing on the roof of a government building during a London air raid so he could see it close up, would indeed lead one to believe that he did indeed feel himself to be protected by a higher power so that the purpose for which he was born could come to pass. (His courage is shown also in his chart by the Mars-Jupiter conjunction.) In fact, when he finally knew for certain that he was the next Prime Minister, a responsibility that would have descended upon most people with profound gravity, he writes that he slept that night with an unusual depth and tranquility! As an example of his wide-ranging perspective and prophetic vision, as well as of the deep philosophical tone of many of his talks, the following quotation from a 1935 speech in the House of Commons is striking for its tone of foreboding regarding the onrushing threat to international peace:

> *When the situation was manageable it was neglected, and now that it is throroughly out of hand we apply too late the remedies which then might have effected a cure. There is nothing new in the story. It is as old as the sibylline books. It falls into that long, dismal catalogue of the fruitlessness of experience and the confirmed unteachability of mankind. Want of foresight, unwillingness to act when action would be simple and effective, lack of clear thinking, confusion of counsel until the emergency comes, until self-preservation strikes its jarring gong—these are the features which constitute the endless repetition of history.*

Another Sagittarius Sun Sign personality, Beethoven, is a perfect example of the Jupiterian tendency to expand and develop extensively beyond the current limits of one's chosen field of endeavor.

> *Beethoven was also a great expander of musical form. The piano sonata, for example, was a form utilised by many composers in the late eighteenth century. Beethoven wrote thirty odd himself but in so doing exhausted the form of its possibilities. It became a worked out vein and very few were written after his time. And there are those who will argue that he also took the symphonic form to its limit, or at least brought it to fruition.*
> *(The Literary Zodiac)*

The "uplifting" quality of both Churchill's oratory and Beethoven's powerful music reminds me of another form of uplift that Jupiter is known for: laughter, humor, and high-spirited joking around. At best, Jupiterians are truly *jovial* in their upbeat attitude and their ability to lift others up from despondency and depression. Although there are many types of humor (such as Venus' pleasant interpersonal harmonies and Uranus' shock-value social critiques), there is no doubt that the humor and perspective provided by Jupiter plays a major role in our feeling good and thus, in our overall health. And, of course, to keep with the spirit of Jupiter, I couldn't resist including a few cartoons in this book.

Jupiter gives us the ability to rise above immediate details and to expand beyond current limitations or pain. It gives us perspective and the ability to bounce back from painful crises, such as psychological shocks or physical surgery, just as Sagittarius follows Scorpio in the zodiac. Jupiter thus may be said to symbolize *recovery*, a path cultivated not only through maintaining a more positive *attitude* but also through working to genuinely *improve* oneself and one's living habits. Once again, we see Jupiter representing the act of bringing one's life more into alignment with an ideal. And of course, Jupiter's connection with laughter and with faith both point to its important role in health and healing.

The connection between laughter and healing has now become a significant field of serious study, with numerous books and scholarly articles having been published in recent years. It has, for example, been suggested through substantial evidence that laughter increases production of endorphins, which in turn have numerous positive effects on our health. In addition, healing through faith, or through a striking renewal of faith, is a phenomenon known throughout the world for millennia. One should never minimize the power of having a surge of strongly focused positive energy flowing through the individual energy field. One cannot really limit the scope of such energy's positive effects. In other words, the high spirits that Jupiter can convey are not only fun, but they actually contribute greatly to our overall state of health! Norman Cousins, in his book *Anatomy of an Illness*, sums up the connection between humor and healing this way:

> *The* Bible *tells us that a merry heart works like a doctor.*
> *Exactly what happens inside the human mind and body as the*

result of humor is difficult to say. But the evidence that it works has stimulated the speculations not just of physicians but of philosophers and scholars over the centuries....Robert Burton, in his Anatomy of *Melancholy, almost four hundred years ago, cited authorities for his observation that "humor purges the blood, making the body young, lively, and fit for any manner of employment." In general, Burton said, mirth is the "principal engine for battering the walls of melancholy...and a sufficient cure in itself." Hobbes described laughter as a "passion of sudden glory."*

Humor also plays a far more important role in problem solving than it is generally given credit for, and the person who can exhibit largeness of heart, bigness of spirit, and a humorous attitude even in the midst of a stressful or dangerous situation is often seen as having extraordinary leadership abilities. Whereas those who over-react to the smallest thing, give in to the negativity of anger or fear, or shake from nervousness in a stressful situation rarely are able to rally other people to their side in major undertakings. As the Roman writer Horace expressed it two millennia ago,

A jest, a laughing word, often decides the highest matters better than sharpness and seriousness.

In fact, developing the ability to rise above the petty annoyances of life is an important part of the great Jupiterian virtue: *wisdom.* As a great American philosopher wrote,

The art of being wise is the art of knowing what to overlook.
—William James

The Jupiterian as Cultural Icon

There is another aspect to the Jupiterian personality that has been little noted in astrological literature, and that is the tendency for the idealism implicit in Jupiter to sometimes be inordinately concretized by a specific person being widely seen as a larger-than-life ideal, a hero, or a cultural icon. Paul Wright brilliantly explores this phenomenon in an article that, at this writing, is not yet published. Hence, I will quote him at length:

We no longer live in religious times, but the human need for the numinous, for something greater, more perfect and more powerful than ourselves has not disappeared. It has, however, taken a perverse turn. Instead of aspiring to the Infinite, we make gods out of mortals. We create 'super-stars' of athletes and artisans. We inflate, glamorise and worship actors, sports people, and musicians. We exalt them in other words. This phenomenon of elevating the ordinary to the extraordinary is a quality of Jupiter and Sagittarius (not so much of Pisces). It emerges at the behavioral level in two basic ways:

1. The mantle of hero or king seems to fall most easily on those strong in Jupiter or Sagittarius.

2. Equally, the Sagittarian/Jupiterian type can have a more than average tendency to idealise and hero worship.

Consider some examples. In music, we have Elvis Presley, often referred to as "The King," and a man who was and still is exalted and celebrated all out of proportion to his real musical talent—a Sagittarian ascendant. Other rock legends, rock icons include: Jim Morrison and Jimi Hendrix (both Sagittarian Suns), Marc Bolan (Sagittarius ascendant), and Bob Dylan (Sagittarius ascendant and Jupiter conjunct Sun). People like Elvis and Jim Morrison have their own shrines; people visit their graves, as people once made pilgrimages in Christian times. Frank Sinatra (Sagittarius Sun) is another who, in my view, is celebrated out of all proportion to his talent (and this lack of proportion is characteristically Jupiter).

In the world of cinema we find James Dean (Jupiter on MC) and Marlon Brando (Sag ascendant). Brando, musing on his own celebrity, was quoted as saying in a recent colour supplement article: "I'm just another son-of-a-bitch sitting in a motor home on a film set, and they come looking for Zeus."*

One man who was subject to a huge amount of adulation was the aviator Lindbergh, somewhat at the expense of other pioneering aviators (like Alcock and Brown, the first to actually fly the Atlantic). Sagittarian Moon and ascendant.

Einstein had a Sagittarian Moon and was the focus of a good deal of banal hero worship that had little to do with the content of his scientific endeavors.

---

* Some estimated charts for Brando give him a Scorpio Ascendant, but even so he would have Jupiter in Sagittarius in the first house.

> *The Soviet writer Solzhenitsyn (Sagittarius Sun) is another cast very much in the role of idol and icon.*

I cannot end this subject without mentioning another cultural icon of the U.S.A., who seemed to many to embody the all-American hero—both athletic and humanly sensitive—New York Yankees baseball star Joe DiMaggio. Although he retired in the early 1950s, over a decade later, in their ode to lost innocence, Simon & Garfunkel asked, "Where have you gone, Joe DiMaggio? Our nation turns its lonely eyes to you" (From "Mrs. Robinson" in the film *The Graduate*). DiMaggio not only played great baseball in the media capital of America and flourished there in spite of his humility and easy-going ways, but he even later married Marilyn Monroe! Perhaps he had begun to believe in his own image as a storybook hero? DiMaggio's chart reveals a stellium in Sagittarius: the Sun at 2°, Venus at 6°, and Mars at 10°, a wonderful signature for an artistic athlete who was noted for the grace with which he did everything, on and off the field. In addition, DiMaggio had the Moon in the other Jupiter sign, Pisces; and he did marry an icon of the Neptunian cinema world.

Although the yearning for an ideal, a goal, or a truth to live by is an essential quality of Jupiter, I may have neglected to emphasize the importance of Jupiter and its symbolism in relation to all forms of travel—both specific journeys on this earth and the journey of life itself as a learning experience and truth-seeking venture. Most people with an emphasis on Jupiter, Sagittarius, Pisces, or the ninth house are strongly drawn toward many forms of travel just for the wide range of experience it provides. I have mentioned earlier the aimless wandering that is sometimes an expression of Jupiter and the two signs that it rules; but on the positive side, travel can provide an arena for risk-taking and adventure. And sometimes Jupiterians feel that exploring the outer world does help them to explore themselves. The old saying, "travel broadens a person," applies to Jupiterians more quintessentially than to any other type of individual.

And finally, we cannot leave this exploration of Jupiterian types without considering one of their greatest concerns—the future. It is probably true to say that, given human nature, for most people everything is lived in relation to the future and our expectations of it. I think it is, however, also accurate to say that Jupiter types of people have this tendency at their very core, and any dissatisfaction with life today for them implies the need to redefine and clarify their vision of the future.

Especially for Jupiterians, experiencing *meaning* today is provided by the anticipation, hope, joy, or thrill of an expected future reward, goal, event, emotion, or satisfying result. The human mind finds it so difficult to remain happily in the present that we are actually dependent upon this future vision to a substantial extent, unconscious though it often is. Of course, for some people or in some cases or during certain phases of one's life, the tendency may be to live almost completely in the past and its resultant emotions, regrets, and longings. In a sense then, we are dependent upon the past and upon our hopes for the future. The present and future are curiously intertwined, however; for our visions and goals for the future mold how we shape our present, just as our actions and thoughts in the present are systematically molding our future. As Carolyn Myss and Norman Shealy, M.D. wrote,

> *What a person believes to be true about life, about God, about other people, about fate or luck, for instance, plays a very powerful role in determining how a person lives. Because what we believe is intimately connected to our emotions, our beliefs influence our emotional response to life. The empowering belief patterns and positive mental attitudes that we possess are, therefore, essential to creating a healthy body as well as a healthy life.*—from *The Creation of Health*

Many spiritual paths teach that living in the present moment is the ideal that we should try to achieve, probably because we can then make more conscious, clear choices that will bear beneficial fruit in the future and not be so obsessed with fantasies about the future that we fail to see what is right in front of us in the present. But we cannot live in such a spiritually enlightened way unless we have that Jupiterian ideal or belief that motivates us to work on it and to develop the art of being in the eternal now. Since the future and our ideals so much impact our lives at every level, it seems remarkably practical to accept our need for a future goal or ideal and thus to explore our natal Jupiter's implications so that we may be at least somewhat more conscious of our future longings and aspirations.

George Washington

George Washington is not only a good example of a Jupiterian personality, but his chart shows how apparently minor astrological factors and themes can converge to create one major theme—in his case, a larger-than-life impression of nobility, eminence, trust, uprightness, and broadminded tolerance of human diversity. Although many North Americans may not realize it, Washington is revered all over the world as a symbol of democracy, and in fact, he put his stamp on the actual form of American democracy, and especially on the office of the Presidency and how it is empowered, far more than is known to most Americans. Even during his lifetime, in his later years, his profile was already being used in a tremendous variety of ways as a uniquely American symbol of virtue and independence. Eventually his image took on a larger-than-life significance, almost equivalent to that of an American Zeus (Jupiter!), although he personally took strong action during his presidency to assure that that office would not in any way become a disguised kingship.

Born on February 11, 1732 according to the old calendar, his birthdate in the modern calendar is February 22nd. The Washington family Bible gives a time of around 10:00 a.m., which yields an Ascendant of the middle degrees of Taurus. This Ascendant makes far more sense to me than would Gemini rising. For example, Washington's success as a General in the Revolutionary War was largely due to his patience, his tenacity, the ability to dig in his heels and avoid costly errors, and to his ability to inspire love and loyalty in his unpaid and poorly equipped troops. A Taurus Ascendant would make Venus his ruling planet, and in his chart Venus is not only exalted in Washington's Sun sign Pisces, but it is widely trine Mars and quite closely conjunct Saturn, which can give a person a sense of responsibility and duty towards others and a solid, enduring loyalty. In addition, since Washington's Jupiter was in Libra, Venus and Jupiter are therefore in mutual reception, greatly amplifying this tone of kindliness and human sympathy. Also, Washington was known for his tremendous attachment to *land*, and he in fact reinvested most of his extra earnings in additional lands over a number of years—surely a natural inclination for a Taurus rising person!

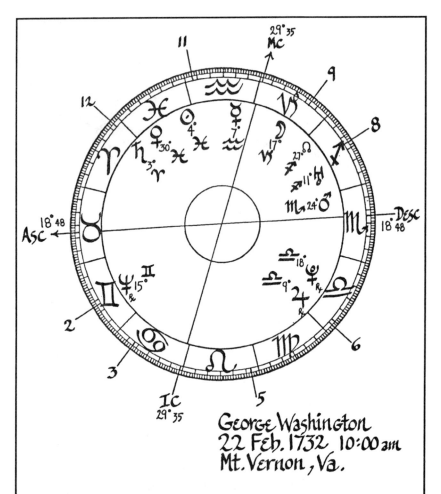

George Washington
22 Feb. 1732 10:00 am
Mt. Vernon, Va.

Other factors contributing to the make-up of this great
Jupiterian personality are:

a) Sun and Venus both in Pisces, a Jupiter (and Neptune)
ruled sign; hence, Jupiter is the dispositor of the Sun and
Venus. His Sun is also quincunx Jupiter.

b) His Capricorn Moon is in the *ninth* house, showing a
practical idealism.

c) His Mercury is quite closely trine to Jupiter. In fact, one
would be hard-pressed to imagine a more apt astrological
structure for a revolutionary leader dedicated to independence

and freedom of thought guided by principles of humane justice than this: Aquarius Mercury trine Libra Jupiter, both of which are sextile Uranus *in Sagittarius*. (One could say that he embodied and understood the currents of independence and human rights that were so fervently debated during that period, symbolized best by Uranus in Sagittarius.)

In fact, it is reflective of this triangular aspect structure between Uranus, Jupiter, and Mercury, that John Adams, who was the second President of the U.S.A. and usually quite critical of Washington, said of him: "He seeks information from all quarters and judges more independently than any man I ever knew." It should also be noted that Jupiter is retrograde in Washington's chart, yet another convincing example of the error of considering retrograde planets to be "weak" or somehow dysfunctional.

Among the evidence that Washington was an especially Jupiterian sort of human being, in the best sense of that term's potential nobility and largeness of vision, are the following facts:

a) Washington was about six feet, three inches tall, a virtual giant in those days. He also had a charisma that was equivalent, as many descriptions of him from the time attest to. All eyes would turn to him when he walked into a room.

b) He took pains to select the most able people for his cabinet, even if they had been political enemies in the past or held different views in major areas of policy.

c) He was adamant about paying his troops, even by personally borrowing and putting himself into great debt. And then, after the Revolutionary War was over, he insisted on paying off all debts, with great difficulty, even though he could have avoided it, as many others were doing in the post-war chaos of inflated currency.

d) He seemed to lead a charmed life that apparently attests to great "luck" or divine protection. Known for his bravery on the battle field, he repeatedly rode to the front lines under heavy fire to guide his troops. Although he had three horses shot out from under him, and bullets penetrated his hat and clothes, he was never actually physically hit during the entire Revolutionary War.

e) Jupiter in his sixth house of public service, as well as the self-sacrificing Pisces planets in the eleventh house (very often indicating political interests) well symbolize why he agreed to serve as President for two terms, even though he dearly wanted to retire to Mount Vernon after the exhausting years of the war.

f) The dignity with which he conducted his activities, even under the most trying circumstances, while various citizens were cooperating with the British armies and the new Congress could not agree on anything or pay his troops, is indeed awe-inspiring.

g) Perhaps most impressively, Washington set a tone of fair play (Jupiter in Libra) and compassion (strong Pisces influence, and Venus in Pisces in mutual reception with Jupiter) in all his dealings that lingers, fortunately, in the national sub-conscious mind. One could in fact make the case that Washington set before the American people an ideal that would later be powerfully symbolized by the Statue of Liberty and internationally respected as a great human ideal (witness the emulation by China's young people during their suppressed demonstrations). This ideal was expressed in Washington's words that the United States should be founded on "this stupendous fabric of Freedom" and on "protecting the rights of human nature" in order to "establish an asylum for the poor and oppressed of all nations and religions." This last line is quintessential Pisces idealism!

—S.A.

*Jupiter energizes and/or teaches wisdom.
From* The Images of the Gods, *by Vincenzo
Cartari, 1571.*

Jupiter's Levels of Expression

Before discussing the specific interpretive guidelines for Jupiter in each of the signs, it is imperative to emphasize that the range of Jupiter's potential expression in an individual's life is tremendously broad. Without dialogue with the person whose chart is being considered, it is extremely difficult to ascertain how that particular energy and function is manifesting. Different people live on different levels of consciousness, and Jupiter likewise can function on a number of different levels. In fact, Jupiter usually operates on at least two levels simultaneously, for Jupiter is far vaster than narrow "this, not that" sorts of analytical categories.

Jupiter thus may manifest on any of the following levels, and conceivably on other levels as well:

a) physical/material level: wealth, worldly success, fame, pride, prosperity.

b) social/psychological level: involvement with causes, large groups, education, law, and other countries and cultures.

c) mythical/archetypal level: the teachings of most spiritual and occult paths; some psychological traditions; religious belief systems.

d) moral/self-improvement level: deeper inner and philosophical development that transcends self-righteousness and conventional categories and that enables one to open up to possibilities of experiencing a vaster, more abundant reality and more profound life truth.

In the following four chapters, I will refer to a wide range of possible manifestations of each sign placement of Jupiter; there is no intention to imply that all such descriptions will precisely fit each person in question. Such ideas and quotations from other authors are primarily to be seen as stimuli to further thought. The reader should refer to the above "levels of expression" as well as contemplating the interpretive guideline phrases at the start of each sign's section in order to reach an in-depth appreciation of a specific person's Jupiter potential.

CHAPTER 4

Jupiter in the Fire Signs: Interpretive Guidelines

Those with Jupiter in any fire sign experience a feeling of unity with life and inner well-being when they express the dynamic energy symbolized by the fire element. A simple yet vital faith usually comes naturally to these people, as does a creative flair which they can add to almost anything they do. Physical vitality is usually strong, even leading to restlessness to a troublesome degree if it is not channeled with some kind of discipline.

Jupiter in Fire Signs

Inner faith comes when one is outgoing, enthusiastic, assertive, and physically active

Opportunities are stimulated when one takes risks to express oneself and try new things

---

These people usually like risk-taking, and they tend naturally to have self-esteem (sometimes even too much, from other people's point-of-view!). Their innate self-confidence is reflected in their living style and appearance, which tend toward flair, demonstrativeness, and liking to be noticed. In fact, these people like style; they like to do things "with style," and they often keep up with the latest styles (while often putting their personal stamp on the style as well) not only in dress but also in many other areas of life.

Generosity usually comes naturally to these folks, reflecting their feeling of inner abundance and their own confidence in the future. They are full of big plans and dreams for the future. At best, they are very idealistic people, but their dreams and ideals are often too unrealistic to be achieved until integrated with practical considerations, continuity of action (rather than chronic impulsiveness), and follow-through.

Jupiter in Aries

Interpretive Guidelines for Jupiter in Aries:

Seeks to grow and to improve oneself through confident, self-assertive activity

Needs to rely on one's own enterprise and energy in order to have faith in life; often has well-developed leadership abilities

Opportunities arise through a single-pointed release of energy toward new experience

Too much aggression, force, and restlessness can lead to over-expansion, taking excessive risks, and missing opportunities for personal development

Has an innate understanding of the importance of courage and faith in oneself

This is perhaps the most fearless risk-taker of all Jupiter positions. In fact, these people usually love risk and challenge; they crave the experience of the new and unknown, and life quickly becomes boring without such stimulation. In fact, they sometimes live in such a way that more cautious types wonder if they are bent on self-destruction! They are naturally rash and impulsive, liking to act quickly and think about it later, if at all. They are frank and honest, but others must be equipped to deal with their directness and bluntness without over-reacting to them emotionally. They don't usually mean any harm; they are merely thoughtless at times. However, there can be a mean streak in Aries, especially if other planets are there also. And almost invariably, there is substantial competitiveness, which serves them well in their natural entrepreneurial activities.

Those with Jupiter in Aries thrive on constant growth towards the new, and they may best express their potential in very independent work situations, such as being self-employed. They do not like to take orders, and in fact they are the epitome of people who can be called "head-strong." They are extraordinarily independent, often to an extreme that may seem to others to be perpetually rebellious. A balanced life is foreign to them (note that Aries is opposite the sign of the balance, Libra), for they are creatures of enthusiasm, and they are physically energetic and vigorous. Mentally, they have an abundance of new ideas, although often not well enough thought out to determine their ultimate consequences. Yet, their intuition into the future is often strikingly apt. They invariably know their future direction, although they may impulsively change it with surprising suddenness. So many new ideas and projects occur to them that many are never pursued long; finishing things may be a problem.

For those with Jupiter in Aries, progress and prosperity depend more on directing and *channeling* their innate confidence and vision than on developing those capacities. These abilities are already there, but cultivating more faith in that inner initiative and intuitive sense of what "I can do" may be the next step for some individuals—such as those who have stressful aspects with their Aries Jupiter or other self-doubting factors holding them back from taking the chances that ultimately will invigorate them.

Carter: *self-willed.*

Hone: *desire to enlarge the scope of personal expression: this may be over accentuated in an aggressive manner.*

Mayo: *self-sufficient, generous (Ebertin agrees), freedom-loving, high-spirited, boastful, bullying, over-optimistic.*

Moore & Douglas: *The forcefulness of Mars can make Jupiter's ambition boundless. Wishful thinking leads to extravagant planning. Consequently, difficulties arise in living up to promises extended in moments of impulsive generosity.*

Moore and Douglas also point out that those with Jupiter in Aries "have the courage of their convictions" and are often inspired by the feeling that they are on a divinely ordained mission. Since those with any number of major factors in Aries are often ahead of their time and pay scant regard to conventional attitudes, it makes sense that they are innovators in a variety of fields.

Courage is not lacking in Aries, and a perfect example of that is Senator Eugene McCarthy from Minnesota, who shocked the political world when in 1968 he challenged Lyndon Johnson for renomination while Johnson was still President and a member of the same party as McCarthy. This was at the height of the Viet Nam War, and the anti-war segment of the U.S. population, which was growing rapidly month by month, desperately needed a spokesman, which neither party was providing. Eugene McCarthy*, who had not only Jupiter but also the Sun in Aries, courageously filled that role

---

*Born March 29, 1916; Watkins, Minnesota, USA; 4:00 AM CST.

in the bold act of announcing that he would run against President Johnson. It was an especially impressive act since Senator McCarthy was widely respected as a thoughtful and loyal politician, one who in fact often acted from broad philosophical considerations, a motivation often found with Jupiter in the Fire signs. McCarthy's action helped to force President Johnson to resign and very likely shortened the war, which unfortunately was still carried on for some time under the next President, Richard Nixon. The courage of McCarthy's act would probably be much more appreciated today, had not Senator Robert Kennedy then entered the race for the nomination, once the way was cleared by McCarthy. Kennedy's later assassination during that time overshadowed much of the credit that McCarthy should have received.

Another person with Aries Sun and Jupiter is John Havlicek, one of the finest basketball players in history. He was known as being "tireless," for he could run endlessly until those defending him were exhausted. In fact, "tireless" might well be a good term for most people with Jupiter in Aries. Havlicek won numerous championships while with the Boston Celtics, and had an unusually long career.

Shirley Temple Black also has Jupiter in Aries, along with Venus and Mercury; her Sun is in Taurus. Not only did she communicate a tremendous vitality to worldwide movie audiences as a child-star (these planets are in the 5th house!), but she subsequently beat all odds by overcoming the cynics with the sheer exuberance of her drive to become a civic leader in many areas and eventually U.S.A. Ambassador to Ghana. Since she has Sagittarius rising (hence, Jupiter in Aries is her "ruling planet"), as well as such a strong 5th house Aries influence, her enthusiasm is evidently so contagious that she conquers all doubters; her chart virtually exudes positive thinking!

Other People Born with Jupiter in Aries

Alice Bailey	Bing Crosby
Clara Barton	Salvador Dali
Fanny Brice	Clarence Darrow
Pearl Buck	Marlene Dietrich
Richard Burton (Orientalist)	Mary Baker Eddy
Frederick Chopin	Gustave Flaubert
Stephen Crane	Jackie Gleason

Hermann Göring	Gregory Peck
Margaret Hone	George Bernard Shaw
Helen Keller	Lily Tomlin
Yehudi Menuhin	Mae West
Jack Nicklaus	Oscar Wilde
Lee Harvey Oswald	Paramhansa Yogananda

Jupiter in Leo

Interpretive Guidelines for Jupiter in Leo:

Seeks to grow and to improve oneself through creative activity, freely expressing one's exuberant vitality, and through warm, supportive encouragement of others

Expansiveness is colored by pride and an urge for recognition; intuitively understands people's needs for attention and self-confidence

Trust in a higher order can be hindered by egotism and an arrogant, domineering attitude, but usually has an innate and irrepressible faith in life

Need to act impressively and be recognized by others leads to confidence in self; has a well-developed sense of showmanship and flair

Expresses faith in life as a drama; feels blessed to be playing one's role in life, but sometimes has excessive faith in the importance of one's own role

At first glance at this combination, one might think that it is too much of a good thing, or at least possibly too much of two big energies. As in all things with Leo, so much depends on sincerity of heart— whether the person is mainly motivated by needs for self-aggrandizement or whether in fact he or she can become a channel for such tremendous love and capacity for vitalizing others that observers may be left in awe. Those with Jupiter in Leo almost always have a strong need for recognition and respect, and they often earn it because they can put out the energy and effort that realistically should be rewarded with some measure of gratitude. They tend to have faith in life and in themselves, but still they do appreciate being noticed.

This is actually a rather puzzling Jupiter position because the range of expression is so vast: for example, from Luther Burbank, who willed and encouraged plants to flourish and who co-created a myriad of new varieties of fruit trees, to President Lyndon Johnson, whose arm-twisting political methods and personal pride (which prevented him from withdrawing from Viet Nam because "I will not be the first American President to lose a war.") doomed him personally and politically. Even some of the great artists who have Jupiter in Leo often have something rather excessive and overblown about them; listen, for example, to Richard Wagner's music.

As Moore and Douglas point out in *The Divine Science*, some people of this attunement "use their organizational abilities to serve others less fortunate than themselves." A perfect example is Eleanor Roosevelt, who was decades ahead of her time in advocating the social causes to which she devoted herself. Moore and Douglas, in fact, have probably summed up Jupiter in Leo's range of potentialities better than anyone else:

> ...the combination may be extravagant or generous, over-bearing or dignified, demanding or altruistic, depending upon the degree to which egocentricity is expanded into consciousness of human need. The key to the character of this individual is the word "nobility." Either there will be the desire to be considered an aristocrat or there will be the elevation of character which marks the spiritual aristocrat whose position is shown by a sense of noblesse oblige.

Leo Jupiter people tend to love risk in all things, except that there is a surprising vulnerability when it comes to their ego and–especially–their heart. They are usually big-hearted people who give spontaneously to all sorts of human beings. But where things get intimate and personal, there they are vulnerable and often feel out of place. They often seem more comfortable in a public show of glamour and affection than in the subtle intricacies of making a relationship work. The perfect example of this is Elizabeth Taylor, whose generosity to social causes is well known, but whose romantic life seems never to attain stability. Another Jupiter in Leo creative person who seems to have constant trouble in romance is singer Diana Ross.

Self-esteem is rarely a problem for these people, and in fact other people often wish they would have less confidence in their own opinions. Witness, for example, the most obnoxious person in the history of TV broadcasting, sports commentator Howard Cosell, whose Leo Jupiter conjuncts his Leo Ascendant and trines his Aries Sun in the ninth house! Surely, there could never be a person who more perfectly fit the adjective "obnoxious"! And yet it was that overly flamboyant style that led to his prominence and success.

People with Jupiter in Leo must use their creativity and breadth of vision in order to feel fulfilled. Film-maker George Lucas, whose futuristic/imaginative visions reflect his Jupiter opposite his Aquarius Moon and square his Taurus Sun, is a good example of this dynamic power. Actor Robert DeNiro was born with Jupiter in Leo conjunct Pluto (and the Sun in Leo also), and it is interesting that, to many people, he is considered somewhat the archetype of an actor. During his long career, he has played many dark roles, including a boxer, a gangster (more than once), and a child-abusing father (Pluto!).

Mayo: *generous, big-hearted, dignified; or over-bearing, intolerant, extravagant.*

Ebertin: *great self-confidence, large-scale planning, a conscious desire to lead is combined with popularity. Love of luxury and pleasure...vanity.*

Moore & Douglas: *propitious for executive work...the self-assured leader. Above all, he wants his life to count for something in the larger scheme of things and he will work ambitiously in order that the world may take note of his presence in it.*

Davison: *enthusiasm for display, righteous causes, good living. Expands magnanimity, extravagance, dignity, desire to lead, and the dramatic sense.*

Hickey: *self-reliance, courage and loyalty, strong vitality, apt to have a big ego and rash judgment.*

Perhaps more than anything, those with Jupiter in Leo need an ideal beyond ego and short-sighted ambitions to motivate them to do and give their best in some field of endeavor that extends far beyond a small circle. They also need to follow their heart toward grand visions of love and giving, extending their talents broadly according to their deepest inner intuition.

Other People Born with Jupiter in Leo

Arthur Ashe	Jean-Claude Killy
Edward Brooke	Alan Leo
Calvin Coolidge	Amedeo Modigliani
Joan Crawford	Nelson Rockefeller
Bette Davis	Sirhan Sirhan
John Denver	Rudolph Steiner
Victor Hugo	George Wallace
Mick Jagger	Duchess of Windsor
Edward Kennedy	Brigham Young

Jupiter in Sagittarius

Interpretive Guidelines for Jupiter in Sagittarius:

Seeks to grow and to improve oneself through aspiration toward a far-off goal and following one's innate faith in life

Trust in a larger order is aided by an optimistic, philosophical orientation

Need to take advantage of opportunities for outer and inner exploration in order to improve self

Too much expansion can lead to over-extension of energy and overlooking the immediate possibilities

Has an innate well-developed appreciation of the importance of the religious dimensions of life

Since Jupiter is in its own sign here, or "dignified," its essential nature can be expressed in a pure form; and it may even be further exaggerated and amplified here since Jupiter, by nature, tends to feed on itself, so to speak, to build expanding momentum, often until it goes completely overboard and then sometimes has to quit because of sheer exhaustion! Going to excess is normal for those with Jupiter in Sagittarius, and the intoxicating feeling of ever-expanding exhilaration that they so readily get caught up in should not be underestimated. If there is some tone of discipline and/or moderation to the chart as a whole, however, such tendencies toward excess will most likely not be a significant problem.

Still, these people thrive on risk in all areas, except that, as with Jupiter in Leo, they are often not comfortable dealing with intimate human emotions. In fact, Jupiter in Sagittarius is usually not at all good at recognizing and coping with the deeper and more downcast human emotions. They would rather remain off in the distant realms of unlimited life that they envision, or in the more abstract mental spheres where they feel comfortable and able to breathe freely. Too much petty detail as well as too much show of emotion bring them down!

Those with Jupiter in Sagittarius are the positive thinkers of the world, par excellence. Witness Dale Carnegie and John Templeton (see Chapter 2). They can also be the great dreamers or visionaries of the world. Examples would be William Blake, the English poet and painter who was not only imaginatively futuristic in his prophetic poems about America, but who also envisioned multiple levels of creation filled with dancing angels and radiant saints in his paintings. William Butler Yeats, the Irish poet, playwright, occultist, and political activist, also worked for years at creating an idealized mythological world of both spiritual and artistic eternal verities. He was also hopelessly inept in trying to have a real relationship with the idealized love of his life, Maud Gonne. Yet another great visionary whose awareness of the swirling energy pervading the creation reflects his Sagittarius Jupiter is artist Vincent van Gogh.

These people are at best very broad-minded, tolerant, future-oriented souls to whom efforts at self-improvement come naturally. They are rarely lacking in either self-confidence or intuitive perception, although they may often need to develop more consistency, sense of responsibility, and the tenacity to finish what they start. "Progress" and "prosperity" may be two of their favorite words, but they need to be sure that the means they use are consistent with the long-term goals that they plan on reaching. As Ronald Davison wrote, they have a tendency to be "self-justifying." They invariably are bubbling over with lots of far-reaching plans and inspirations! And they usually love travel and in fact anything international.

Another "celebrity" who has not only Jupiter but also the Sun in Sagittarius is TV talk-show host, Phil Donohue, who later in his career also began to assume the role of political and social commentator on cable TV stations. His TV personality seems to me a good example of the arrogance and hypocrisy that, as mentioned earlier in this book, is often found in certain types of Jupiterians and Sagittarians. While pretending to be a crusader for truth, he seems

Carter: *a high-spirited, liberty-loving, generous, good-natured person; often reckless; lacking in concentration of effort.*

Mayo: *optimistic, philosophical, jovial, liberal-minded; or extravagant, boastful, lawless.*

Ebertin: *wastefulness, speculation; a noble character.*

Hickey: *outdoor type, fond of sports and willing to take a chance on anything. The more highly evolved are interested in metaphysics, religious philosophy and humanitarian pursuits.*

Moore & Douglas: *regardless of whether theirs is a religious bent, most people having this combination tend to be prophetic and inspirational. They have a capacity to impress others with their vision of how much better everything might be.*

to be mainly a crusader for high TV-viewer ratings by artificially cultivating controversy whenever possible. His adopting a "high moral tone" of disapproval while simultaneously providing tremendous publicity to the very people and activities that he so condescendingly sneers at makes his "moral indignation" transparently false.

How the Sagittarius Jupiter combines with the rest of the chart is of especially great importance, since it will greatly amplify anything it touches. It thus has a profound power for positive action, or potentially, for wasting innate talents or for exploiting others through misuse of the gift for publicizing–and encouraging others to seek–the truth. Since the book *Astrology, the Divine Science* is, as of this writing, out of print, it is worth quoting a concise paragraph that sums up some of the qualities of this Jupiter placement.

Here in its own sign, genial Jupiter rules handsomely over the domain of travel, metaphysics, serious literature, and sports– all of which imply the luxury of a fair degree of leisure and prosperity if they are to be properly enjoyed. The affairs which come under the aegis of Sagittarius lead beyond the cares and anxieties of the struggle to earn a living. They enlarge man's mental horizons and add zest and interest to his earthly sojourn. Jupiter is the planet of hope, and the games and intellectual divertissements associated with Sagittarius set the goals people require to keep their hopes in high gear.

Other People Born with Jupiter in Sagittarius

Maria Callas	Barbara Hutton
Truman Capote	Sandy Koufax
Maurice Chevalier	Henri de Toulouse-Lautrec
George Clemenceau	Sidney Poitier
Nicolas Copernicus	Prince Charles
Doris Duke	Robert Redford
Helen Hayes	Pierre Auguste Renoir
Hermann Hesse	Adlai Stevenson
Charlton Heston	Antoine de St.-Exupéry

Woody Allen

Born Allen Stewart Konigsberg in New York, Woody Allen is now known worldwide as both a comedian and as a film actor and writer-director who has constantly experimented with new types of movies. With Sun, Mercury, and Jupiter all in Sagittarius, it is not surprising that philosophical themes and references occur throughout his movies. Even in the comedies, there are often amusing one-liners and diverting dialogues that center on philosophical questions or which make fun of over-intellectualized philosophizing. The constant urge to expand his film-making repertoire and range of mastery likewise reflects the Sagittarius attunement. In addition, his Sagittarian/Jupiterian nature is further accentuated by the Jupiter-Sun conjunction, as well as by the Sagittarian Mercury, which is the "ruling planet" of the chart since it rules the Virgo Ascendant.

Furthermore, Jupiter is closely square the Ascendant, while Uranus in the ninth (Jupiterian) house almost exactly trines the Ascendant, a perfect symbol for a creative and innovative person who projects (literally in this case, via film projectors onto vast screens) to the public his vision of life. Saturn (which is closely square Jupiter) also strongly aspects his hard-working Virgo Ascendant, providing an apt symbol of a perfectionist who is widely known as a workaholic who does not easily relax.

Allen's conjunction of Mercury and Jupiter is indicative of his widely-respected writing talent, both in film scripts and in the genre of short stories. He has even had a best-selling book that is a collection of his stories, which also combine humor with philo-

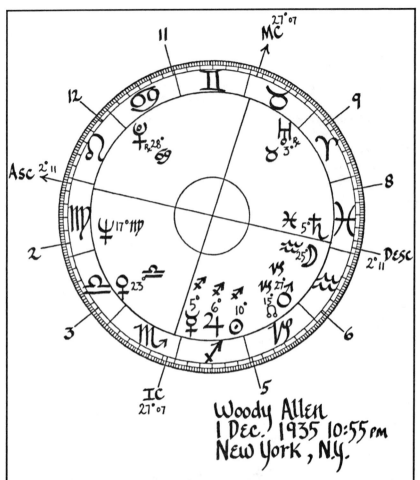

Woody Allen
1 Dec. 1935 10:55 PM
New York, N.Y.

sophical themes and absurdities. In the early years of his career, he
was a successful writer of jokes for famous comedians. Much of his
work explores the interplay between reality and fantasy, and
between the ideal and the prosaic, which are common Sagittarian
themes in literature.

Although Virgo rising gives him the image of a self-conscious,
rather humble, anxiety-ridden person who has few pretenses, his
way of handling the controversy over his bitter break-up with Mia
Farrow, the custody battle over children, and his affair with a
virtual stepdaughter has revealed what has been to many fans a
surprisingly offensive arrogance and a shocking degree of pander-

ing to the public through the media for one who usually comes across as a retiring, private sort of man. This kind of arrogant self-righteousness is indeed often found in those who have Sun/Jupiter aspects. It simply became more apparent when his family life exploded, as one would predict since the conjunction is in his fourth house. The fourth house location of his Sun, Jupiter, and ruling planet Mercury are likewise apt for one who never wants to leave his birthplace, New York, unlike most who have such strong Sagittarian and Jupiterian emphasis, for whom travel is a powerful urge. In addition, his fourth house emphasis is shown by his continual use of music from the twenties, thirties, and forties in all his films; such a comfortable feeling with the past is often seen in those who have major emphases in Cancer or the fourth house. He has likewise intentionally emulated the styles of his most admired film director idols, such as Ingmar Bergman, and he has also experimented with black-and-white films, both of which show an adherence to tradition and the urge to pay homage to predecessors— again, fourth house matters.

His seventh house Saturn is in square not only to Jupiter but indeed to all three of his fourth house Sagittarian planets, as if there is a great tension between his need for self-expression and privacy on one hand and a stable, serious relationship on the other. In fact, he has had a succession of relationships with actresses (Saturn in the seventh shows possible relationships revolving around work or career), but no relationship seems to satisfy him for more than a few years. In *Astrology in Action*, Paul Wright explores further this seventh house Saturn:

> He seems to have an affinity for Saturnian mates. Two women he has enjoyed serious relationships with are Mia Farrow and Diane Keaton. The charts of both are given in The Gauquelin Book of American Charts. The first shows Sun in Aquarius, Mars in Capricorn, and Moon in Capricorn opposing Saturn; the second shows Sun in Capricorn opposite Saturn, and Moon in Aquarius. His taste in women is perhaps a reflection of Saturn conjunct his 7th house cusp, and his own Aquarian Moon.

—S.A.

CHAPTER 5

Jupiter in the Earth Signs: Interpretive Guidelines

A feeling of unity with life for those with an earth sign Jupiter usually means experiencing a oneness with nature. A sense of inner well-being cannot really be attained until one's basic material needs are comfortably fulfilled. Naturally skeptical about "impractical dreams" and unproven schemes, these people are the least idealistic of all Jupiter placements; but they do specialize in getting things done–in other words, they hold, and act upon, practically achievable ideals.

Jupiter in Earth Signs

Inner faith comes when one tunes into practicality, dependability, and the experiences of the senses

Opportunities are stimulated when one works hard, assumes responsibilities, and tunes in to nature and its rhythm

---

A steady reservoir of physical vitality is usually present. In fact, *steadiness* is one of the chief virtues of this group of people. Accordingly, they engage in steady, systematic planning in all areas of life. They have a conservative bent and need to *contemplate* on their options *slowly* to reach a comfortable understanding. They are averse to impulsive risk-taking; any risk-taking must fit a preconceived practical plan, and the risk-reward ratio must be seen as prudent.

These people usually have well-developed practical skills, even if they are not fully confident of that fact. They need to *earn* self-esteem, as practical achievement allows confidence to grow over time. To those with Jupiter in the earth signs, appearance and image are moderately important. They do not need to show off like Jupiter in the fire signs does, but they are fond of looking dignified and being respected.

Jupiter in Taurus

Interpretive Guidelines for Jupiter in Taurus:

Seeks to grow and to improve oneself through productivity, steadiness, and reliability

Urge to connect self with a larger order is fulfilled through deep appreciation of the physical world; has a highly-developed sensuality

Attempting to improve life solely through money, possessions, and luxury can lead to an overly-materialistic attitude and wastefulness

Has a broad and tolerant understanding of human nature and basic human needs for pleasure

Trust in life is enhanced by communication with nature and a simple existence; expresses the more noble and generous qualities of Taurus

An appreciation of nature, textures, colors, and physical forms comes naturally to those with Jupiter in Taurus, so much so that they often seem intentionally to slow down some of their actions and descriptions of beautiful things just so they can savor them longer! These people are born with even more patience than Jupiter in the other two earth signs. Generally, they hesitate and dig in their heels if risk is called for; they prefer the "slow but sure" approach in life, love, and building security.

These folks have a large capacity for enjoyment and living in the present, as well as a depth of appreciation for the small, beautiful things of nature and the pleasant moments of simple physical life. In fact, they can get great satisfaction and contentment from small things. In my experience, they are rarely greedy, as might be expected from some descriptions of this combination, although they are usually somewhat possessive of what (and whom!) they "have." They do love comfort and pleasure in most instances, but they generally are not obsessed with acquiring more and more money or goods. In fact, these people tend to have a *faith* that they'll be provided for. And they are often quite generous with those they love, even at times extravagant, not only giving them *things*, but also doing things for them. Tightness with money is observed in many of these people, but they still may periodically go on a binge to indulge themselves in a high-quality purchase.

Physical pleasure and beauty are invariably important to this group of people, and a few of them can act lazy and self-indulgent; but their steadiness, reliability, and supportiveness towards others is still usually evident. I have never seen a person with this position who did not relish good food. In fact, in my experience, the women who show the greatest appetite for good food and feel not the slightest bit of culturally-conditioned self-consciousness about it all have Jupiter in Taurus. And none of them are particularly overweight, as might be assumed by some astrologers.

President Franklin D. Roosevelt is an excellent example of Jupiter in this sign. Taurus is a particularly productive sign, and Roosevelt naturally envisioned (Jupiter) the potential power and natural productivity of the American people, who were mired in a seemingly hopeless depression when he took office. Likewise, he envisioned the potential for growth and success of Western Europe's peoples, if only they could be liberated from fascism. As Eleanor Roosevelt remarked, "That sense of continuing growth and development was always keenly present with him." (See Chapter 8 for his complete birth chart.)

Mayo: *Sound judgment, good-hearted, reliable; or self-indulgent, self-opinionated, exploitative.*

Moore & Douglas: *Their philosophy of finance can be summed up in the words of the millionaire who said, "Money is like manure. Spread around it does a lot of good, but piled in one heap it makes an awful stink."*

This last quote from Moore and Douglas reminds me that, contrary to what some traditions would lead one to expect, these people do not necessarily accumulate much wealth, at least not in their younger years. They "spread it around," and their faith is such that they often don't bother learning about money or investing and even sometimes resist doing so. *Security* is important to them, but not necessarily abundance. Glancing at the list of well-known people at the end of this section will reveal a great range of experiences with and attitudes toward wealth. Three of those people inherited considerable wealth, quite a few others amassed wealth during their lives, and two (Gandhi and de Chardin) took vows of poverty! Mao Tse-tung also based his communistic philosophy on the redistribution of material wealth.

With Jupiter in Taurus, the mind and beliefs can be quite conventional, but are usually sympathetic to human needs and tolerant of human imperfections. A "down-to-earth" philosophical nature is prevalent, such as is evident in many of the themes of Bob Dylan's songs, who has Jupiter in Taurus (see Chapter 9 for a detailed description of his chart). Whatever form their life philosophy takes, it must be practical and–most of all–sufficiently satisfying that they do not have to sacrifice the present for some far-off, uncertain goal.

The road to prosperity for these people is slow but sure. The fixed sign Taurus provides a strong inner confidence, which can be tuned into further by exploring the enduring values that they live by. And some of their most perceptive intuitions may derive from their special understanding of human nature and from their remarkably deep capacity for giving.

Other People Born with Jupiter in Taurus

Joan Baez	Mao Tse-tung
Jack Benny	Dean Martin
Teilhard de Chardin	Henri Matisse
Mohandas Gandhi	Aristotle Onassis
Audrey Hepburn	Louis Pasteur
Howard Hughes	Pablo Picasso
John F. Kennedy	Franklin Roosevelt
Martin Luther King, Jr.	Jean-Paul Sartre
Bruce Lee	Ringo Starr
John Lennon	Richie Valens

Jupiter in Virgo

Interpretive Guidelines for Jupiter in Virgo:

Seeks to grow and to improve oneself through spontaneous helpfulness, dutiful service, and a disciplined approach to self-development

Humbly stays open to grace from a higher power, and naturally trusts the value of regular work and self-discipline

Expansive need for perfection motivates openness to self-improvement

Over-attention to detail can inhibit connection with a larger order, but usually has a well-developed critical faculty without excessive pettiness

Has an innate understanding of the appropriate use of one's analytical and discriminative abilities

Although Jupiter in Virgo (being in a sign opposite one which it rules–Pisces) is known as being in "detriment," I personally find that it is far more common to see Jupiter elevating and expanding the critical, analytical, linguistic, and intellectual faculties of Virgo than to witness Virgo dominating Jupiter, thus theoretically squeezing out all personal expansiveness and generosity. Attention to detail is certainly present in abundance in these people, but excessive pettiness is in my experience rather rare. They do, however, need periodically to clarify their larger vision of the future so that they know toward what goal they are working, and so they do not become lost in details and short-sighted concerns.

There is usually a technical attunement, if not intellectual, and *craftsmanship* is usually evident in whatever field they pursue, sometimes with a remarkable attention to minute detail. I feel a perfect image for Jupiter in Virgo craftsmanship would be the work of the great Japanese artist Hokusai, who had a number of planets in Virgo; he was reputed to be able to draw a perfect sparrow on a grain of rice! Self-confidence is rarely excessive (unless perhaps the person's Jupiter is conjunct the Sun in Virgo), and these people gain self-esteem over time through their work and practical accomplishment. Self-improvement is a lifelong mission for those with Jupiter in Virgo.

Those with Jupiter here have an analytical outlook on life and a tendency not to put themselves forward aggressively nor to try to be especially prominent. Unlike Jupiter in many other signs, they rarely promise others more than they can deliver. If anything, they understate their abilities and underestimate their talents. Because of such an orientation, it should be emphasized that, in pursuing personal and professional progress and all levels of prosperity, they should be careful not to sell themselves short. They seem to feel that their worth will manifest and prove itself through practical accomplishments and results, not through boasting; and this innate humility and eagerness to be useful is often expressed in the helping and health professions, service vocations such as teaching, or civil service. In virtually every arena of life, Jupiter in Virgo doesn't like risk, but–after systematic analysis–they will take risks deemed to be prudent.

Coleman: *This indicates that opportunities will come to you throughout life as a result of your willingness to render practical service to others. However, you demand extraordinary integrity of detail and often exhibit a moralistic concern for perfection which annoys colleagues.*

Carter: *Kind, but narrow in the affections.*

Ebertin: *The urge to learn, the ability to teach.*

Hickey: *Strong discrimination, but if afflicted, critical, irritable and petty.*

Moore & Douglas: [The following quote seems to describe Jupiter in Virgo at its worst, those people who can always find a reason *not* to believe in anything transcendent. I personally have seen few people with Virgo Jupiter who are this sort; but it is evident to me that this quotation concisely sums up an almost archetypal attitude among certain people in Western technocratic culture.—S.A.]

This pseudo-expansive outlook is typified by the science fiction writer who considers himself to be extremely imaginative in conjuring fantastic visions of life as it might be on stars, light years removed from Earth, yet who cannot conceive of anything beyond the strictly mechanistic view of the cosmos left over from nineteenth-century materialism. By projecting his own small shadow upon the

---

> *backdrop of the universe, he creates bigger and better monsters, but little that touches the heart or uplifts the mind.*

Other People Born with Jupiter in Virgo

Daniel Berrigan	George Patton
Claude Debussy	Prince Philip
Ralph Waldo Emerson	Mickey Rooney
Mia Farrow	Kate Smith
Dorothy Hamill	Peter Ustinov
Harry Houdini	Giuseppe Verdi
Mario Lanza	Walter Winchell

Ralph Waldo Emerson

"We live in succession, in division, in parts, in particles. Meantime within man is the soul of the whole; the wise silence; the universal beauty, to which every part and particle is equally related; the eternal One."

In these serene words, Ralph Waldo Emerson expressed the heart of his transcendentalist philosophy. With a first house Jupiter in Virgo, Emerson was especially attuned to perceiving the wholeness that is implicit in "every part and particle." But the serenity of this vision of life was forged from struggles with illness, religious doubts, and personal tragedies. To explore the humanity of Emerson is to uncover the Virgoan path (both the Ascendant and Saturn are in Virgo, as well as Jupiter) that refined Emerson's spirit and gave birth to a deeply life-affirming philosophy. His work has had a widespread influence on both American culture and the world for over a century. And the power of his personal presence was attested to by his friend John Muir, who wrote: "Emerson was the most serene, majestic, sequoia-like soul I ever met."

Early in life, Emerson wrestled with two dilemmas that are often associated with the Virgo experience: he suffered from chronic illness, and he grappled intensely with, to use his words, "a humiliating sense of inferiority." (Pluto in the sixth house square to the Sun also points to these issues.) While in his thirties, Emerson watched two of his brilliant and ambitious brothers

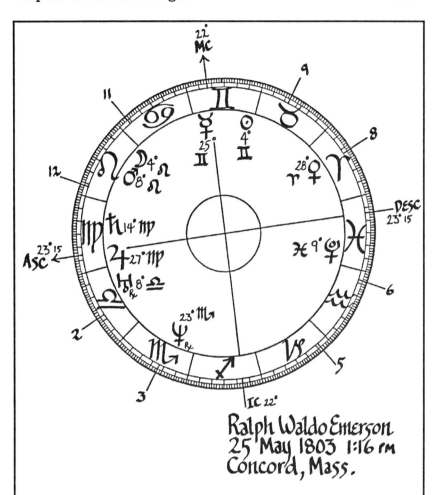

Ralph Waldo Emerson
25 May 1803 1:16 rm
Concord, Mass.

fatally succumb to tuberculosis (a disease that had already claimed his father at the age of forty-two, when Emerson was only eight). Emerson, too, struggled with tuberculosis and other physical limitations throughout his life. Emerson's other Virgoan quandary, his self-criticism, was exacerbated by the Saturnian voice of excessive family expectations. Born in the family of a highly renowned Boston minister, Emerson and his brothers experienced great family pressure to succeed at exceptional levels. Emerson felt inadequate to meet these demands. His self-denigration can be seen in his journal writing and is evident in this comparison (from a letter) with one of his brothers: "My own manner is sluggish; my speech flippant, sometimes embarrassed and ragged; my actions (if I may so) are of a passive kind. Edward always had a great power of face. I have none. I laugh; I blush; I look ill-tempered, against my will and against my interest."

How Emerson came to terms with his sense of inferiority and physical limitations reveals the uplifting influence of Jupiter. From hesitant beginnings, he went on to become an electrifying lecturer in constant demand and a brilliant essayist and poet, fulfilling the promise of Sun in Gemini in the ninth house and Mercury in Gemini near the Midheaven. The words of Emerson scholar Lewis Leary (in *Ralph Waldo Emerson: An Interpretive Essay*) are remarkably apt for describing how the Jupiter in Virgo placement fostered Emerson's development: "He was beginning to suspect now that these imperfections of his might be ballasts, defenses against excess, anchors to sanity. A man might make a virtue of his imperfections. For every weakness could there not be some compensating strength?" Leary adds that "Emerson spent the rest of his life devising an attitude toward living that could be satisfying to a man crippled as he was. He outlines it in expansive detail [Jupiter in Virgo!], but not for our imitating....He invites recognition that every person is somehow crippled, and no two in quite the same manner. Yet he would have them confident that each is capable of finding a way toward truth." To Emerson, our limitations can become Jupiterian guideposts that point the way towards our own particular genius.

After emerging from the abyss of self-negation, Emerson expressed his first house Jupiter in Virgo by becoming a lifelong advocate of deep trust in oneself and of responsible discriminating one's own truth. He urged individuals to take the risk of questioning accepted dogmas: "The faith that stands on authority is not faith. The reliance on authority measures the decline of religion, the withdrawal of the soul." (No doubt Emerson's first house Uranus bolstered this radical willingness to stand independently of society's expectations. And he lived it out when, during his first Saturn return, he resigned as minister of a Boston church due to disagreements on church doctrine.) The central message of his essay "Self-Reliance" still rings powerfully today: "Trust thyself: every heart vibrates to that iron string....Nothing is at last sacred but the integrity of your own mind. Absolve you to yourself, and you will have the suffrage of the world."

Emerson expressed an all-encompassing spirit of optimism—not surprising given his strongly Jupiterian nature. (Emerson had Jupiter not only near the Ascendant, but also in major aspect to Mercury, the ruler of both the Virgo Ascendant and the Gemini Sun—the Sun also placed in the Jupiterian ninth house). Some have even accused him of a "facile optimism." But in fact, it was through tragedies such as the deaths of both his beloved first wife (from tuberculosis within two years of marriage) and of his first son (at age five) that Emerson discovered, in the midst of his grief, the presence of God within. This revelation became the bedrock of his life, illuminated all of his writing, and resulted in a profound faith in, as Lewis Leary says, "the operation of a great and beneficent law in the universe." Emerson affirmed "that the soul of man does not merely...contain a spark or drop or breath or voice of God; it *is* God." He emphasized this core belief by writing later in his journal: "In all my lectures I have taught one doctrine, namely the infinitude of the private man." His emphasis on self-reliance springs from this experience of an indwelling guiding force, and is an apt expression of the influence of a *first house* (self-oriented) Jupiter. (Note also that, with Sagittarius on the I.C., Jupiter is the ruler of the fourth house of the private, interior life of the individual.)

It is important, in exploring Emerson's spiritual experience, not to lose track of the earthy nature of a Virgo Jupiter (and Ascendant). While his ninth house Gemini Sun sought out transcendent realms of thought, Emerson's Virgo side stayed grounded in the everyday experiences of children, gardening, long walks in nature. In Leary's words (and quoting from Emerson): "He delighted in plain, solid, substantial things: 'I embrace the common, I explore and sit at the feet of the familiar, the low.'" Another writer, Larzer Ziff, noted: "No philosophy is so drenched in the common natural scenes of daily life as is Emerson's, and none has so powerful a sense of these as constant revelations rather than ordinary events."

One last quote, from Emerson's essay "The Over-Soul," conveys particularly well his fine integration of wide-lensed Jupiter with microscopic Mercury (planets which are in a highlighted square, with Jupiter at the Ascendant and Mercury at the

Midheaven): "We see the world piece by piece, as the sun, the moon, the animals, the tree; but the whole, of which these are the shining parts, is the soul. Only by the vision of that Wisdom can the horoscope of the ages be read, and by a falling back on our better thoughts, by yielding to the spirit of prophecy which is innate in every man, we can know what it saith."   —B.McE.

Amelia Earhart & John Glenn

The lives of both Amelia Earhart, record-setting pilot in the early days of aviation, and John Glenn, U.S. Senator and the first American astronaut to orbit the Earth, prove that the adventurous potential of Jupiter is not necessarily limited by the often cautious nature of the sign Virgo. In fact, the Virgoan ability to give patient and thorough attention to technical details is a prerequisite for success in the risk-filled, pioneering ventures they both undertook. The two share other Jupiter in Virgo traits: eager participation in exploring new developments in technology and a lifelong concern for improvement of society. The aspects and house placement of Jupiter for each tell the story of their contrasting expressions of the same chart factor.

During World War I, the twenty-year old Amelia Earhart served as a nurse's aid, and her fascination with flying was ignited by the stories she heard from wounded military pilots. Within a few years, while also pursuing a career in social work, she took flying lessons, received a pilot's license, and bought an airplane. In 1928, a year after Charles Lindbergh's historic solo flight across the Atlantic Ocean, Earhart became the first woman to fly over the Atlantic as a passenger, accompanied by a male pilot and mechanic. With Jupiter exactly conjunct Mars, Earhart was abundantly courageous and filled with a love for risky adventures. Before leaving on the dangerous trip (more than a few had died attempting it), she said: "I have tried to play for a large stake, and if I succeed all will be well. If I don't, I shall be happy to pop off in the midst of such an adventure." These words would prove prophetic when her plane disappeared over the Pacific Ocean on an around-the-world flight just nine years later.

After the success of the 1928 flight, Earhart found herself in a

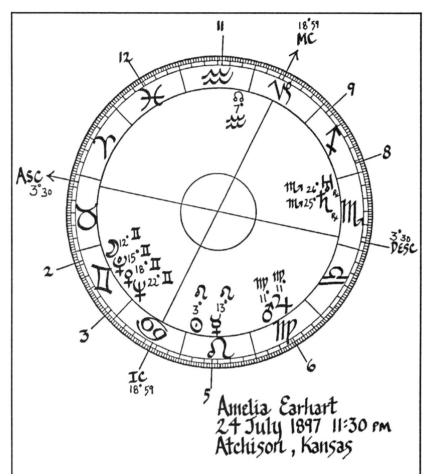

Amelia Earhart
24 July 1897 11:30 PM
Atchison, Kansas

whirlwind of public acclaim and celebrity, which enabled her to embark on a daring life of record-setting flights. (Jupiter, the principle of superlatives–"the biggest, the fastest, the longest"–is probably the planet most closely correlated to "record-setting" achievements.) In 1932 she became the first woman to fly solo across the Atlantic Ocean, assuaging her discomfort about (as she said) feeling like "a sack of potatoes" on the 1928 trip that brought her so much fame. (Jupiter amplified her Martian urge to prove herself *on her own*.) She completed the flight in record time, and was the first person since Lindbergh to fly it solo. In 1935 she was the first person, male or female, to make a solo flight from Hawaii to the mainland.

The *fifth house* dimension of Earhart's Mars-Jupiter pursuit of flying is clear in her words after the flight: "I flew the Atlantic because I wanted to....To want in one's heart to do a thing, for its own sake; to enjoy doing it; to concentrate all one's energies upon it—that is not only the surest guarantee of its success. It is also being true to oneself." (In addition to the fifth house influence, the integrity and focus of a fourth house Leo Sun shows here.) It is fitting that the title of one of her books about her exploits was: *The Fun of It*. For Earhart, flying was a fifth house affair of the heart–something she loved doing and a way to express her adventurous spirit.

Earhart's Mars-Jupiter conjunction is square to the Moon-Pluto-Venus Gemini stellium (that also includes Neptune) in the second house. To provide the second house financial backing for her flying (the expensive fifth house hobby), she launched into a round of Geminian speechmaking, writing, and radio commentaries. The alternating sides of these square show up in statements like: "It's routine now. I make a record [Mars-Jupiter in the fifth house] and then I lecture on it. That's where the money comes from [Gemini stellium in the second house]. Until it's time to make another record." Her husband, publisher G.P. Putnam, captured well the more taxing side of the Gemini squares to Mars-Jupiter in Virgo in his reference to "the sheer, thumping hard work of conscientious heroing." In 1935 alone, Earhart made 135 stage appearances.

Earhart's passionate concern was the empowerment of women (Moon-Pluto-Venus-Neptune stellium) to cultivate their talents and capabilities in whatever arena they chose (Jupiter-Mars in the fifth). With the reformist urge of Jupiter in Virgo, Earhart used her fame and achievements to promote her message: "I, for one, hope for the day when women will know no restrictions because of sex but will be individuals free to live their lives as men are free." Two tributes to Earhart attest to the fact that in her short life she achieved some of what was closest to her heart. From President Herbert Hoover (in words that well describe the capability of Jupiter conjunct Mars in Virgo): "You have demonstrated not only your own dauntless courage, but also the capacity of women to match the skill of men in carrying through the most difficult feats of high adventure." And, from her close friend Eleanor Roosevelt: "She helped the cause of women, by giving them a feeling there was nothing they could not do." (All quotes are from the book *Still Missing* by Susan Ware.)

Like Amelia Earhart, John Glenn took flying lessons while still in his twenties, and then led a life centered around flying. Interestingly, both birth charts have Venus in Gemini square to Jupiter in Virgo: the airy affinity for flight connected with a comprehensive mastery of complex technology. The Virgoan side of flying was noted by author Richard F. Fenno, Jr. (in *The Presidential Odyssey of John Glenn*) when he had the opportunity, as did other reporters covering Glenn, to take a flight with him: "None failed to be impressed–as I was–with the incredible concentration and attention to detail he exhibits during the flights. There was the checklist to be gone through at every stage, the multiple indicators to be constantly monitored, the constant cross-checking with people on the ground, the anticipatory commentary on atmospheric and airport conditions." Earhart's Virgo talents also undoubtedly served her well in this way.

While Earhart's Virgo Jupiter conjunct Mars in the fifth house placed her in the cockpit as a record-breaking aviator who flew for the love of it, Glenn, with a Virgo Jupiter conjunct Saturn at the Midheaven, flew in that most structured of environments–the military–as a marine fighter pilot. He flew missions in both World War II and the Korean War, serving for sixteen years before joining the Project Mercury astronaut program. He also worked on aircraft design, as a military test pilot, and in 1957 set a speed record when he made the first transcontinental supersonic flight. (No doubt the sextile of Jupiter to Mars and Pluto bolstered Glenn's courage and supported his success in these endeavors.) In 1962, exactly thirty years after Earhart's pioneering flight over the Atlantic Ocean, Glenn was launched into his historic solo three-orbit flight around the Earth. (Such an unprecedented "long voyage" is fitting for a Sagittarius rising individual, whose chart ruler, Jupiter, is in the ninth house, close to the Midheaven, and in opposition to Uranus, planet of radical breakthroughs.) Glenn's dramatic space flight, in which he took manual control of the capsule after a malfunction, made him one of America's great heroes, just as Earhart became a beloved heroine as a result of her exploits.

As we've seen, for Earhart, the Jupiterian call to adventure was combined with the individual initiative and personal drive of Mars;

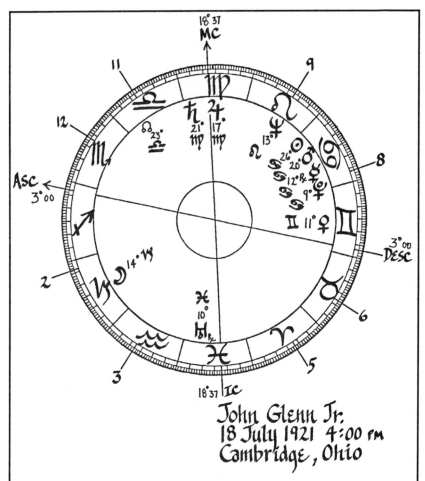

John Glenn Jr.
18 July 1921 4:00 PM
Cambridge, Ohio

while for Glenn, the Jupiterian adventurous quest is wedded to the sense of duty and social responsibility of Saturn. John Glenn has said repeatedly, "I look upon my entire life as service to my country." In recent years, he has continued his commitment to this tenth house-Virgoan public service orientation in his career as a U.S. Senator. About his choice to run for the Senate, Glenn said: "I didn't want to do it as an ego trip. The challenge is to make a better place for the people still to come."

It is remarkable how clearly Glenn's reputation has been shaped by the Virgoan Jupiter-Saturn at the Midheaven. He is known as a hard worker and respected for "impeccable integrity."

Other quotes from Fenno's book illustrate this Virgo influence: "In contrast to his studious concentration on issue-related detail, he displayed an equally distinctive inattention to self-promotional publicity seeking." "He's very effective. But he's self-effacing." And a critical lobbyist made the ultimate Virgo statement: "'He doesn't see the forest or even the trees, only branches and twigs.'" John Glenn is highly respected for his technical expertise, cultivated over so many years of involvement with aviation. "His intellectual and visceral commitment to scientific and technological activity flows naturally from his years of commitment to space exploration and from the faith he imbibed there in the ability of scientists and engineers to solve problems." That last line, from Fenno's book, precisely describes Glenn's manifestations of the Jupiter-Saturn conjunction in Virgo.

Clearly the detail-oriented sign of Virgo did not narrow the Jupiterian horizons of Amelia Earhart or John Glenn. In appropriate Virgo fashion, their aeronautical achievements made the world a "smaller place" by stitching together distant locales, even encircling the globe. Earhart and Glenn moved both aviation, and the human venture, forward.

—B.McE.

Jupiter in Capricorn

Interpretive Guidelines for Jupiter in Capricorn:

Seeks to grow and to improve oneself through hard work, discipline, and steady progress.

Need to express qualities of self-control and confident conservatism in order to improve self; has innate sense of authority that inspires trust from other people

Optimism and expansion can be squelched by an overly serious, fearful attitude

One's faith and trust is based on reality, experience, and one's innate understanding of the value of history and tradition

Opportunities come through one's ability to be reliable, responsible, and patient—qualities that are usually well-developed

In Capricorn, Jupiter is opposite Cancer, where it is especially well placed and therefore traditionally considered to be "exalted"; in Capricorn, Jupiter is in its "fall," a position where its innate qualities are not so easily expressed. However, that does not mean Jupiter's power should be underestimated here, as we shall see in this section. Nothing in Capricorn comes quickly or easily, although at times one must wonder why these people make things unnecessarily difficult for themselves. As Isabel Hickey wrote, those with Jupiter in Capricorn are "too cautious for their own good."

The extreme caution with which these folks approach everything, from close relationships to handling money, is of course typical of the sign Capricorn. Those with Jupiter here don't trust anything that is not "proven" or validated by traditional acceptance. The skeptical streak in their minds is pervasive, but they are not without practical *ideals!* Witness, for example, Walt Disney, Robert E. Lee, Robert Kennedy, and Edgar Cayce! The fact is that tradition plays a large part in molding their ideals. They will look at the history of any action or ideal that they are evaluating and will slowly test it to determine how much risk there really is. They are not fools and don't ever want to appear to be such; dignity is immensely important to them. They feel that knowing the risks in advance is simply practical. They have little need for the sheer excitement of taking risks, as so many people do; once they have determined that there is little risk, or at least that it is acceptable for the goal being pursued, they can act decisively.

However, those with Jupiter in Capricorn will take extra risks *in order to gain authority*. Examples of this are Richard Nixon, Margaret Thatcher (see details of her chart in this section), Robert Kennedy, and Adolf Hitler, who staged the infamous Munich Beerhall attempt to gain control of the government. Oftentimes, those with Jupiter here seem to attract especially powerful enemies, because of their power or prestige. This is true, although in varied manifestations, for all the following Jupiter in Capricorn people: Thatcher, Nixon, Hitler, Robert Kennedy, Robert E. Lee, as well as Charlie Chaplin and Charles Lindbergh. This Jupiter certainly inflates the ambition, and the result is well described by Moore and Douglas:

> *Having achieved the position of eminence for which they have labored, they may be obliged to pay the price once more in a sense of isolation and loneliness. Then they should try to forget their dignity and enjoy the simple pleasures of life without worrying about an image to be maintained or an impression to be made.*

The resourcefulness of these people should never be underestimated, nor should their determination. They may well simply outwork those endowed with more cleverness or imagination, and their sense of duty and responsibility is legendary, as, for example, the life of General Robert E. Lee attests. (Lee placed his duty to his native Virginia ahead of the duty to the Union in the U.S. Civil War, even though President Lincoln offered him the command of the Union army.) They can of course be austere and heavy-handedly judgmental; a Jupiter in Capricorn evidently often becomes rigid and easily lapses into self-righteousness. Carter, Mayo, and Davison all use the term "conscientious" to describe this person, and Ebertin relates Capricorn Jupiter to "consciousness of goal," which I take to mean the innate ability to patiently act with a view to long-term plans.

Carter: *Reticent, self-controlled, righteous.*

Mayo: *Enthusiasm for duty; expands ambition (autocratic) and organizing ability.*

Ebertin: *A sense of responsibility, trustworthiness...qualities of leadership, hypocrisy, egotism.*

Hickey: *A tendency to be miserly with the expression of loving feelings, as well as with money.*

This last quotation brings to mind the inherent conflict with Jupiter in Saturn's sign; it can create a tension between thriftiness and extravagant arrogance, or the need to be recognized and respected for being generous while at the same time wanting to maintain one's financial security by not spending unnecessarily. Although they are more concerned with appearances and being "respectable" than are Jupiter in Scorpio people, those with Capricorn Jupiter are quite similar in that they may alternate between penny-pinching and spending prolifically. They do not like waste, but they may invest huge sums in either business ventures or in goals that they deem to be in accord with their higher values.

Essential qualities of the Jupiter-Capricorn personality are precisely captured in Moore and Douglas' following comments:

Jupiter-Capricorn people work in a practical and conservative manner without the inclination to indulge in risky speculation. They conduct their affairs according to the tried-and-true rules of tradition and are satisfied with slow growth and gradual gain. Generally, they flourish in business and when given the opportunity to manage established enterprises of proven merit, they justify the faith invested in them. They want to know precisely where they stand financially and to feel that the ground is solid beneath their feet.

This position is conducive to a career in government, politics, or large corporations where business is carried on impersonally and strictly according to protocol.

Other People Born with Jupiter in Capricorn

Warren Beatty   Elizabeth Browning
Willy Brandt   Art Buchwald
Emily Brontë   Richard Burton (actor)

Albert Camus   André Malraux
Johnny Carson   Karl Marx
Sammy Davis   Paul Newman
Emily Dickinson   Jack Nicholson
Manly Hall   Arthur Rimbaud
Jimmy Hoffa   Carl Sandburg
Dustin Hoffman   Peter Sellers
William James   Upton Sinclair
Rudyard Kipling

Margaret Thatcher

It would be hard to find a better example of a Jupiter in Capricorn person than Margaret Thatcher, the most dominant Prime Minister of England since Churchill and one of the most powerful and influential women leaders in the last two centuries. Her entire chart is interesting, but here we need to be concerned primarily with Jupiterian and related factors. Obviously, her extraordinary rise in power from modest middle-class roots could only have happened if she were, in fact, extremely determined and ambitious; for she was not only fighting the British class system, but also the bias against her sex because of the dominant "old boy" network. Her Capricorn Jupiter clearly reveals far-ranging planning and broad ambition, augmented further by Saturn conjunct her Ascendant. She was known for being extremely rigid and authoritarian, heavy-handed and domineering. Known as the "Iron Lady," she also expressed a "paternal" (many felt it was patronizing and pompous) attitude toward the average citizen, even causing a bit of a controversy when she stated publicly that most citizens were like children who had to be told what to do.

Regardless of what one thinks of some of her tactics, attitudes, and personality, there seems little doubt that her Jupiter in the 2nd house gave her an instinctive understanding of the ability of money and financial security to motivate people to work harder. She increased incentives for entrepreneurial activity, lowered taxes, and empowered thousands of people to purchase their first homes from the government's stock of houses. In many ways, she reinvigorated capitalism in a country (and in fact in the entire European community) that had grown increasingly socialistic since 1945.

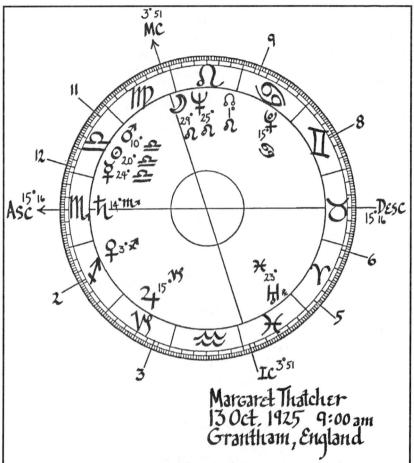

Margaret Thatcher
13 Oct, 1925   9:00 am
Grantham, England

Much of her ability stemmed from the inspirational, Jupiterian qualities that she had and the confidence in herself and in her ideas that she was able to project. We can briefly list such factors as:

- Jupiter is square to her Sun and Mars, revealing confidence (perhaps excessive pride) and her combative nature.

- Venus in Sagittarius, showing clearly her directness of expression.

- Moon and Neptune are in the 9th house, traditionally associated with Jupiter.

—S.A.

CHAPTER 6

Jupiter in the Air Signs: Interpretive Guidelines

Those with Jupiter in the air signs are born with a broad curiosity about people and ideas, and the process of discovering new ideas and exploring new intellectual and relationship dimensions is the key to their happiness and sense of well-being. There is often a sense of unity with all human beings, and their contributing to or participating in some purposeful social and/or intellectual activity gives them a sense of protection and inner freedom. In addition, they need upbeat contact with people to encourage their vitality; intellectual work alone can sometimes exhaust them, especially if taken to excess that leads to a state of nervous strain. Their intellectual energy, nevertheless, is usually formidable and often amazes others not similarly endowed.

Jupiter in Air Signs:

Inner faith is stimulated through exploring new ideas, communicating with new people, and social improvement

Opportunities come when one expresses ideas enthusiastically and interacts with others for a future goal

---

Self esteem for these people grows from successful relationships, social involvement, and intellectual development and exploration. It is in these areas of life that the individual will be willing to take risks most readily, although in general these folks are relatively adventurous. (Libra, however, is quite a bit more conservative than the other two air signs.) While there's a natural ability to be adventurous socially, Jupiter in the air signs can lack depth and commitment in relationships and other involvements because the urge is so strong to continue exploring.

Also, the air sign Jupiter individual is so mental and detached that there may be an avoidance of emotional engagement, as well as a tendency to be out of touch with the physical body (unless other personal planets offset this). These people are carried away easily into far-off realms beyond body and emotions, and even close relationships may be dealt with in an abstract manner unless great communication is established. But ideally, these people are true "life-long learners" with a capacity to contribute dynamically to society's improvement.

Jupiter in Gemini

Interpretive Guidelines for Jupiter in Gemini:

Seeks to grow and to improve oneself through communication, developing a wide range of skills, and broad learning

Faith comes through immediate perception and verbalization of all connections; wide-ranging interests contribute meaning to life

Optimism is sometimes hindered by changeable curiosity and excessive thinking and worrying

Need to develop intelligence and reasoning power in order to experience trust in oneself and in life; an urge to connect with a larger order that is rational and logical

Has an innate understanding of the importance of good communication and a desire to benefit others by being a source of information

Although traditional astrology designates Jupiter in Gemini as being in "detriment," since it is in a sign opposite one that it rules (Sagittarius), generations of readers can only be grateful that some people are able to tell fantastic stories with a myriad of details that yet impart larger meanings. At best, Jupiter in Gemini can weave a large-scale creation through correlating many diverse details and facts. One example would be Charles Dickens, whose novels were originally published in serial form in newspapers. His writings had a major impact on public enthusiasm for social reform. In fact, those with Jupiter in Gemini often have a sense of the public's emotions and aspirations and can appeal to the public in original ways. Arthur Conan Doyle, the author of the Sherlock Holmes stories, also had Jupiter in Gemini and was ultimately the most popular and well-paid author of his time. In fact, with Jupiter in his first house, Conan Doyle established through his detective character the virtual archetype of the analytical mind, which objectively analyzes all facts and does not want to be distracted by emotions (see *Introduction* for more on his chart).

Those with Jupiter in Gemini don't generally consider that they are taking any risk in their intellectual endeavors, but certainly many of these people readily take risks in frank communication and in *exploring* ideas that are not generally considered conventional.

There is an innate openness to the new and an endless curiosity. At worst, they are unfocused and have no discrimination about ideas or people. Yet, they remain constantly busy. They usually have great instinctive communication ability (and linguistic ability) with a wide variety of people. They tend to be glib and easily exemplify the "gift of gab," but also—unlike many people with Sun or Mars in Gemini (more aggressive Geminian expressions)—they find others' ideas not only interesting but worthy of being listened to! Those with Jupiter in Gemini are often good listeners and perceive quickly what the other person *really means*, even if one can see that they have to make an effort to bite their tongue long enough to let the other person finish speaking!

Rashness of speech is not unknown in these people, but at best their easy way of sharing ideas and trading observations with a variety of people makes them extraordinary in professional pursuits that emphasize exchange of ideas, sales, design of communication media, publicity, etc. After all, positive (Jupiter) thinking (Gemini) is widely accepted as the key to successful sales and promotional efforts! Like Jupiter in the other Mercury sign, Virgo, these folks can always find a reason *not* to believe in something, but at best, they have an ability to express abstract ideas and ideals concisely and energetically.

Mayo: *Highly intelligent, varied talents, broad-minded; or crafty, diffuse and scattered interests, indiscreet.*

Ebertin: *Versatility in obliging others, an aptitude for making social contacts...a love of change, the desire to have many connections. A carefree attitude towards life, superficiality.*

Hickey: *Fond of travel. Does well in the travel business or any occupation that involves selling, communication of ideas or teaching.*

It would be too large an omission to fail to mention the importance of Jupiter in Gemini's cleverness and ingenuity, on a number of levels. Such remarkable inventors as Thomas Edison and Alexander Graham Bell had Jupiter here. Naturally, since both Jupiter and Gemini are related to teaching and education, it should come as no surprise that the founder of the Montessori method of education, Maria Montessori, had Jupiter in Gemini, in the 11th house. It was also opposite Saturn in Sagittarius in the fifth house; this seems to me a striking symbol of future-oriented (Jupiter in 11th) educational innovation (Saturn in Sagittarius in the creative 5th house).

A couple of other especially interesting examples of Gemini Jupiter are Jacqueline Kennedy Onassis and Arthur Schlesinger, Jr. "Jackie," who obviously had all the money she would ever need, still chose to pursue her own private path to personal growth and development by taking a job as an editor with a major New York publishing house. Obviously, "prosperity and progress" meant something different to her than material wealth.

Arthur Schlesinger, Jr. has Jupiter in Gemini in the 10th house, and, through his writings, his reputation as a historian gained momentum at a relatively early age. He has won two Pulitzer Prizes and gained his greatest prominence by being an advisor and *speechwriter* for a Gemini Sun President, John F. Kennedy. Shall we ever know whose words were those which made JFK's speeches famous? (See Chapter 10 for more on Schlesinger's chart.)

Many writers have had a Gemini Jupiter, although since Gemini likes to do two things at once, a great many of those have also had other careers: Theodore Roosevelt, Dane Rudhyar, Anne Morrow Lindbergh, and—an author whose moral impact reached a remarkably large number of citizens at a crucial time in American history— Harriet Beecher Stowe, author of *Uncle Tom's Cabin*. In virtually all people who have Jupiter in Gemini, mental exploration and growth is a key to their self-improvement agenda.

Other People Born with Jupiter in Gemini

Mohammed Ali	Graham Nash
Adolf Eichmann	Gamal Nasser
Indira Gandhi	Clifford Odets
Greta Garbo	Giacomo Puccini
Kahlil Gibran	Barbra Streisand
Grace Kelly	Duke of Windsor

Babe Ruth

Born George Herman Ruth on February 6, 1895, "Babe" Ruth dominated baseball from the time he was 18 yeas old, first as one of the best three pitchers in the professional league and then as the most prolific power hitter the game had ever known, or was to know in future decades. He is one of many Aquarius Sun sportsmen who reached a level never before seen in their sport, thus *revolutionizing* (Aquarius!) the sport. (Hank Aaron, who broke Ruth's career home run record, Michael Jordan in basketball, and Wayne Gretzky in hockey are some others.)

The most famous American of his time, according to numerous historians, and the best-loved by all age groups (at least until Jupiterian Charles Lindbergh), was born with Jupiter (most likely close to the Ascendant) in Gemini *retrograde!* (Another example which dispels the common astrological misconception that retrograde planets are somehow weak or not effective in the outer world.) Since I believe Ruth had an early Cancer Ascendant, which certainly agrees with his appearance, childlike temperament, and nickname "Babe," he therefore has an especially prominent Jupiter, since it was part of a stellium of Jupiter, the Ascendant, and the Moon. Ruth was always one of the highest paid players in baseball, and he in fact set salary precedents, in addition to earning a large number of testimonial and advertising fees. He had a huge income for almost twenty years; and he was also an extravagant spender who always went to excesses in everything: spending, eating, bar-hopping, etc.

His superb natural physical coordination, although he obviously broke all rules of physical training, is well symbolized by:

a) Venus closely conjunct Mercury in Pisces (a Jupiter/Neptune sign), both trine Saturn.

b) Jupiter conjunct his Moon (which was either late Gemini or early Cancer).

c) Mars in Taurus (which was reflected in his physical appearance) in exact square to the Sun and opposite Uranus, forming the explosive T-Square configuration that erupted in 714 home runs.

I should state that the emphasis on Mercurian factors (Venus conjunct Mercury, as well as Jupiter in Gemini and possibly a

Gemini Moon) confirms further the results of research I have done previously regarding athletes: the coordination and quickly-responding nervous system shown by such factors should never be overlooked.

—S.A.

Jupiter in Libra

Interpretive Guidelines for Jupiter in Libra:

Seeks to grow and to improve oneself through a balanced and objective attitude, fair-mindedness, and a diplomatic approach

One's faith is enhanced through a balanced, impartial, broadminded attitude

Opportunities arise through one's close relationships, and the capacity for sincere one-to-one interchange is usually well developed

Urge toward a larger order is expressed through sharing, cooperation, and encouraging others—sometimes through art or beauty

A need to weigh all sides of a question may undermine confident expansive actions and decisive thinking

Although Libra is a rather conservative sign (note that Saturn is exalted in Libra), those with Jupiter in Libra will quite often take risks in those areas of life that are of greatest concern to Libra. One might say that, in general, moderate, sensible risks are worth considering for individuals with Jupiter in Libra; but they will tend to risk more in romance, in artistic and humanitarian activities, and for the sake of key relationships or a sense of fairness.

These folks almost always have a pronounced romantic and/or artistic streak in their natures, even though they may not show romantic feelings publicly. In fact, they usually show little emotion, except through their artistic expression or in very private circumstances. After all, Libra is an *air* sign, and it is not very expressive of emotion. (The creative work of George Gershwin and Judy Garland—both of whom had Jupiter in Libra—are excellent examples of how romanticism can be channeled into an art form.) In most cases, these people have a well developed capacity to strongly support a partner, in work, marriage, or creative ventures, and they also need a reciprocal inflow of energy from their partners.

When one looks at the well-known people who have this position of Jupiter, one is struck not only by the fact that they are so often artistically gifted, but also by the fact that they seem always to have a special focus on one-to-one relationships or on their marriage or working partnership, even if the public is not aware of it. For example, in the life of actress Katharine Hepburn, her relationship with Spencer Tracy had a profound impact, both personally and professionally—a clear reflection of her Libra Jupiter. Those with Jupiter in Libra also have an ability to encourage others; they are responsive to others and are often good listeners and counselors. In any case, they cannot live for themselves alone. They often stand behind their partner's success or they draw upon their partner's strength and support to give a lift to their own enterprises. My research concludes that, unlike the commonly drawn image of Jupiter in Libra, they are not always super-social people by any means, although they do invariably have excellent social skills and instincts. Still, they are most comfortable and effective in one-to-one situations rather than in groups.

Carter: *Just, sociable, artistic or scientific.*

Mayo: *Sympathetic, just, charitable, hospitable, or conceited and lazy.*

Ebertin: *A sense of justice, the enjoyment of social contact, popularity, a striving for public work.*

Davison: *Enthusiasm for partnership, but may be overly anxious to please others.*

Hickey: *Refinement and idealism strong. Impartial, friendly and outgoing in nature. Loves art and beauty.*

Some interesting examples of this Jupiter position are Winston Churchill, C. G. Jung, and George Washington. Churchill always acknowledged his reliance on his wife Clementine. Although there is evidence that she felt quite neglected, her supportiveness and consistent loyalty were crucial to his being able to do his impossible war-time job. Churchill also had a mutual reception of Jupiter and

Venus, with Venus not only in Sagittarius, but also sextile Libra Jupiter. One might call this an amplified mutual reception! And it cannot be denied that the poetic beauty and cadences of his speeches did indeed inspire the entire free world with visions (Jupiter) of classic beauty and idealism (Venus). In fact, it has become known in recent years that Churchill actually wrote out some of his speeches in large stanzas reminiscent of the lines of classic epic poetry. In addition, he was a gifted painter who completed hundreds of impressionistic canvases.

George Washington was discussed in Chapter 3, and that section could be referred to again in relation to Jupiter in Libra. But certainly, he was one of the earliest champions of democracy and social justice. And, as even his often-times enemy John Adams said, "He seeks information from all quarters and judges more independently than any man I ever knew." This seems a perfect definition of Jupiter in Libra!

Carl Gustav Jung is rather a different expression of Jupiter in Libra than politically-involved people, although he did write many articles in professional journals analyzing various social trends from a psychological viewpoint. Jupiter in Libra for Jung seems to have manifested especially as a strong focus upon the importance of one-to-one relationships. His life-long marriage to his wife Emma not only lasted and produced numerous children, but ultimately resulted in Emma's doing her own writings in archetypal psychology. Jung emphasized for decades the importance of the quality of the therapist-patient relationship and the fact that that quality, as well as the personality of the therapist, had a profound impact upon the potential effectiveness of their interchange. Jung also published important writings on the psychology of "transference," studies which concerned the importance and results of the patient's natural proclivity toward *projecting* various values and images upon the therapist. In addition, Jung's more advanced works on alchemy and its psychological meaning bring out his interest in the concept of the *soror mystica* (a mystical sister who helps one with the inner development process) and various explorations along those lines regarding self-knowledge methods that were virtually inconceivable in his time and place. Jung also cultivated a deep long-term relationship with Toni Wolff, his *soror mystica* who gave him considerable support and inspiration.

In short, those with Jupiter in Libra prosper psychologically and materially as they establish relationships that help them work towards a definite goal and future direction. They develop confidence through living and sharing in such relationships, and often it seems that they can improve themselves most effectively by working within the context of a one-to-one relationship.

Other People Born with Jupiter in Libra

Steve Allen
Paul Cezanne
Jacques Cousteau
Henry Ford
Yuri Gagarin
Judy Garland
Joseph Goebbels
Katharine Hepburn
Sophia Loren

Martin Luther
Thomas Mann
Liza Minnelli
Bill Moyers
Wolfgang A. Mozart
Percy Bysshe Shelley
Van Cliburn
Swami Vivekananda

George Gershwin

George Gershwin is virtually an archetypal expression of Jupiter in Libra. In addition, the fact that Jupiter was in his Libra Sun Sign amplifies this quality all the more in every dimension of his life. (One published chart also gives him Sagittarius rising, which further emphasizes Jupiter since it would then be his ruling planet!) Those not familiar with the details of his life and work would be amazed to hear the huge number of popular songs and other musical works that he created. His popular songs were often upbeat, some even playfully happy, while at the same time virtually no one has ever written so many strikingly poignant romantic songs. He was virtually the epitome of *romantic* song-writers; he worked his entire life in writing *partnerships* (most notably with his brother Ira); and—when one examines the lyrics of his songs— one notes that he very often expressed the woman's point of view in the sentiments expressed...all of which are specifically Libran characteristics.

George Gershwin died just before age 40, and it might well be said that he was the most productive genius in American music, given the vast array of works he completed in so few years, ranging

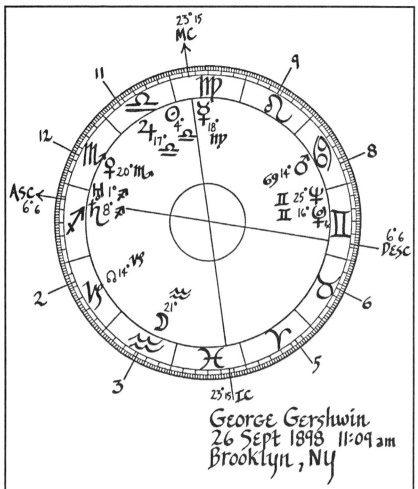

George Gershwin
26 Sept 1898 11:09 am
Brooklyn, NY

from *Rhapsody in Blue* (which perfectly captures the "jazz age" and America's vitality in that period) to *Porgy and Bess* (the first opera to focus on black people and their unique musical rhythms). It is also compellingly interesting to note that another song-writer who achieved great fame and wealth at an early age (as did Gershwin) and who died young also had the Sun in Libra and Moon in Aquarius: John Lennon. With their Aquarian Moons, both were amazingly attuned to the feelings and hopes of the masses, an ability which Gershwin's Libra Jupiter trine Pluto also augmented.

Gershwin's early fame and wealth and his enormous output

reflect the Jupiter square to his Cancer Mars, symbolic of an extremely driven person whose efforts know no bounds. (The position of Mars in the archetypally feminine sign Cancer may also indicate why he so readily wrote songs from the woman's viewpoint.) The Mars-Jupiter square's tendency toward *overdoing* may also be a reason why he died of a brain hemorrhage!

—S.A.

Jupiter in Aquarius

Interpretive Guidelines for Jupiter in Aquarius:

Seeks to grow and to improve oneself through humanitarian ideals, intellectual development, and daring experimentation.

Optimism can be deflected by an overly-detached, uninvolved attitude, but usually generous toward others

One's faith is eccentric, individualistic, unorthodox, and unique to oneself

Trusts in the unity of all humanity and all knowledge, and has a broad tolerance for a wide variety of free expression

Since Aquarius is co-ruled by the risk-taking, rebellious planet Uranus, it is not surprising that those with Jupiter here are usually quite comfortable taking risks in many areas of life. In fact, social, political, intellectual, and creative risks are stimulating to them and even necessary for them to feel alive. In the area of human relationships, they will also take chances as to the form, structure, and definition of their relationships; but perhaps it is the Saturn co-rulership of Aquarius that introduces a strong disinclination toward risk-taking as soon as they enter the domain of *emotions* in those relationships. Free and easy, tolerant, unconventional they can be, so long as they are not made to deal with or express emotions. Those with Jupiter in Aquarius are often quite unaware of some aspects of down-to-earth life and human feelings, which is understandable since they seek to rise above emotions and to seek well-being in *detachment*. They easily place their trust in large ideas and plans, but remain uncomfortable with the subtler nuances of human relationships, unless perhaps they have personal planets in water signs. This of course should not be surprising since Aquarius is an air sign, not a water sign. But this is a particularly aloof air sign and more detached and cold than Gemini or Libra.

These people often cultivate extreme ideas and beliefs, sometimes vacillating between quite contradictory concepts. They are very independent people, even to the point of being so willful as to be described as downright contrary.

As Walt Whitman, who had Jupiter in Aquarius, put it so well:

Do I contradict myself?
Very well then
I contradict myself, I contain multitudes.

Whitman is also an example of both the humanitarian impulses and the flaunting of social conventions that come naturally to those with this placement. Not only was his lifestyle completely unconventional in almost every way, but he served as a nurse during the Civil War. He rebelled against the strictures of narrow sexual roles in a number of areas of his life.

Another Jupiter in Aquarius man who, although well known previously as a poet and translator, gained his greatest fame through his explorations and promotion of various unconventional concepts of masculinity is Robert Bly. The humanitarian impulses of this position are also clearly seen in the chart of comedian Jerry Lewis, born March 16, 1926. The driving force behind the fund-raising activities of the Muscular Dystrophy Association since 1966, Lewis was born with an almost exact conjunction between Venus and Jupiter in Aquarius; a more perfect symbol of altruistic love for humanity would be hard to imagine. In addition, his Pisces Sun is conjunct Uranus almost exactly, giving yet another impetus toward humanitarian service to those in need.

In all fairness, however, it should be stated that some people with Jupiter in Aquarius express a sort of ivory-tower humanitarianism, sometimes with a streak of arrogance and even acting condescending to "less intelligent" people. This must be what Jeff Mayo observed, which led him to the comments in the first quote below.

Mayo: *Rudely tactless and intolerant. [At best] impartial and broad-minded.*

Carter: *Just, humane, often gifted in science.*

Davison: *Enthusiasm for humanitarian causes, reform. Expands originality...imagination, philosophial interests.*

Hickey: *Makes a good scientist interested in large projects and reform. Expands interest in group endeavors and can work well with others. Keen judgment and good intellect. Gives originality and ability to implant new ideas in other minds. Make good diplomats, labor relations experts, personnel managers and organizers.*

Moore & Douglas: *These individuals have inventive minds which are well adapted to promoting comprehensive programs of a philanthropic nature....often becomes involved in the handling and distribution of money in the interest of social, scientific, or charitable enterprises.*

These folks are often drawn to government service and are what Marcia Moore called "the ideal democrat with a knack for handling groups of people." This perfectly describes the role that Dwight Eisenhower (with Jupiter in Aquarius) played during World War II, as he worked to coordinate a vast number of nationalities and power centers. Charles de Gaulle was also a champion of democracy, refusing to submit to the Nazi demands and actively reorganizing a French army in England for an eventual invasion. With both Mars and Jupiter in Aquarius, de Gaulle did exemplify some of the "know-it-all" arrogance that can sometimes be observed in this placement, but he also displayed the courage and risk-taking propensity—based on a vision of the future—that so centrally characterizes an Aquarian Jupiter.

In fact, those with Jupiter here are *focused on the future*. Rarely materialistic, their sense of prosperity and confidence comes from exercising their unique breadth of vision. As Moore and Douglas put it, their "broadened viewpoint produces new patterns of perception." Witness the following examples of those who achieved scientific and/ or creative breakthroughs:

● In science, Marie Curie, Tycho Brahe, and Albert Einstein.

- In the arts, Gustave Courbet, Edouard Manet, Michelangelo, and the composer Erik Satie.

- Bridging both fields, Lewis Carroll was renowned as a mathematician, but also wrote *Alice in Wonderland* and other superb exercises in imagination.

Other People Born with Jupiter in Aquarius

Helena Blavatsky	Hedy Lamarr
Governor Jerry Brown	Grant Lewi
Tom Dooley	Herman Melville
Isadora Duncan	Thomas Merton
Elizabeth II	Marilyn Monroe
Alec Guinness	Vaslav Nijinski
Immanuel Kant	Ed Sullivan

Albert Einstein

The life and work of Albert Einstein provide a particularly illuminating example of the dynamics of Jupiter in the revolutionary sign Aquarius. He has an undisputed place in the highest pantheon of those scientific geniuses who have transformed our basic assumptions about reality: "In the history of the exact sciences, only a handful of men—men like Nicolaus Copernicus and Isaac Newton—share the honor that was Albert Einstein's: the initiation of a revolution in scientific thought. His insights into the nature of the physical world made it impossible for physicists and philosophers to view that world as they had before." (quoted from Roger H. Stuewer, in the *McGraw Hill Encyclopedia of World Biography*)

The innovative, tradition-shattering quality of Jupiter in Aquarius is given vastly more voltage by the opposition to Uranus in the third house. This aspect indicates the way Einstein's process of thinking took unprecedented intuitive leaps. (Physicist J. Robert Oppenheimer referred to Einstein's 1905 papers on the theory of relativity, written when Einstein was only in his mid-twenties, as "paralyzingly beautiful.") The profound impact on society of Einstein's discoveries, and their penetration into some of the deepest mysteries of physics, is shown by the placement of Pluto in the *eleventh house* (of social change and scientific inquiry) at the

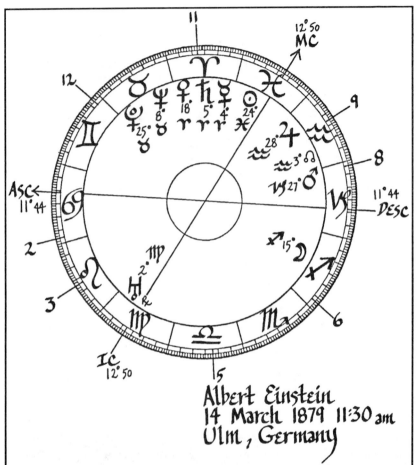

Albert Einstein
14 March 1879 11:30 am
Ulm, Germany

apex of a T-square to the Jupiter-Uranus opposition. This transformational influence burst upon the world's awareness when headlines in the November 7, 1919 *London Times* trumpeted: "Revolution in science, New theory of the universe, Newtonian ideas overthrown." (quoted by Roger Highfield and Paul Carter in *The Private Lives of Albert Einstein*) The news stories confirmed that British scientists had found empirical evidence for Einstein's theories. During 1919 the forty-year-old Einstein was experiencing transiting Uranus opposition natal Uranus; and in November, transiting Uranus was exactly stationary conjunct Einstein's natal Jupiter in the ninth house!

Some years before this, Einstein was employed at the Swiss

Patent Office in Berne. In his biography of Einstein, Kenji Sugimoto writes that the young man, "who was known for his lack of concern for appearances and for his casual dress, often appeared in the office in green slippers trimmed with flowers." This humorous detail illustrates an important facet of Einstein's character: his Aquarian indifference to what others thought, and his insistence on pursuing his own unique path. His friend Antonina Vallentin (quoted by Hilaire Cuny in Louis de Broglie's *Einstein*) noted: "He puts himself to much trouble and mischief to defend himself against the intrusion of the conventional in his existence." Einstein's birth chart is, in a sense, "triply" Aquarian/Uranian: Aquarius, Uranus, and the eleventh house are all involved in the aspect configuration discussed above. And Aquarius is the "subtone" for the Jupiter-disposited Pisces Sun as well as for the Sagittarius Moon, which is the chart ruler. Aquarius themes appear prominently both in others' observations of Einstein and in his own writings. Stuewer writes: "Both in his scientific and in his personal life, he was utterly independent, a trait that manifested itself in his approach to scientific problems, in his unconventional dress, in his relationships with family and friends, and in his aloofness from university and governmental politics (in spite of his intense social consciousness)."

The capacity for Aquarian intellectual detachment gave Einstein the ability to look at the enigmas of physics from entirely fresh vantage points. But, as the following quote from his *Autobiographical Notes* makes clear, for Einstein the Aquarian quest, in an expanded Jupiterian sense, shaped his entire life path. From an early age, he writes, he felt the urge

> to free myself from the chains of the 'merely personal,' from an existence dominated by wishes, hopes, and primitive feelings. Out yonder there was this huge world, which exists independently of us human beings and which stands before us like a great, eternal riddle, at least partially accessible to our inspection and thinking. The contemplation of this world beckoned as a liberation, and I soon noticed that many a man whom I had learned to esteem and to admire had found inner freedom and security in its pursuit. The mental grasp of this extra-personal world within the frame of our capabilities presented itself to my mind, half consciously, half unconsciously, as a supreme goal.

The airy Aquarian/Uranian focus on the impersonal was evident also in Einstein's relationships, although first-hand descriptions do pick up on the watery sensitivity one would expect of a Pisces Sun with Cancer rising. A son-in-law (quoted by Cuny) observed the vivid impact of Einstein's appearance and said: "This power resides in the kindness of his expression which envelopes his whole being with a kind of radiant softness." But a friend (quoted by Highfield and Carter) "remarked on the paradoxes of Einstein's behavior. Here was a man who could seemingly sympathize 'deeply and passionately with the fate of every stranger,' yet on closer contact 'immediately withdrew into his shell.'" Of course Einstein, a Nobel prize-winning scientist (with a jam-packed tenth house), acquired enormous fame; and, with Venus in the tenth trine to the Sagittarius Moon, his popularity was wide-ranging. It is understandable that he would need to protect his privacy (a Cancer rising instinct anyway!). But Einstein himself acknowledged the deeper Aquarian/Uranian detachment that colored his relationships:

> *I have never belonged wholeheartedly to any country or state, to my circle of friends, or even to my own family. These ties have always been accompanied by a vague aloofness, and the wish to withdraw into myself increases with the years....I lose something by it, to be sure, but I am compensated for it in being rendered independent of the customs, opinions, and prejudices of others, and am not tempted to rest my peace of mind upon such shifting foundations.* (quoted by Highfield and Carter)

Both of his marriages were problematical. He referred to marriage as "an undertaking in which I twice failed rather disgracefully." (quoted by Abraham Pais in *Einstein Lived Here*) And his relationships with his two sons also were strained. However, Einstein had lifelong friendships, and showed particular compassion to his sister, who was disabled in her later years. In his wider social circles, the egalitarian, free-spirited side of his Aquarian behavior was evident; and it was perceptively noted by his stepdaughter (quoted by Cuny) who "asserts that Einstein's interest—or his disinterest—in an individual never depended on the individual's title or social class, and a poor beggar could be retained for hours while an 'important personality' might find himself rudely rejected."

It was the larger "global family," more so than his personal one, that was of most concern to Einstein. Not surprisingly, Einstein's Aquarian Jupiter (as well as the tenth house Pisces Sun and eleventh house outer planets) found expression in wide-ranging humanitarian social concerns, including pacifism, efforts toward international cooperation, and—after firsthand experience of Nazi anti-semitism (including assassination threats)—active campaigning for Zionism. (In 1952 he was offered the presidency of the young state of Israel, but turned it down.) He also joined other scientists, after the atomic bombs were dropped on Japan in 1945, in speaking out against the use of atomic weapons. Einstein stated that he felt a sense of obligation to use his fame, and the generalized authority that had been accorded him, to protest injustice in society—even at the risk of his reputation.

In Einstein's life, we see the effort to integrate a Piscean yearning for a sense of transcendent meaning with a ninth house Aquarian Jupiter insistence upon a belief system compatible with scientific inquiry. The friction between these two needs emerged during an overtly religious stage of Einstein's boyhood. In his *Autobiographical Notes* Einstein writes:

> *I came—though the child of entirely irreligious (Jewish) parents— to a deep religiousness, which, however, reached an abrupt end at the age of twelve. Through the reading of popular scientific books I soon reached the conviction that much in the stories of the Bible could not be true. The consequence was a positively fanatic orgy of freethinking coupled with the impression that youth is intentionally being deceived by the state through lies; it was a crushing impression. Mistrust of every kind of authority grew out of this experience.*

Interestingly, when Einstein was twelve, transiting Uranus made a station at 27 degrees Libra—exactly trine to the natal Jupiter in Aquarius.

Despite this disillusionment, Einstein did not divorce himself from the value of religious perspectives, although he rejected anthropomorphic notions of God and orthodox dogmas in general. (He was, in fact, denounced by conservative religious authorities for, in their view, promoting atheism and for turning "science into a God.") His union of the Piscean and Aquarian impulses was expressed in such statements as: "I am of the opinion that all the finer speculations in the realm of science spring from a deep religious feeling, and that without such feeling they would not be fruitful" (quoted by William Lawhead in Dennis Ryan's *Einstein and the Humanities*); and in this famous line from Einstein's essay "Science and Religion": "Science without religion is lame, religion without science is blind." Einstein used the words "cosmic religion" to differentiate his outlook from that of traditional religions, and given his "mistrust of authority," it is not surprising that he would feel an affinity with heretics (who are innately Aquarian!):

> *The religious geniuses of all ages have been distinguished by this kind of religious feeling, which knows no dogma and no God conceived in man's image; so that there can be no church whose central teachings are based on it. Hence it is precisely among the heretics of every age that we find men who were filled with this highest kind of religious feeling and were in many cases regarded by their contemporaries as atheists, sometimes also as saints. Looked at in this light, men like Democritus, Francis of Assisi, and Spinoza are closely akin to one another.* (quoted by Pais)

Einstein's spiritual concerns would seem to point towards a Jupiter-Neptune interaction, in addition to the Jupiter-Uranus and Jupiter-Pluto already noted. In fact, Jupiter is at the apex of a triangle formed by *quintiles* to both Neptune in the eleventh house and to the Moon in Sagittarius in the sixth house. Neptune and the Moon form a bi-quintile to each other. In a mind with the subtlety and complexity of Einstein's, we could expect that these quintiles would not remain dormant. Bil Tierney's description of the quintile aspect (in *Dynamics of Aspect Analysis*) is remarkably apt for Einstein: "The general opinion concerning quintiles is that they are indicative of uncommon facets of human capacity expressing a notable degree of creative genius, rare insight, and mental artistry." Einstein's Aquarian Jupiter quest for scientific understanding was infused with a Neptunian sense of wonder and a heightened aesthetic perception (Neptune in *Taurus*) of the beauty inherent in the organizing principles of the universe. His sixth house Sagittarian Moon aided his intuitive formulation of his vast perceptions and shaped them (with the help of Mercury-Saturn!) into the shorthand notation of physics.

A moving statement from Einstein's "My Credo" sums up the spiritual perception that gave rise to his revolutionary scientific work:

> *The most beautiful and deepest experience a man can have is the sense of the mysterious. It is the underlying principle of religion as well as of all serious endeavor in art and science. He who never had this experience seems to me, if not dead, then at least blind. To sense that behind anything that can be experienced there is something that our minds cannot grasp, whose beauty and sublimity reaches us only indirectly: this is religiousness. In this sense I am religious. To me it suffices to wonder at these secrets and to attempt humbly to grasp with my mind a mere image of the lofty structure of all there is.*
> —B.McE.

CHAPTER 7

Jupiter in the Water Signs: Interpretive Guidelines

Those with Jupiter in water signs usually have strong intuition, both applied to understanding other people and in sensing where future trends are leading. Such intuition will, of course, only be accurate if the individual has overcome any tendency toward wallowing in fear or letting the memories of past hurts cripple objectivity. A sense of well-being and self-confidence often takes time to develop for these introverted souls, and the key to achieving it is to tune in on one's hidden emotional reserves and the strength that emanates from one's inner life.

> ### *Jupiter in Water Signs:*
>
> Inner faith is stimulated through depth of emotional experience and through positive expression of one's compassion and imagination
>
> Opportunities come when one is sensitive and caring toward others, and when one intuitively follows one's inner yearnings

These people idealize emotional experience somewhat, leading often to disillusionment and even bitterness. However, once they learn not to rely on others treating them kindly and sensitively but rather to depend on their own inner emotional strength, they can at best grow to express and experience human oneness and compassion. They do have abundant emotional reserves which both they and others can draw upon, especially in emergencies or in trying times.

Those with Jupiter in water signs are disinclined toward risk in almost all areas of life, but they are usually happy once they have engaged in substantial emotional risk-taking, thus enabling them to overcome their natural fears and thereby eventually gaining more self-confidence. Since they so intensely live within themselves, they usually care little for outer appearances.

Jupiter in Cancer

Interpretive Guidelines for Jupiter in Cancer:

Seeks to grow and to improve oneself through development of family values and emotional supportiveness

Opportunities come through one's expression of protective empathy and instinctive nurturing

Need for sensitivity to others' feelings in order to have confidence in self; this emotional sensitivity is usually well-developed

Reliance on a higher power can be dampened by excessive reserve, fears, or self-protection

Has an innate understanding of the human need for security, and usually expresses the more giving, generous side of Cancer

The fact that Jupiter is exalted in the sign Cancer has been discussed earlier in this book. I also explained what a unique and encouraging combination this is. However, the fact that Cancer is the Sun sign of the U.S.A. seems to me to have a special relevance. The theme of "family values" is a political measuring stick for many conservatives in the U.S.A. as this is written, and the reference to "family values" in the guidelines above was actually written in the late 1980s, before it became such a political "buzzword." Further, those with Jupiter in Cancer in their natal charts seem to have an especially strong resonance with the popular culture of the U.S.A., for the birth chart of the U.S.A. has not only the Sun in Cancer, but also Jupiter conjunct Venus in Cancer! The names seem veritably to leap out at me as I scan my research, for they constitute an *amazingly* popular group:

a) Humanitarians who gave abundantly to the country's cultural resources, such as Paul Mellon and Andrew Carnegie, who are discussed at length in Chapter 2.

b) Great athletes who electrified the crowds in the "American pastime" baseball, Jackie Robinson and Willie Mays, perhaps the two most exciting players of their era. And of course, Robinson had a profound impact on the entire society as well as on his sport through his courageous confrontation with racism.

c) Extraordinarily popular actors such as Sean Connery and James Dean, who are also favorites of women worldwide.

d) Musicians who seemed invariably to have their finger on the pulse of the public's emotions: Paul McCartney, Liberace, Nat King Cole, and Leonard Bernstein, whose Jupiter conjunct Pluto in Cancer manifested as his extraordinarily dramatic style of conducting vast symphonic works, while also teaching the masses about classical music. (Franz Liszt, who also had Jupiter in Cancer, was also hugely popular in his era and captivated audiences throughout Europe.)

e) Neil Armstrong, the first man to land upon the Moon, had not only Jupiter in Cancer, but also Moon in Sagittarius; hence, he had a mutual reception of the Moon and Jupiter, a great symbol of lunar exploration!

f) The writings of author James Michener have enjoyed enormous long-term popularity, most of which delve into the *history* of various countries or regions of the U.S.A. but often express this history from the *subjective* viewpoint of specific characters' experience.

g) The evangelist Billy Graham has drawn a huge following, which has now grown to be quite extensive even in foreign countries, appealing as he does to the emotions of his listeners. He became in the 1970s and 1980s rather a *de facto* national chaplain and counselor to Presidents of the U.S.A.

h) William Jennings Bryan was a great favorite of many U.S. citizens for many years. Not only was he a Presidential candidate more than once, but he also argued for "traditional values" in the famous "monkey trial" regarding the teaching of evolution in the schools.

In short, those with Cancer Jupiter seem remarkably often to have extraordinary popular appeal. They are able to express old-fashioned feelings and often to remind others of kinder, safer, simpler times.

Although those with Jupiter in Cancer work especially well with the public, they are also usually quite private people. Indeed, they are *responsive* to others, but they also insist upon their right to privacy and inner peace. A good example is J.D. Salinger, author of

Catcher in the Rye and other best-sellers, who so prizes his privacy that he has sued to preserve it numerous times. "Beatle" George Harrison likewise carefully measures out his public appearances and is known for cultivating his inner, private life through gardening, meditation, and humanitarian concerns such as his concert for Bangladesh. The painter Paul Gaugin also yearned for a simpler life and privacy to the extent that he moved to the South Seas. In short, those with Jupiter in Cancer seem to be "old-fashioned" in some major way and to yearn for *traditions* wherein they can find security. They need to feel simultaneously a sense of belonging and emotional freedom, whether in values, relationships, or religion.

Mayo: *Kindly, protective, charitable; or extremely touchy, too conscientious.*

Davison: *Expands sympathies, business acumen, acquisitiveness. Mind is practical yet imaginative.*

Moore & Douglas: *People with Jupiter in Cancer generally are genial hosts and hostesses who are well suited to coordinate the many facets of social protocol with the culinary complexities that contribute to the making of a festive occasion. They are often found in clubs, hotels, bars, and restaurants, dispensing refreshments in an attractive setting.*

Those with Jupiter in Cancer are often instinctively more risk-averse than people with most other Jupiter placements, but they will give of their emotions to care for those they are close to or sympathize with. In fact, it is in this area of emotional expression that they may achieve some of their greatest potential. They can take chances in this area of life because they tend to have faith in people, especially in old friends or relatives. And their own sense of confidence can grow simultaneously with their encouraging others to develop.

Although closely tied to the past, these people are often gifted with a special vision of the future and how it will develop from past and present trends. They often have an intuitive and expanded understanding of how vast concerns affect the lives of individuals, families, and communities. And pursuing that future vision is usually a key to their own prosperity.

Other People Born with Jupiter in Cancer

Richard Alpert (Ram Dass)
Annie Besant
Robert Browning
Margot Fonteyn
Edmund Hillary
Jeddu Krishnamurti
Princess Margaret Rose

Benito Mussolini
Sir Laurence Olivier
Margaret Sanger
Harry Truman
Mark Twain
Leslie Uggams

Jupiter in Scorpio

Interpretive Guidelines for Jupiter in Scorpio:

Seeks to grow and to improve oneself through transmutation of desires and compulsions and by unusually thorough understanding of life's inner workings

Opportunities come through one's ability to shrewdly judge people and situations—a well-developed sense of resourcefulness and opportunism

Optimistic expansion and developing faith can be hindered by fear, secrecy, and the inability to open up emotionally; but Jupiter often expresses the nobler and more elevated qualities of Scorpio

Urge to connect with something greater than self is expressed through intensity of experience and depth of feeling; trust in a higher power comes through seeking and confronting that intensity

Need to tap into a powerful transformative energy in order to have confidence in self

Over the years, I have come to express Scorpio's nature as one of "emotional extremes," and Jupiter's manifestations through the sign Scorpio are no exception. In fact, since Jupiter itself is given to excess, it should come as no surprise that this combination quite often is expressed in powerful and contradictory ways that could indeed be characterized as extreme. For example, these people need risk in order to have the intensity of experience that they crave, but they are also fearful of being vulnerable and even feel terrified of life getting "out of control." And yet, if things remain calm for too long, they often instinctively stir up conflict, problems, or at least start new projects or tackle new challenges.

This is a placement of strong and deep emotions; it can be expressed as resentment and extreme pettiness, *or* through ennobled emotions and loyalty to people and causes. And the same person may contain all these diverse tendencies! These folks crave deep involvement with whatever they do. Superficiality is not a familiar concept to them. Marcus Aurelius, whose Jupiter was in Scorpio, gives us a great watery image of finding goodness (Jupiter) in the depths (Scorpio):

> *Dig within. Within is the foundation of good,*
> *and it will ever bubble up, if you will ever dig.*
> *—Meditations*

Those with this Jupiter position often like to expand and explore in the "taboo" areas of experience and knowledge, such as the occult, sex, death, deeper psychological motivations, and various metaphysical laws. In any case, they are research-oriented and may investigate natural laws, financial operations, military strategies, or criminal behavior with equal thoroughness. Moore and Douglas concisely summarize some of the essential qualities of this position:

> *He knows how to think big and at the same time is willing to dirty his hands by undertaking the practical work of the world. His talent for converting natural resources into useful products may attract him to fields connected with chemistry, engineering, and pollution control. He may also be a discerning psychologist who can assist people who are endeavoring not only to adjust to the circumstances of the world, but to reconstruct themselves from within.*

> *Jupiter and Scorpio combine to give a flair for business and finance. Frequently, these people prosper because they are willing to take the trouble to dig out necessary information, to get down to essentials, and to bide their time until a situation is ripe for development. They amass wealth because they so strongly desire and expect success in all their enterprises. Theirs is an almost mystical faith in the power of money to breed more money and, consequently, more power. Forceful Scorpio and farseeing Jupiter blend in the hard driving, efficient executive who, despite having his nose to the grindstone, is quick to catch the*

scent of new and promising markets for his products. There may be an almost sublime self-confidence which transcends ordinary egotism...

Those with Jupiter here often feel the need to be possessed by a cause, a greater power, another person, or a sense of mission. In any case, they are often seen by others to act as if they are "possessed" by a passion or energy which they cannot fully control, which is especially obvious if they also have other Scorpio or strong Pluto factors in their chart. This "something beyond them," however, also gives them a great ability to tune into extra reserves of power or into an intelligence that transcends conscious logic. They often have shrewd hunches, and "they think with their guts." This uncanny intuition also enables them to see the core of truth or value in a person, thing, investment, or situation, which most other people have completely given up on. Hence, they can revivify seemingly dead situations, products, companies; and likewise, with people, they can help them to heal or reform themselves, even if the condition seems desperate.

Carter: *Reserved, dignified; sometimes reckless or self-indulgent.*

Davison: *A resourceful, subtle mind; can be suspicious. Expands passions, devotion, magnetism, will-power, and pride. Can be self-absorbed.*

Hickey: *Courage strong. Very secretive. Can give healing power.*

Ebertin: *Ruthless striving for possessions and pleasures...overly pronounced sexual life.*

Ebertin's reference above to the emphasis on the sex life should probably be clarified and elaborated. Marcia Moore wrote that there is a tendency with this placement either to "repress or over-express the erotic impulses," which is generally true for many other planets in Scorpio as well. I think it is most accurate to say that those with Jupiter in Scorpio will strive to broadly *understand* eros and sex, probably to experiment with it, but at least to exhibit a strong and wide-ranging interest in the sexual energy, its manifestations, and theories about it. In some people, it remains primarily a *mental* interest. In other words, by no means do all those with this placement act out their curiosity. It depends on the rest of the chart, and

I have personally seen a number of people of both sexes with Jupiter in Scorpio who exhibit a fairly low physical sex drive and not at all an inordinate interest in sex and eros, but yet who seem to have an instinctive understanding of the role sex can play in human life and motivation.

Many well-known people who have Jupiter in Scorpio focused on passionate emotional expression or on emotional tension in their creative work, such as Elvis Presley, Alfred Hitchcock, Auguste Rodin, and Tennessee Williams. Others expressed in their work grand and wide sweeps of emotion, such as in the music of Ravel, Tchaikovsky, and Richard Strauss. Various others explored the underside of human life, such as author Joan Didion, Mata Hari, and Aleister Crowley.

Other People Born with Jupiter in Scorpio

Konrad Adenauer	Jean Harlow
Julie Andrews	Ernest Hemingway
Lucille Ball	Norman Mailer
Napoleon Bonaparte	Ronald Reagan
Charlotte Brontë	Albert Schweitzer
Charles E. O. Carter	Gloria Swanson
George Washington Carver	Leo Tolstoi
Diane Von Furstenberg	Emile Zola

Jupiter in Pisces

Interpretive Guidelines for Jupiter in Pisces:

Seeks to grow and to improve oneself through living one's ideals, expanding one's sympathies, and generosity of spirit

Need to be compassionate and sensitive in order to feel faith in oneself

Acting on the need for self-improvement can be hindered by unfocused, noncritical attitudes and escapism

Openness to grace is based on one's compassion toward all that suffers

Has a well-developed trust in a higher power; understands the importance of devotion to an ideal and openness to the spiritual dimension of experience

As one might expect when Jupiter is "dignified" in Pisces, the sign of compassion and devotion, there is a considerable idealism and desire to be of service to the helpless. Abraham Lincoln is the best example of this, for his writings even before he became President testified to the empathy he felt for the plight of the slaves. Chief Justice of the U.S. Supreme Court Earl Warren also had this placement, and his views profoundly affected all of society by liberalizing and opening up traditionally closed segments of American life. Walter Mondale, Senator, Presidential candidate, and Ambassador to Japan, was also known for his liberal political views and for his activist definition of government, slanted toward benefiting the have-nots, the working class, and organized labor. (See Chapter 9 for more details of his life and his chart.) Also, Dr. Benjamin Spock, who wrote the most influential book on baby and child care, is credited with *softening* child-rearing practices throughout the country, although in later years he was accused of helping to raise a generation of undisciplined, spoiled brats!

In all of the people mentioned above, one can see the Pisces Jupiter need to take risks—and even bear severe criticism—in order to promote a greater cause, goal, or vision. There is often an image of nobility and dignity that these people exude, an aura which very likely helped Sidney Poitier and Harry Belafonte not only to fame but to relatively easy acceptance by white American society during the 1950s, when segregation was still the norm in much of the country. Orson Welles was another actor who had Jupiter here and who could emanate a large, expansive, impressive energy. His directorial efforts in numerous breakthrough films which are now regarded as classics are especially indicative of the imaginative and inventive abilities found in this placement. Dramatic and emotionally evocative jazz singers Ella Fitzgerald and Billie Holiday both have Jupiter in Pisces in their charts. For further examples, Leonardo da Vinci had Jupiter here, as did the greatest of all German poets, Goethe. And one should not fail to mention the many people with Jupiter in Pisces who made great contributions to science, such as Johannes Kepler, Isaac Newton, and Charles Darwin.

Carter: *Pleasant, easy-going, friendly; devoted to philanthropy and public work.*

Ebertin: *Altruism, kind-heartedness, contentment in modest circumstances, a love of solitude and quiet happiness... impressionability.*

Davison: *Enthusiasm for public welfare, healing; a mind that is sympathetic, receptive, impressionable (vacillating).*

Hickey: *Interest strong in occult and psychic laws. Can work well with people for there is a deep understanding of their needs. Emotion and sympathy must enter into his work or he will not be happy.*

Moore & Douglas: *The Piscean influence toward introspection is not incompatible with Jupiterian expansiveness. The lesson of this combination is that real growth must imply an evolution of consciousness...and that inner and outer processes are carried forward simultaneously.*

Mayo: *Benevolent, genial, humorous; or extravagant, unreliable, over-imaginative.*

The tendency just mentioned by Mayo toward possible extravagance can indeed manifest in a minority of cases as an over-inflated ego, sometimes leading to quite destructive consequences. Keeping one's feet on the ground may be the hardest challenge for those with this position. They can float away into dreams of personal glory (e.g., General Douglas MacArthur); they can become lost in self-aggrandizement posing as big-heartedness (Joseph Stalin); or they can indulge themselves in exaggerated, mythologized versions of their lives (Friedrich Nietzsche and Henry Miller). In some cases of more ordinary mortals, they can "go to pieces" if their lifestyle, marriage, or job to which they have been devoted disintegrates, resulting in disorientation, escapism, and difficulty coping with reality.

Self-esteem and confidence for most of these people, however, slowly develops over time as they align themselves with a spiritual, social, or artistic ideal. As Moore and Douglas implied in the quote listed earlier, growth, personal progress, and improvement are for them intimately connected with the development of higher and/or broader consciousness. These folks are usually future-oriented people, and almost invariably they have some kind of special imagination, intuitive understanding of life, or breadth of vision that can inspire themselves and others, and which they need to act upon throughout their lives if they are going to feel prosperous and successful. As Moore and Douglas explain, "success" for those with Jupiter in Pisces has little to do with money or material goods:

> *...considerably less money-minded than those with Jupiter in earth signs. They are not as likely to see life in terms of material failure and success because they care too much for their own serenity to sell their souls to the jealous gods of commerce. They want to know what life means, and if the earning of money is less meaningful to them than having the leisure to enjoy what nature has gratuitously given, they will turn disdainfully from the struggle to accumulate possessions to the search for inner fulfillment.*

> *Periodically, these types of people need to escape from themselves altogether and return to nature. Music, open spaces, and beautiful scenery benefit their health more than any tonic. A sea voyage or a vacation by the water may also restore their jaded nerves. They should habitually set aside times of peace and solitude for quiet meditation.*

Other People Born with Jupiter in Pisces

Evangeline Adams	Bob Hope
Louisa May Alcott	Edgar Allen Poe
Abdul Baha	Franz Schubert
Sarah Bernhardt	Frank Sinatra
Benvenuto Cellini	Leon Trotsky
Sigmund Freud	Paul Verlaine
Arthur Godfrey	Lawrence Welk
Haile Selassie	Stevie Wonder
Isabel Hickey	

Michael Jordan

Basketball superstar Michael Jordan, born February 17, 1963, is probably the most widely-known sports celebrity in history, surpassing even Babe Ruth (see Jupiter in Gemini section) because of the far greater extent of electronic media exposure worldwide in modern times. Jordan is one more Aquarius Sun sportsman whose level of skill is simply on another plane compared to his competitors. Others are Ruth himself, Hank Aaron (who broke Ruth's home run record), and Wayne Gretzky, the ice hockey star known simply as "The Great One."

Jordan's Jupiter is in Pisces, and it is therefore dignified since it is in a sign that it co-rules. It is also especially strong since it is the ruler of his Moon Sign Sagittarius; and in fact Jupiter may also square his Sagittarius Moon, depending on the exact birth time. If it does, that would make his Moon (the "public") doubly colored by Jupiter's beneficent energies. This would certainly be appropriate for the most famous and the richest (according to *Forbes* magazine) athlete in the world. His fame is so extensive that, in sporting circles, he is referred to simply as "Michael." In fact, if "Magic" Johnson had not earned that nickname, I think it would have been awarded to Jordan. I say this because he is known for doing the *impossible*, as if he possessed a kit of magic which he could draw upon. It seems significant that so many factors in his chart relate to Jupiter and Neptune, the big magicians of the mythical planetary pantheon:

- Jupiter in Pisces (a sign co-ruled by Jupiter and Neptune)
- Jupiter trine Neptune
- Neptune stationary at his birth, an indication of an inordinately powerful attunement to that planet
- Moon in a Jupiter sign and probably square Jupiter
- Jupiter is semi-sextile Saturn, an indication of a potentially perfect balance between relying on one's divine gifts and on one's personal efforts and discipline. It is well known that Jordan is one of the hardest working athletes.

I should also briefly mention a couple of astrological facts that deflate traditional astrological superstitions. First, Jordan's Mars in Leo is *retrograde!* This must be the most conclusive proof ever discovered that the concept of retrograde planets as being "debilitating" is a prime candidate for the astrological scrap-heap. Also, Saturn in Jordan's chart is in his Sun Sign Aquarius, which obviously has not symbolized any sort of worldly failure! In fact, I find that Saturn aspects of this type are commonly found in those who succeed in their chosen fields through sheer effort and determination.

—S.A.

CHAPTER 8

Jupiter in the Houses

Ideals are like the stars–we never reach them, but like
the mariners on the sea, we chart our course by them.
—Carl Schurz

Since the houses are far more abstract than the specific *energy* that one can feel and directly experience from a planet's placement in a sign, it might be a useful exercise to visualize the image expressed above by Carl Schurz's quote and to envision what ideals or dreams of the future one consciously or unconsciously dwells upon that are symbolized by the house position of one's Jupiter. An alternative approach might be to reflect upon what areas of life and fields of experience one tends to habitually *idealize*, whether constructively or perhaps excessively. The guidelines given later in this chapter will further provide clues as to potential meanings of each person's house placement of natal Jupiter.

First, however, I want to make it absolutely clear that, as we proceed into the murkier realm of trying to understand the houses, it is virtually impossible to know with confidence that a specific, sharply-defined interpretation of Jupiter in a certain house is completely reliable*, especially for those with whom we are not quite familiar. With our own chart and the charts of those people we know well, we can in time determine a general range of action and meaning for Jupiter, especially after we observe the natal Jupiter being activated by transits and progressions over a period of years. During those times, Jupiter's potentials will be energized, future plans will come to the surface, opportunities will appear, and strong urges for

---

* ED. NOTE: The reader should refer to the Note on Example Charts after the Prologue at the beginning of this book in order to review various issues that relate not only to the houses as discussed herein but also to the style of charts depicted in this book. Most importantly, the reader should be aware that a planet conjunct a house cusp (or even placed a few degrees prior to the cusp) very likely manifests through that specific house, whether or not it also is expressed through the previous house to some extent.

expansion, improvement, and going to excess will be felt and sometimes acted upon. Observing such developments will enable an experienced astrological practitioner to determine more reliably what Jupiter does mean and will mean in the future. But still, Jupiter invariably implies movement, change, improvement, and going beyond the *status quo*, so it can indeed be a planet of surprises–not so shocking as those of Uranus, but nonetheless not a factor in any chart which can confidently be interpreted rigidly with predetermined assumptions.

Why do I begin a chapter on Jupiter's meaning in the houses by immediately referring to how uncertain such interpretation is? I do so for a number of reasons, which have been explained in my previous books (for example, see the chapter on the houses in my *Chart Interpretation Handbook*). But just to summarize a few reasons as briefly as possible:

a)   Most birth times are at least somewhat inaccurate, making all house cusps less reliable.

b)   Many different house systems are used worldwide, some of which seem to work better in different latitudes; each system changes the positions of the eight intermediate house cusps.

c)   Even if one is happy with a specific house system, one must learn how to use it effectively. For example, many experienced astrologers have concluded that the house cusp is *not* the beginning of a house, but that the house seems to start perhaps 6° before the cusp, thus making many planets "act" as if they are in the next house compared to how they may appear at a superficial glance in traditionally-drawn charts. (This is explained in detail on page 127 of my *Chart Interpretation Handbook*.)

d)   The sign position of and aspects to a planet are so dominant that trying to interpret a planet's house position in isolation is a dubious venture. It is far more useful to employ reliable guidelines, like those we will outline in this chapter, and then to determine the individual's values, ideals, background, and future plans in a dialogue of discovery.

The houses, after all, represent vast fields of experience, both inner and outer. The rich symbolism of the houses, on many different levels, must not be eliminated in an attempt to make them fit into neat, narrow little theories, such as the old "departments of life" idea implied. Such a traditional approach was extremely rigid and resulted in "readings" that left many individuals depressed and despondent about their evidently immutable fates! The houses' symbolism *must serve us*; we need not limit ourselves and our potential to try to fit into restrictive "rules" of interpretation! As astrologer/author Noel Tyl wrote in an article, if we try in a rigid way to relate a client's life only to our understanding of astrological rules, we "run the risk of *confining* the life to what we know about astrology....Our craft takes us well beyond textbooks and lessons. What we know about life becomes a lot more important than what we know...about the tools of astrology." Hence, we should view the houses as tools for exploration of reality, inner and outer–not rigid boxes into which everything must "fit." After all, don't most experiences and activities in life bridge more than one house and echo through, perhaps, three or four fields of experience? So, the guidelines in this chapter should be viewed as jumping-off points for reflection, inquiry, honest self-analysis, and discovery of personal meaning and potential.

The reader will notice that I am repeatedly using a system of keywords for each house, which sometimes align with and sometimes are varied from the traditional meanings of each house. This keyword system, which I have used for over twenty years, is explained in depth in my books *Astrology, Psychology and the Four Elements* and *Chart Interpretation Handbook*. I refer the reader to those books for the rationale behind those keywords, but suffice it to say that those keywords are based on the fact that there are "fiery" houses, "earthy" houses, "airy" houses, and "watery" houses–paralleling the twelve signs. And, just as there are signs called cardinal, fixed, and mutable, so there are corresponding houses labeled "angular," "succedent," and "cadent," each of which connotes a certain orientation of Jupiter in this lifetime.

Interpretive Guidelines for
Jupiter's House Placement

> NOTE: If the reader will consider each of the guidelines listed below and then give some thought, with some depth and reflection, to how that guideline might apply to the specific Jupiter position in his or her chart, a number of them will jump out as being particularly suited to understanding Jupiter for each individual. Naturally, I am assuming that most readers already understand the traditional meanings of the twelve houses, but–for those who do not–the subsequent part of this chapter should explain some of those meanings as well as giving examples of well-known people who have Jupiter in each house.

a) Whatever house Jupiter is in, it is there that one can develop a comprehensive and broad understanding, assuming that one accepts the challenge to explore that area of life with courage and unblinking honesty.

b) Wherever Jupiter is placed, it is in that realm where one can most *immediately* experience faith, trust, inner confidence, and a sense of well-being and prosperity.

c) Jupiter's house can point toward a field of experience that gives one hope for the future, optimism, and a feeling of inner strength and resiliency.

d) Jupiter's house position reveals where one has an intuitive mode of learning, and an instinctive sense of future trends, which can take one rapidly toward one's goals. Because of this natural attunement, it shows an area of life where, with some effort, one can achieve fast growth and substantial improvement on many levels, worldly and personal.

e) Jupiter expands the amount of attention one must pay to the field of experience symbolized by its house placement. If other planets are also in that house, invariably one must focus quite a bit of conscious attention and energy toward the areas of life symbolized.

f) Jupiter's house reveals an area of life where one continually seeks the truth and desires to explore new horizons. There is often an instinctive feeling that "the truth shall make you free" and that this truth will help you to find meaning and direction in life; hence, there is a persistently strong urge toward openness and honesty in those spheres of activity.

g) Jupiter's house indicates a field of action and experience wherein one should take risks in order to develop more confidence and self-esteem, trusting in one's inner potential and God-given talents.

h) Jupiter's house shows an area of life where one is continually motivated to *improve* the current situation and where rapid development and expansion are likely–even sometimes surprisingly and abundantly successful. The house placement of Jupiter therefore also reveals where there is an opportunity to *give* of one's own inner abundance.

i) Jupiter's house position represents an urge toward a larger order or toward connecting with something greater than one's small ego-self in the area indicated; this partly explains why one often feels a release from pressure and fear (and feels able to breathe freely, expand, and express oneself in new ways) when enthusiastically involved in those activities symbolized by Jupiter's house.

Jupiter in the First House
Keywords: IDENTITY IN ACTION

Good vitality, an optimistic outlook, and an up-beat temperament characterize most people with this placement. Confidence in action is usually observed, even for retiring sorts with Pisces rising! (See Walter Mondale and Ringo Starr biographies in Chapter 9.) When such a dynamic planet is found in a "fiery" house, one can naturally expect a certain amount of energetic self-assertion and rather an easy way of making an impression on others. Jupiter in this house usually gives good energy, vitality, and thus good health; the first house is perhaps more indicative of vital health than is the sixth house, as Charles Carter observed in *Essays on the Foundations of Astrology* (p. 168). However, Jupiter in Gemini or Virgo may tend to siphon off some of the natural energy and exuberance into mental channels that can affect the health; it all depends on the person's lifestyle and overall chart.

Traditionally, one cannot have a much better placement in one's chart, for it is presumed to present many opportunities for success and popularity (partly because the person exemplifies a certain high-minded or noble quality in many cases). The overall attitude toward life is usually cheerful and broadminded, which naturally makes the person more content and more likeable. Good luck and material abundance often come easily according to tradition, and I have seen little to contradict this rule. There can be a certain pomposity or superiority in the demeanor, but even those people are often quite generous and well-meaning. There is usually quite a lot of innate confidence in self, although often also a touch of arrogance and self-centeredness. After all, the first house is the house of Aries–the sign that is the most me-me-me oriented of all.

Especially if Jupiter is *conjunct the Ascendant*, within even 6° or 7°, whether on the first house or twelfth house side of the Ascendant, one can be inordinately proud of one's own beliefs and their "rightness," and even their nobility. This can inhibit some aspects of close relationship, but even most of these people are still interested in others and encourage communication. Jupiter in the first usually manifests as expanded worldly ambition, or at least as quite an extroverted orientation toward society at large.

Taking on large goals may come naturally to them, such as Arthur Conan Doyle's international crusade to convince the world of the reality of the spiritual dimension of life. (See the Introduction for more on this and his chart.) And their large-scale undertakings may in fact go remarkably far, partly because they make such an impression of enthusiasm and integrity upon the public at large. Jacques Cousteau, for example, who has Sun in the ninth house and Jupiter conjunct the Ascendant (and whose chart is reproduced in this chapter) undertook vastly expensive underseas investigations, somehow got them financed with increasingly wide sponsorship, and ultimately had a tremendous international impact in raising the consciousness of the world regarding oceanic ecology.

Hermann Hesse, author of numerous internationally popular and influential books, also had Jupiter in the first house. (See his chart and biography in Chapter 9.) Other well-known people with this position are Albert Schweitzer (see Chapter 10 for his chart), Toulouse-Lautrec, Uri Geller, Van Cliburn, Marlon Brando, Dustin Hoffman, Marc Edmund Jones, and Hal Holbrook (whose greatest fame as an actor came from his portrayal of Sagittarian Mark Twain).

A few other well-known personalities with Jupiter in the first house seem to all share the theme of creating controversy by being outspoken or by expressing things that were previously hidden or

Jacques-Yves Cousteau

"To earthbound man he gave the key to the silent world." These words were inscribed on the National Geographic Society's gold medal presented to Jacques Cousteau by President Kennedy in 1961. In a life devoted to penetrating the mysteries below the surface of the ocean, Cousteau has been the consummate explorer. He opened up the vast continents of the "undersea world" and, through his award-winning films, television documentaries, and books, brought millions of people along with him on his expeditions.

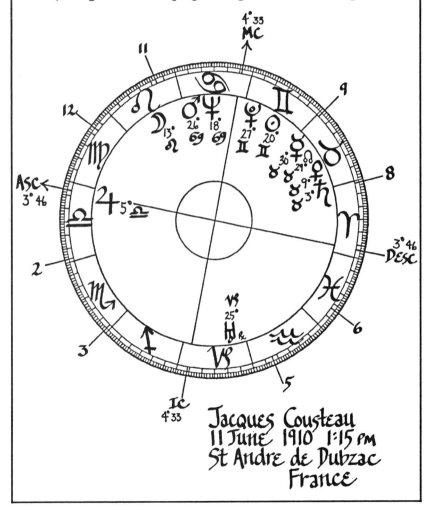

Jacques Cousteau
11 June 1910 1:15 PM
St Andre de Dubzac
France

With Jupiter in the first house, just one degree from the Ascendant, Cousteau has met the world through the adventure-beckoning, horizon-expanding energy of that planet. His life has been a sequence of pioneering exploits with ever-widening impact. Axel Madsen (in *Cousteau*) conveys the Jupiterian thrust of Cousteau's life: "The most remarkable thing about Jacques Cousteau is his evolution, his progression from navy officer to conscience of a fragile planet, from gee-whiz filmmaker to visionary of a global *terra amata*."

With his identity permeated by the future-oriented first house Jupiter, Cousteau has spent his life envisioning possibilities–and creating them. In Cousteau's words (quoted by Madsen): "Ever since Jules Verne, and lots of people before him, the informed human imagination has projected what is to come." Following in the fictional footsteps of Verne (whose book *Twenty Thousand Leagues Under the Sea* he carried aboard his ship), Cousteau ventured into the previously unexplored depths of the ocean. And, like Verne, he was fascinated with potential technological inventions that could extend the reach of his explorations.

In the early 1940s Cousteau co-invented the "aqua-lung" (called "scuba" by the British: "self-contained underwater breathing apparatus"), the device that made his underwater adventures possible. It is one of those whimsical astrological literalisms that a *Gemini* Sun would invent a "lung," a way to carry one's own air supply into the watery world that was so attractive to the Mars-Neptune in Cancer side of Cousteau's nature. Appropriately, transits both from and to Jupiter played a role in this invention that proved so crucial to the unfolding of Cousteau's life path. In late 1942, when Cousteau developed the first working prototypes of the aqua-lung, transiting Jupiter made a station at twenty-five degrees Cancer, exactly triggering the inventive and innovative Mars-Uranus opposition. Just weeks earlier, transiting Uranus made a station at four degrees Gemini, exactly trine to his natal Jupiter at four degrees Libra. It is remarkable that in June 1943, when refinements had produced a fully operational aqua-lung, transiting Jupiter and Uranus were again at twenty-four to twenty-five Cancer and four to five Gemini respectively. And, with watery Cancer and airy Gemini involved, what else but an *aqua-lung* could have been invented!

In later years Cousteau developed a one-man jet-propelled submarine (his "diving saucer"), and experimented with the first manned undersea colonies (called "Conshelf," short for "Continental Shelf Station"). Showing affinity again with far-thinking Jules Verne, he also predicted the evolution of *Homo aquaticus*–humans with adapted lungs that enable them to live below the sea. Cousteau never abandoned his optimistic, Jupiterian expectation that the seemingly "impossible" can become reality.

While Cousteau's oceanographic expeditions have provided a wealth of scientific data, it is the *aesthetic* translation of these ventures onto film that captured the attention of a worldwide audience. Cousteau's Jupiter and Ascendant are in Libra, and from the time of his initial dives underwater, he was concerned with the artistic portrayal of the dazzling, colorful world he was uncovering. During the same transits that accompanied the inventing of the aqua-lung, Cousteau made his first underwater films. These gained immediate recognition and were awarded prizes at the Cannes Film Festival. Eager to enhance his depiction of undersea beauty, Cousteau made use of the newly developed color photography for his mid-1950s film "The Silent World," which won both the Cannes Festival's "Palme d'Or" and an Academy Award. But it was the medium of television that was the most satisfying to the Jupiterian and Sun-in-the-9th-house missionary zeal of Cousteau: "Television is for me the greatest reward there is. Making films and writing books is good but not as thrilling. With television, you know that on one evening 35 to 40 million people are going to see dolphins." (quoted by *Current Biography* from the *New York Times*) The TV series "The Undersea World of Jacques Cousteau" brought sharks and manatees, coral reefs and sunken treasure into a vast number of living rooms.

The personal impact of Cousteau's first house Jupiter is clear in this quote from Madsen: "He had a way of infusing ideas with enthusiasm, of connecting seemingly unconnected facts, of overwhelming by drawing the big picture." While Cousteau's first house Jupiter describes his role as the chief promoter and central guiding figure–"the Captain"–of all his enterprises, the sign Libra points towards the emphasis he has placed on *collaboration with others*. Also, his skillful use of Libran diplomacy has been essential to garnering support and financial backing. For example, the purchase of the *Calypso*, the retired mine sweeper which was redesigned to serve as Cousteau's research base at sea, was funded by a British philanthropist (during the 1949-50 transit of Uranus conjunct Cousteau's Midheaven and square to natal Jupiter). And for decades, Cousteau has benefited from a loyal and enthusiastic crew aboard the *Calypso*. Both of Cousteau's sons, Philippe (until his tragic death in a 1979 plane crash) and Jean-Michel, have been significant contributors to Cousteau's work. Cousteau's wife Simone, one of his greatest Libran blessings, had a sense of adventure equal to her husband's and accompanied him on almost every expedition. Jean-Michel referred to her as "the permanent and original source of *Calypso's* spirit." (quoted by Madsen) Cousteau summed up his Libran Jupiter philosophy this way: "The only way to find happiness is through an expansion of yourself. You must love and share and work for others. Concentrate too much on yourself, and you will be miserable." (quoted from the *Christian Science Monitor*)

The sensitivity to relationship symbolized by Libra is raised to a more comprehensive, even global, level by Jupiter's placement there. In Paul Wright's words (in *The Literary Zodiac*): "The redemptive vision of Libra is one of otherness and interdependence, for there is the subliminal awareness that some sacred web of harmony was destroyed when man became ego-centered and put himself above all else." Through his marine explorations, Cousteau has become acutely conscious of the "broken web" of life, the destruction of ecological balance. At a U.S. congressional hearing (quoted by Madsen), he said: "People do not realize that all pollution ends up in the sea. The earth is less polluted. It is washed by the rain which carries everything into the oceans, where life has diminished by forty percent in twenty years. Fish disappear. Flora too." This dimension of Cousteau's Libran Jupiter was expressed in his founding the Cousteau Society to educate the public and world leaders on the urgency of environmental concerns and the necessity for global cooperation in facing them. It is fitting that Jacques Cousteau, captain of the *Calypso*, has brought his prophetic first house Jupiter vision to bear on the fate of a larger, space-venturing vessel—the Earth itself: "However fragmented the world, however intense the national rivalries, it is an inexorable fact that we become more interdependent every day. Now as never before, the old phrase has a literal meaning: We are all in the same boat." (quoted by Madsen)

—B.McE.

suppressed. The following examples are listed without commenting on the rightness or wrongness of their stance:

Governor George Wallace of Alabama, who prominently expressed the segregationist sentiment of the southern USA and who ran for President, shaking up the political establishment.

John Dean, a White House aide to President Nixon, who came forth publicly to reveal the "cancer growing on the presidency" through Nixon's devious and illegal tactics.

Lenny Bruce, a comedian in the USA whose acerbic social commentary, spiced with obscenities, evoked considerable outrage, but also helped to get his point across.

Elisabeth Kübler-Ross, whose Aquarian Jupiter exactly on the Ascendant revolutionized society's and the medical world's attitude toward death and dying, as she did not shrink from the controversy that her breaking the social taboo about death elicited.

Jupiter in the Second House

Keywords: MATERIAL SECURITY

Jupiter's position here in an "earthy" house and the keywords of "material security" do seem at first glance to confirm the narrow traditional meanings of the second house: money, possessions, wealth, etc. However, this house has a far broader meaning in general, and when Jupiter is located in it, its range is stretched further still to a vast spectrum encompassing deeper values, a faith that the earth will provide what one needs, and a profound appreciation of nature and its bounteous creative powers.

Over forty years ago, Margaret Hone wrote that Jupiter in the second house could indicate a "contentedness with possessions," which is surely a different image than that of greed for masses of money, which is the impression that students of astrology get from so many basic textbooks. There is often an inner faith that one will be provided for, but in perhaps half the cases, the person will use this faith as a reason not to save for a rainy day nor to exercise prudence with his or her assets. In some cases, a notable wastefulness is apparent, with a tendency to spend every dollar they receive. Perhaps some people can "tempt fate" in this regard, but I have seen cases where the individual has been forced into a financial corner that is exceedingly uncomfortable by relying completely on faith while simultaneously spending or wasting rather large amounts of assets that came to them easily.

Invariably, when Jupiter is in this house, it will expand this area of focus in life. Sometimes, it will manifest as what Marcia Moore and Mark Douglas call "an instinctive regard for Earth's bounty" with the person sometimes prospering through what they call "the carefully planned development of natural resources." In a broader view, Charles Carter was, as usual, way ahead of his time when in 1947 he wrote in *Essays on the Foundations of Astrology* that "psychologically...the 2nd has much to do with one's contentment and ability to enjoy life." From this perspective, I would say that–come what may financially–those with Jupiter in this house are always wealthy!

Among well-known people who have this Jupiter position, we have already discussed Margaret Thatcher in Chapter 5, whose second house Jupiter manifested as a profound understanding of how "selfish" ownership motives had to be recognized and harnessed to revitalize a stagnant, socialistic economy in 1980's England. She encouraged home ownership and economic entrepreneurship in a country where "selling" and "economic ambition" were regarded as unfashionable. But, coming from a middle-class background where she experienced the daily struggles of economic life that affected much of the general public, she didn't care if it did not "look right" to actively recognize the value of wealth accumulation once again in England. Always controversial, she nonetheless provided the bitter medicine that a severely ailing economy needed at that time.

Another English Prime Minister, Winston Churchill, also had Jupiter in the second house–in fact, conjunct his second house cusp. He was continually in the habit of spending far more than he earned, which supported his vast capacity to enjoy himself. His income also primarily came from such Jupiterian activities as book royalties, speaking tours, jobs as an international correspondent for newspapers, as well as Chancellor of the Exchequer (Treasury Department).

William Jennings Bryan championed the cause of having the U.S. dollar backed by precious metal, in addition to fighting publicly for many other traditional causes. Composers Debussy and Mozart had Jupiter in the second house (which has a Venusian dimension through its correlation with Taurus); and both created intricate musical *textures* that were stunningly original and–to many listeners over the decades–extraordinarily uplifting and inspiring. Michelangelo is also an excellent example of this Jupiter position's expression of an appreciation for *form* and for vast, inspiring images, as both his sculptures and his paintings reflect. Certainly, Michelangelo exemplifies second house Jupiter's desire to give *concrete shape* to inspiring philosophical or religious ideals.

Jupiter in the Third House

Keywords: **LEARNING ON THE SOCIAL & INTELLECTUAL LEVEL**

This house is preeminently the field of experience of learning, categorizing, and communicating concepts and facts of all kinds, whether or not they are related to each other or to a specific theme or purpose. Endless curiosity is the rule for those born with virtually any planet or planets in this house; and, the more planets in this house in the natal chart, the more energy that is focused consciously toward satisfying this curiosity through reading, analyzing, talking, traveling, listening, and observing others.

Compared with the other "airy" houses (the seventh and eleventh), this is the most airy in the sense that it represents the mutable processes of the mind itself, which is constantly moving and changing, like the wind. As Carter wrote in *Essays*, "The Third House has much to tell of the mental activities and of the actual mental ability of the native, being in this respect at least as important as Mercury." (p. 169) Jupiter in this house augments interest in a wide range of learning and communicating, with a substantial ability to make use of all opportunities for education, travel, and mental development. An idealistic, goal-oriented tone of mind can often help this person to distinguish between the meaningful and the superficial; but in order to achieve this, the person needs to have a relatively clear philosophy of life or set of standards. Without such guidelines, Jupiter in the third house can prompt the person to gather too many unrelated details and a multitude of quite meaningless facts. At best, scholarship, lecturing, or writing along philosophical, sociological, or idealistic lines may come naturally. In any case, knowledge can be virtually the "great goal" of life for these people, and sharing it with others may be felt as absolutely imperative for a fulfilling life.

One finds many people with a third house Jupiter who have had a strong influence on social trends through their writings or other forms of communication. They are often active in the media, and finding various social commentators or would-be reformers with this position is as common as is the case with Jupiter in Gemini. Although in this group one does find Josef Goebbels, the official Nazi propaganda minister who was, unfortunately, far ahead of his time in understanding how the masses can be readily manipulated through the media, most of the well-known third house Jupiter people who made their mark by catching social trends are far more positive contributors to society. For example, Upton Sinclair*, who was extremely popular in his day and won the Pulitzer Prize for literature, wrote social criticism that ultimately influenced the enactment of new laws promoting social justice. Controversy naturally followed such an outspoken advocate of social change, and this increased when he put his Jupiter in Capricorn in the 3rd house to work by running for California Governor and Senator, although unsuccessfully. Nonetheless, these political races gave him even more of a forum for expressing his ideas. His third house Jupiter was trine his Sun/Mars conjunction in Virgo in the politically-oriented 11th house.

As already noted, many prominent writers were born with Jupiter in the third house. One popular author who was concerned with social reform was John Galsworthy, who won the Nobel Prize in 1932. Although not discussed much today in the U.S.A., he was the author of the later-filmed series *The Forsythe Saga* and attained tremendous popularity in the United Kingdom and elsewhere. When his Nobel Prize money was awarded, he gave it away in support of social causes. In early America the most popular author was Washington Irving, whose novels and stories caught the current social trends and popular state of mind so much that he was eventually one of the most widely-read U.S. authors internationally. Other authors with Jupiter in the third that are notable include Ernest Hemingway, perhaps the most popular novelist of his time in the U.S.A., whose works often captured the international social changes that were occurring, and French poet Arthur Rimbaud, whom some consider

---

*Born September 20, 1878; Baltimore, Maryland, USA; 9:00 AM; died 1968.

the preeminent, almost archetypal poet of his era.

Other curious examples of Jupiter in the third include: Johnny Carson, whose Moon/Jupiter conjunction in the third house evidently emanated a message of "talk with me; I am your neighbor" as his "Tonight" TV show ran for over two decades to a loyal following; Leonardo da Vinci, whose wide-ranging curiosity has resulted in his being known as the quintessential "Renaissance Man"; and rockstar Cat Stevens, who wrote numerous philosophical songs and who eventually abandoned fame for a religiously-dedicated life (Jupiter in Sagittarius!). Another notable pair with Jupiter in the third are singers Julie Andrews (with a Scorpio Jupiter and a Sagittarius Mars in the third) and Barbra Streisand (with Jupiter and Mars both in Gemini in the third). Not only have both been regarded as especially vocally gifted in the range and expressiveness of their singing, but also have been extraordinarily involved in social improvement commitments—Andrews with the international relief agency Project California and Streisand with substantial contributions to liberal political causes and candidates.

Jupiter in the Fourth House

Keywords: **ACTION ON THE EMOTIONAL & SOUL LEVEL**

Although quite a private house, fourth house placements become at once more publicly attuned (because Jupiter is so outgoing) and more confidently action-oriented when Jupiter is found here. The self-confidence is often quite strong, emanating as it does from the depths of the person's being, although it is not flaunted. Just as Jupiter is exalted in Cancer, so it is also quite at home and prosperous in the unpretentious fourth house—a conclusion one must draw after considerable research. It seems that many people with this Jupiter placement are not fooled by the superficial allurements of the outer world and instead remain quite comfortably rooted in an inner security that they are born with. An inner generosity of spirit is often also apparent, and—with Jupiter's tendency to broaden the scope of everything it influences—this largeness of spirit is not limited to family, as one might expect. As Charles Carter wrote, psychologically the fourth house "probably rules the depth and sincerity of the affections, especially those arising from family ties."

But with Jupiter there, one might expect that such feelings would not be confined only to a small circle of people.

These people do need time alone to explore their inner world, and their religious orientation may well be strongly influenced by their upbringing. With the prophetic planet Jupiter in a "watery," psychically-sensitive house, one should not be surprised to find people with considerable psychic sensitivity and intuitive abilities. And, as Isabel Hickey writes, they are usually "openhearted and generous." Although some of these people do become well-known, there is still something very basic and "down home" about them that persists and which the public sees and likes. As Marcia Moore and Mark Douglas wrote, those with Jupiter in the fourth house "want to feel a sense of belonging to the community in which they reside and would rather lead a rich and full life than struggle for worldly fame."

A certain loyalty to and comfort with past traditions persists throughout the lives of those with this placement. For example, in the case of Woody Allen, whose chart is discussed in detail in Chapter 9, a number of manifestations of his fourth house Jupiter are evident, without even having to refer to his upbringing and the influence of his parents on him. Throughout his many films, he has made light of (Jupiter) old fears and anxieties (fourth house). He has emphasized privacy and the need of a full life over mere fame, as, for example, when he sent word that he could not be at the Academy Awards ceremony when he won the Oscar for *Annie Hall* because that was his regular night to play clarinet in a local band. He has almost always used music from the 1920s through 1940s as the scores for his films, and he has also done a number of innovative black and white films during an era when color was not only the rule, but when older films were being "colorized"–an artistic travesty against which he testified in the U.S. Congress. Also, his fourth house Jupiter is demonstrated in the way that he has made films in various styles in homage to those directors whom he considers to be his predecessors and his cinematic "gurus."

The fourth house's connection with patriotism, or at least with the spirit of a society or culture, may be seen in such people as Johann Goethe, whom many consider to be the preeminent writer in Germany and who has in *Faust* expressed the soul of that nation. American World War II hero General George Patton was a fanatical patriot and also believed deeply in reincarnation and karma, which are ideas to which Jupiter in the psychically oriented fourth house might gravitate. And, in a somewhat smaller arena geographically, singer John Denver gained fame by singing a number of songs which described the joys of his Rocky Mountain homeland.

Another example of a fourth house Jupiter person who exemplified a feeling of unity with his country or the spirit of his society is American writer Carl Sandburg*, one of America's best-loved and most widely read poets. With Jupiter exactly conjunct the fourth house cusp (the I.C.) as well as within one degree of conjoining his Capricorn Sun, his Jupiterian expression through a fourth house focus is profound and powerful. An entire chapter could be devoted to detailing how this energy attunement was expressed, but we can summarize briefly:

a) He was known for a lifelong devotion to his country and to the common people, for whom he felt a deep sympathy and respect.

b) As *Current Biography* states, he "for some sixty years proclaimed faith in the collective wisdom of the American people."

c) A folksy poet who wrote in a simple language, he was deeply interested in folklore, folk songs, and other traditions from his country's story-telling past.

d) He also wrote a famous six-volume biography of Abraham Lincoln, presenting him as the embodiment of the American spirit. This prodigious work won the Pulitzer Prize in history (1939).

e) In addition, he published a collection of children's stories in 1922, another example of fourth house interests.

The importance of children's stories shows up also in the life of another fourth house Jupiter writer, Antoine de Saint-Exupéry, who wrote *The Little Prince*, one of the world's most famous children's stories. And in addition, Saint-Exupéry was known for his profound feeling of duty to his country and in fact lost his life during World War II during a reconnaissance flight. Another author who stands out as an example of a fourth house Jupiter is French writer Marcel Proust, whose multi-volume *Remembrance of Things Past* is a reflection of his obsession with and yearning to understand the memories and hidden motives of life.

---

*Born January 6, 1878; Galesburg, Illinois, USA; 12:05 AM; died 1967.

Jupiter in the Fifth House

Keywords: **IDENTITY SECURITY**

Since all of the "fiery" houses have a major impact on one's attitude toward life itself, one would be correct in assuming that having Jupiter in this house (the house correlated with the Sun and Leo) would indeed motivate a person to have a strongly philosophical–and usually optimistic–attitude toward life. There is in this placement of Jupiter a powerful urge toward *significance*–toward "being somebody" (as in show business), toward expressing something significant creatively, or toward making a significant contribution to society. It is not surprising that Jupiter in the fifth house is not known for a humble expression of one's self and beliefs, for such a big planet in such a powerful, dynamic house cannot be squelched or ignored.

The upbeat, optimistic quality of Jupiter is expressed well through the fifth house, with little inhibition, and in fact sometimes life is seen or felt to be a show, a drama, or an arena for spontaneous and enjoyable play. Traditionally, the fifth house rules speculation, and–with Jupiter in this house–risk-taking of all kinds is accentuated. Risking hurt by giving one's heart (fifth house) in love; risking financial loss through speculative investment; risking disapproval by appearing on stage in the hope of public approbation; or launching out into the world a creative work, thus risking criticism, rejection, or sheer neglect–all of these are fifth house ventures closely tied in with one's identity. All are a result of revealing and projecting publicly one's innermost self, as is also having children, another reflection of one's self (or at least, so many parents seem to think!). So what does such extensive risk-taking have to do with "Identity Security," this house's keywords? Simply that, by taking risks in a wide range of activities and modes of personal expression, we can grow more secure and gain confidence that we do indeed have something to contribute; and thus our awareness of our inner self and creative purpose (beyond mere personality) can be expanded.

In Indian Vedic astrology, the fiery houses (1, 5 & 9) are known as *dharma* houses and are thus connected with *right action*. The fifth house specifically is known for symbolizing "creative intelligence," which is not intellectual ability but rather a more intuitive perception with a creative flair. All the fiery houses have to do with *projecting dreams into the physical world* in the hope of seeing them manifested; but the fifth house especially–being the most creative house of all–represents a strong need to see an effect on the world at large through one's creative ventures and self-expression. With Jupiter in this house, this urge tends to be even more persistent and powerful than with most other placements in the fifth house. This house, in fact, has more to do with true creativity than with fame; many creative pioneers have various planets in this house but are relatively unknown. If I wrote about such individuals in this book the reader wouldn't have the vaguest idea about who they are!

Creative expression can take so many forms that we should not fall into the trap of seeing "creativity" only as expressed in a few artistic or entertainment fields, for Jupiter in this house can indicate an entrepreneurial streak as well, creatively building a business through the power of vision into the future. Or one can find people who encourage others to grow or to express themselves, especially those who work with children. One can also find unique examples of creative expression, such as Helen Keller, whose Aries Jupiter was in the fifth house and who overcame being blind and deaf to write popular books and lecture worldwide. Jupiter in this house can also manifest as being *outspoken* in a creative way, thus having a strong impact on society. Examples are such diverse people as Sigmund Freud, who challenged social convention through his emphasis on sex (as well as emphasizing the impact of children's upbringing–

Helen Keller

Helen Keller* is perhaps one of the best examples of Jupiter in the fifth house. Her fifth house Jupiter was in Aries, trine Mars in Leo in the ninth house, and thus was expressed with a rare fearlessness and dynamism. She even wrote a book entitled *Optimism*, which expanded on such Jupiterian inspirations and thoughts as the following:

Life is either a daring adventure or nothing.

Delight is essential to growth and self-improvement…. He who does not see that joy is an important force in the world misses the essence of life. Joy is a spiritual element that gives vicissitudes unity and significance.

*Born June 27, 1880; Tuscumbria, Alabama, USA; 4:02 PM; died 1968.

another fifth house matter) and Tom Smothers, a comedian who challenged the government establishment during the Viet Nam war in a wildly popular TV show that the network was pressured to cancel.

Extraordinarily popular comic actor Peter Sellers, although not known for his outspoken comments but rather for his widely publicized series of love affairs with beautiful young actresses, also had Jupiter in the fifth; his most famous characters, Dr. Strangelove and Inspector Clouseau, were transparent creations of an actor merely *playing* at the roles with a gleeful detachment. Another fifth house Jupiter example is Maurice Chevalier, who became internationally known as the virtual archetype of an "entertainer," his worldwide fame no doubt helped along by his Jupiter conjunct both Mars and the fifth house cusp in Sagittarius.

Because the fifth house is known for taking risks, and especially so when Jupiter is posited in it, we have to mention the tendency toward going to excess through taking too much risk. As Charles Carter wrote about the fifth house in *Essays,*

> *Thus it would not be too much to postulate that the term "the house of self-undoing" is much more applicable to this sector than to the maligned 12th house, which more often points to trouble through other people. Those who have ruined themselves through self-indulgence and recklessness...will usually show in their nativities an involvement of the 5th house....*

Good examples of this observation, with Jupiter in the fifth house, would be President Nixon's aides John Mitchell and H. R. Haldeman, both of whom were conspirators in the famous Watergate cover-up; both acted with supreme over-confidence and arrogance.

Other well-known people who have Jupiter in the fifth are writers Joan Didion, O. Henry, and James Hilton; actors Sidney Poitier and Derek Jacobi; and three men who combined athletics or physical conditioning with show business–Arnold Schwarzenegger, martial arts expert Bruce Lee, and Johnny Weissmuller, who won an Olympic swimming medal and went on to play Tarzan in many films. Cinema child stars Shirley Temple Black and Jackie Coogan also have Jupiter in the fifth house, as do Hector Berlioz and Richard Strauss, both of whom were conductors as well as composers of symphonic music.

Jupiter in the Sixth House

Keywords: **LEARNING ON THE MATERIAL LEVEL**

Jupiter in the sixth house gives not only a prodigious capacity for work, but also the ability to carry out one's duties and daily routines with an unusually cheerful outlook. Daily work, or at least being of practical use in the world and/or of service to others, is inordinately important to these folks, so much so that they may–in their boundless optimism–take on far too much for their constitution to bear.

Howard Sasportas summarized Jupiter in the sixth as follows in *The Twelve Houses*:

> *Those with Jupiter in this house seek (or should seek) to experience meaning in life through work and service to others. Self-purification and the refinement of their skills and abilities afford them a greater sense of well-being and satisfaction.*

I personally have seen this placement expressed as that most rare of qualities: the ability to balance enthusiasm with humility. (Even Leo Sun individuals seem to express themselves in a more humble way when their Sun is in the sixth house!) These people usually feel optimistic about their daily routines and are eager to help. As Charles Carter wrote in *Essays on the Foundations of Astrology*, those with Jupiter in this house exemplify a "cheery or philosophical outlook"; and he goes on to explain another one of his original insights into human psychology: that the sixth house has "a very strong (but apparently overlooked) relation with the disposition, especially one's moods, temper and manners." Carter connects the sixth house not only with the traditional meanings that we find in all the textbooks, but also with the *temperament*, even overriding the Ascendant to some extent. I would add that it is especially the temperament and moods as expressed in performing one's daily routine duties that are illuminated by the sixth house; but of course most of us spend the majority of our waking hours performing just such activities. The connection of the sixth house with Virgo, and hence with the nervous system, further confirms his insight; we have all noticed how a person with "afflicted Virgo planets" can be "cranky," peevish, or overly critical toward others. The same nervous tension may be indicated by 6th house planets whose aspects are less than harmonious.

The Virgo connection with this house also manifests in other little-known expressions of planets in this house. For example, craftsmanship is often notable in those with an emphasis on the sixth, and Bob Dylan is a perfect example of Jupiter in the sixth in this respect in the way that he crafted his prodigious output of songs. (See Chapter 9 for his complete chart.) This house is also known for an analytical focus of the mind, and a good example of Jupiter in the sixth in this regard is Henry Kissinger, former Secretary of State and winner of the Nobel Peace Prize, whose analyses of world conflicts and strategies are still valued enough for him to be paid huge consulting fees by governments and corporations. (Note that Kissinger's Jupiter is in Scorpio, trine to a first house Pluto, a superb symbol for in-depth research and strategy.)

Technical expertise and enthusiasm for scientific developments are often shown by Jupiter in this house. The chart and life of French author Jules Verne, whose full chart and details of his life are included in this section, provide a good example of this expression. Moore and Douglas connect Jupiter in the sixth with "loyal and devoted service." We can find a superb example of this in George Washington, whose Libra Jupiter in the sixth impelled him to continue his public service even after he dearly wanted to retire from the limelight. Another example, although more controversial these days, is J. Edgar Hoover, who was a workaholic in his dedication to building up the FBI (and his authority within it) and whose public persona while still in office was that of a completely self-effacing public servant!

The sixth house is also traditionally known for having a major concern with one's health, and as Sasportas points out in *The Twelve Houses*,

> *Although Jupiter in the 6th is normally associated with excesses of food and drink, I have noticed the extremes of Jupiter just as frequently operating the other way–week-long fasts eating nothing but grapes, for instance.*

A tragic example of this is Mario Lanza, probably the greatest natural tenor ever born in America, whose continual bouts with overeating and weight problems led him ultimately to try absurdly radical "health treatments" which led to his early death. One might say concisely that Jupiter in the sixth should encourage the person to take care of his physical (and nervous system's) health enthusiastically, but that–as always with Jupiter–some kind of moderation should be used.

Jules Verne

The French author Jules Verne is a superb example of numerous Jupiterian factors, which together culminated in his being internationally renowned as a futurist/visionary author of prodigious output who simultaneously maintained both literary quality and scientific feasibility. One could easily write at least a hundred pages about Verne's life and how it reflected his birth chart–a reliable chart from the Gauquelin records. Although his books are not much read today, hundreds of millions of people worldwide will remember watching the fabulous Disney film *20,000 Leagues Under the Sea* (how perfect a title for a Jupiter conjunct the Moon in Scorpio!) and the enchanting mega-hit movie on extra-wide

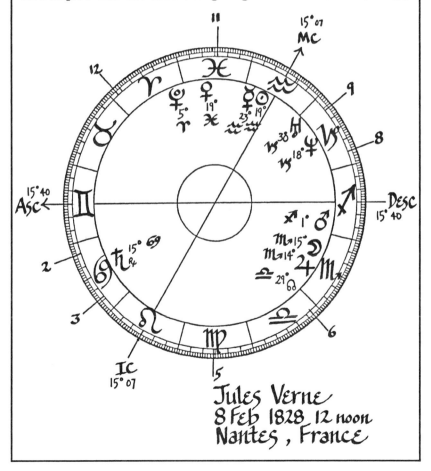

Jules Verne
8 Feb 1828 12 noon
Nantes, France

screen *Around the World in Eighty Days*, both of which were based on Verne novels. In fact, Verne's worldwide popularity began in the 1860s and continued for many decades. Many years before the movie was made, a play based on *Around the World in Eighty Days* ran for fifty years!

Today, Jules Verne is primarily known as the first exponent of scientifically credible science fiction. However, what is not focused on today is that his works often contained a substantial tone of idealism and of questioning the moral value of scientific progress, which he emphasized in his later works. His moral idealism earned him a personal audience with Pope Leo XIII in 1894, and he once wrote: "If I am not always what I ought to be, my characters will be what I should like to be." His awareness of the social dangers of uncontrolled technological advance are a reflection not only of his strong prophetic qualities, which we will explore further below, but also of his substantial involvement in social betterment and government, as shown by his Aquarius Sun conjunct Mercury in the 10th house, and his Venus and Pluto in the politically and socially oriented 11th house. In fact, Verne was quite involved in local politics in France, and he was elected to the City Council of Amiens in his later years.

It would be difficult to imagine a chart that is more indicative of the ability to be prophetic of future technological developments. Let me enumerate some of the principal factors in his chart:

1) Jupiter in the 6th house, conjunct the Moon closely. The 6th house (and Virgo) is known for an orientation toward technology. Verne envisioned the future of science and technology.

2) In addition, Mars is in Sagittarius (known for prophecy and for projecting one's energy and vision into the future) and is in the 6th house. (The packed 6th house could also be the explanation for his prodigious output of nearly eighty books, for the 6th house is known for an addiction to work!)

3) The Mars in Sagittarius is especially important since it is the dispositor of his Jupiter and Moon in Scorpio; in other words, there is a Sagittarian sub-tone to his Jupiter and Moon, coloring the sixth house planets further with a future-oriented perspective.

4) The Jupiter-Moon conjunction is also part of a grand trine in the

intuitive water element, the grand trine also involving Saturn in Cancer and Venus in Pisces. With Saturn involved and so many of these planets placed in "earthy" *houses*, it is no wonder that so many of his "fantastic" visions of the future were so based in the physically possible realm that many have come true.

5) Uranus is in the 9th house, another perfect symbol of the ability to tune in prophetically regarding many scientific inventions; for he envisioned and published (both in ninth house) those visions of the worlds that science and inventions might create.

6) Gemini rising is not only an apt sign for a writer, but Gemini almost always has a flair for and interest in the latest technology and gadgetry.

7) The Sun and Mercury in Aquarius, with Venus and Pluto in the 11th house, combine for a major futuristic emphasis in his consciousness, breaking with tradition without much hesitation. And, not only are Aquarius and the 11th house known for a future-orientation, they are especially known for a concern regarding the future trends of society, which Verne came to focus on more and more as he got older.

To substantiate the above facts, we have only to look into some of his writings to see the vast number of prophetic insights and explorations that he wrote about. It is important also to note that he termed a series of his books *voyages extraordinaires*, and the majority of his works are *explorations* of distant lands or unknown, distant parts of the earth or the solar system. His work was thus a clear and focused reflection of his strongly Jupiterian/Sagittarian nature.

In his personal life, Verne was also an active explorer, purchasing a series of yachts that enabled him to travel to ever more distant ports of call: Southern Spain and Algeria, Italy, and north to Scotland, Denmark, Ireland, Sweden, Norway, and into the Baltic.

Among the most remarkably prophetic items in his vast creative work are these:

a) He described space travel in which weightlessness was experienced by the "astronauts," who were launched from Florida in the USA!

b) His submarine *Nautilus* predates the first successful power submarine by over a quarter century, and its self-sufficiency was an anticipation of the modern submarines that can run underwater for longer periods, performing experiments and studying the sea's potential as a source of food, medicine, etc.

c) Not only did Verne pre-vision the helicopter (although da Vinci had also done so!), but he also seemed to prophesy the artificial satellite and the rocket-propelled guided missile.

d) Passages in *For the Flag* suggest that he had an inkling of atomic energy.

e) He predicted instant communications similar to modern-day fax and electronic mail a full century before they came into common use. In an 1863 manuscript entitled "Paris in the 20th Century," which was just discovered and published for the first time in 1994, Verne wrote: "Photo telegraphy allowed any writing, signature or illustration to be sent far away....Every house was wired."

—S.A.

The prodigious capacity for work is also shown in another way when one considers the chart of Mark Spitz*, whose seven swimming gold medals in the 1972 Olympics ranks as one of the most amazing achievements in sports history. Spitz dedicated years of disciplined work into the sports-loving Jupiter in the sixth house, and anyone who has ever been involved in competitive swimming knows that the training is not only horribly boring but requires a machine-like efficiency, as well as a tremendous capacity for sheer, painful work. Another Olympic champion who also exemplified a similar capacity for practice and discipline is figure skating gold medalist Dorothy Hamill, whose Virgo Jupiter in the sixth is expressed through the technical expertise and precision which competitive figure skating requires.

Craftsmanship as well as a sizable productivity are evident in the work of Vincent Van Gogh, whose large output is remarkable considering his personal problems and his short life. Jupiter conjunct the Moon in Sagittarius in the sixth house symbolizes the fiery intensity of his emotions which were projected into his work. Craftsmanship, as well as a precision in the use of language, is evident in

---

*Born February 10, 1950; Modesto, California, USA; 5:45 PM PST.

numerous writers who have Jupiter in this Mercurian house. American adventure writer Jack London wrote about the Jupiterian outdoors and wilderness and, like Jules Verne, produced an enormous amount of work–forty-three books in sixteen years! French novelist Gustave Flaubert (whose analysis of manners and psychological motivation in *Madame Bovary* was considered groundbreaking) had Jupiter conjunct Saturn in the sixth and, as quoted by Lois Rodden, "worked tirelessly to create an exact, realistic style, taking years to perfect a novel." Percy Shelley, perhaps the epitome of the idealistic, romantic poet, showed a remarkable mastery of his craft at an early age; his idealism and yearning for a spiritual experience of transcendent beauty is well symbolized by his stellium of Jupiter, Mars, and Neptune all in Libra in the sixth.

Jupiter in the Seventh House

Keywords: **ACTION ON THE SOCIAL & INTELLECTUAL LEVEL**

Although much influenced by other people, especially close partners, those with Jupiter in the seventh house themselves usually express a strong optimism and confidence in all their actions. Their confidence, however, does rise noticeably when supported by an enthusiastic partner or when approved of by the public. This position gives a sensitivity to the trends of society and to what will appeal to the public taste. Note that this is the house corresponding with Libra, and although intellectual activities are indicated by Jupiter here, they often bear an artistic coloration as well. A good example would be film producer David O. Selznick, whose masterpiece *Gone with the Wind* combined history, cinematic beauty, and tremendous popularity with the public. The artistic dimension of this placement can also be seen in writer F. Scott Fitzgerald and composer Erik Satie, both of whom produced work of elegant beauty and awe-inspiring simplicity.

Charles Carter points out how placements in the seventh house can lead to personal publicity, and the number of famous Jupiter in the seventh people who have enjoyed unusually high and sustained levels of popularity is virtually endless. Such diverse individuals as baseball great Willie Mays, actor Burt Reynolds, and pianist Liberace all share this placement; as do the following public figures who have been not only extraordinarily popular but who also project an aura of classiness and dignity: actors Sean Connery and Rex Harrison, and two-time American Democratic presidential candidate and later United Nations delegate Adlai Stevenson, who was noted for his broadmindedness and humane future-oriented political and social principles.

One should not lose sight of the fact that, as the keywords indicate, there is a strong urge toward various sorts of intellectual activity, often focused toward key issues in society and one's culture. There is also often a strong desire to promote ideas that they believe in, whether through communications media or through politics. We just mentioned Adlai Stevenson as an example of such Jupiterian expression (Stevenson in fact had Jupiter conjunct Uranus *in Sagittarius*). Pioneering social theorist Machiavelli also had Jupiter in the seventh, an apt symbol of questioning how society and government work.

Moore and Douglas use the keywords "profitable partnerships" for this placement, and it is an accurate designation in more ways than merely the narrow traditional notion that one will gain wealth through the partner. Those with Jupiter here have an enthusiasm for *sharing* life and concepts with others. They gain from close associations not only materially but also intellectually, philosophically, and in character development. These folks seek mutual understanding in human associations, and they are often adept at encouraging others to express themselves and to grow from self-discovery. The nobility of Jupiter shines through in many cases, often expressed as dependable honesty in relationships, and as an ever-expanding broadmindedness as the understanding of human nature develops. As Moore and Douglas wrote, "these people tend to give people the benefit of the doubt."

One-to-one interaction comes so instinctively to these individuals that they are often natural counselors to whom others go for advice. They are good listeners, and they are often so adept at understanding the other person's point of view that they may also achieve notoriety as speakers or writers, since they will be able to express what others are thinking. Popular writer and psychologist Rollo May has Jupiter in Virgo in the seventh house, and his analysis of therapeutic interaction resulted in his book *The Art of Counseling*, as well as in other volumes inquiring into the mysteries of human love (Jupiter in the relationship-oriented seventh house trine a Taurus Sun in the second house).

I suspect that Jupiter in the seventh is often found in the charts of the spouses of famous and extraordinarily prominent people, even if the spouse keeps quite a low profile. In other cases, one will experience a launch into more prominence through the partner. For example, long-time USA Senator Margaret Chase Smith*, who had Jupiter in the seventh house in Libra, suddenly had the opportunity to run for (and was elected to) Congress when her husband, the Representative from Maine, suffered a heart attack and urged her to fill in for him. She went on to serve eight years in the House of Representatives, 24 years in the Senate, and later became the first woman to be nominated for the Presidency by a major political party. (For 24 years, she was the only woman in the U.S. Senate.) Just as the old traditions suggest, if Jupiter is in one's seventh house, the life partner will most likely reflect various Jupiterian qualities. At best, he or she will be inspiring, encouraging, tolerant, and generous; I will leave it to the reader's imagination what a Jupiterian partner (or partners!) might express in his or her less attractive manifestations.

One last dimension of the relationship field of experience must be mentioned. Although Jupiter in the seventh is considered generally to be a "fortunate" position in any chart, it should be recognized that Jupiter's scope of action and arena of exploration tends to be much broader than the more intimate, personal Venusian domain of the seventh house. There may be extensive social interests and involvements for those with Jupiter here; much depends on Jupiter's sign. But in most cases, those with Jupiter in the seventh need to have a broadminded partner who is not particularly demanding or controlling. Once again, Howard Sasportas has provided us with a concise summary of this particular issue, which is so essential for understanding those with this chart placement:

> *Jupiter in the 7th suffers from a classic freedom-closeness dilemma. They want their independence to explore different facets of life, and yet they want their security as well. (On an archetypal level, spirit as symbolized by Jupiter yearns to be free of the restrictions of matter represented by Hera, and yet spirit needs matter through which to express itself.) Ideally, those with*

---

*Born December 14, 1897; Skowhegan, Maine, USA; 11:30 AM EST.

Jupiter in this house do best with partners who share and understand their urge to have other interests outside of the relationship.   (The Twelve Houses)

Jupiter in the Eighth House

Keywords: **EMOTIONAL & SOUL SECURITY**

The above keywords encompass the innumerable modes of expression that eighth house energies take. Generalizations are difficult to make when discussing eighth house factors for it is a rather daunting task to attempt a summing up of such a profound field of experience that can manifest on so many levels. In addition, the nature of the eighth house is so private, not to mention intentionally secretive, that finding prominent people with this placement has not been the easiest of tasks. Although such individuals seek power and/or deeper knowledge, they do not generally seek publicity.

These people tend to have an enthusiasm for exploring the deeper laws of life, even if their search leads them to confront "taboo" areas of experience. In fact, far from having any fear of the eighth house matters which so fascinate–but also terrify–most people (sex, death, power, psychic and occult laws, etc.), these folks deliberately and honestly face these taboo subjects and often feel an exhilaration and inner freedom from having done so. They have an inner conviction that they are morally *right* to follow their individual path of discovery, even if society frowns on it. And their optimism about confronting the dark side of life is often remarkable. For example, in her later years, one older lady with Sagittarius rising, and her ruling planet Jupiter in the eighth house conjunct the Sun and Neptune, told her daughter, "Dying sounds like a great adventure, doesn't it?"

Those with Jupiter in the eighth house need time alone to explore things that are hidden, whether involved with their own inner life or various types of research or investigative work. They are dominated by overriding *yearnings* to find well-being through a search into the deeper forces that seem to them (depending on their level of consciousness) to be at the core of life's processes: physical laws (such as chemists, doctors, engineers or surgeons have to learn); psychic or occult laws; biological/emotional energies (sex and concomitant emotional urges to merge with another); financial/ economic laws; or universally true religious principles.

In fact, the religious needs of those with Jupiter in the eighth are never completely orthodox. Their religious yearnings are satisfied only by deep inquiry. C. G. Jung* is a perfect example of this tendency, including the eighth house orientation toward wide-ranging research and exploring such "taboo" subjects as astrology and alchemy. Jung's search for meaning pervaded his entire life. In fact, one of his most accessible books for the general public is entitled *Modern Man in Search of a Soul*. This search for Jung encompassed all world religions, mythologies, folklores, and artistic and dream symbols; the worldwide breadth of his inquiries is an apt expression of Jupiter's universalism. He also uncovered the deeper psychological significance of *religion* and of religious rituals and symbols, including all forms of "occult" and esoteric traditions. Another explorer of universal religious and occult traditions was Helena Blavatsky†, worldwide promoter of theosophy. Like Jung, her Jupiter is in the eighth house, according to Blavatsky's own best estimate of her birth time.

One unifying factor that explains something of the eighth house's mystery is once again found in the writings of Charles Carter. He points out that the Ascendant has much to do with the vitality, the sixth house with the "tissues" (and–I would add–the general state of health, especially as an expression of attitude and the nervous system), and the eighth house with the state of health of the "large aqueous content of the body." This is perhaps a far more profound statement than Carter even realized when he wrote it. For example, the impact on the overall health of the *emotions* has only really been explored in the latter half of the 20th century. Carter goes on to observe that the eighth house, somewhat like the sixth, influences the *moods* and the general temperament. Carter's connection of the eighth with the aqueous (or watery) element in human nature correlates perfectly not only with the intuitive expressions of the eighth house, but also with the profound "urge to merge" with others that one finds in those with an eighth house emphasis, whether that urge is manifesting through sexual expression, emotional experimentation, or devotion to some esoteric path.

In *The Twelve Houses*, Howard Sasportas also makes some key

---

*Born July 26,1875; Kesswil, Switzerland; 7:32 PM; died 1961.
†Born August 12, 1831 N.S.; Ekaterinoslav, Russia; 2:17 AM; died 1891.

observations which illuminate how many people experience Jupiter in this house:

> *For Jupiter, sexual intimacy can be understood symboli-*
> *cally as two people merging to become something greater than*
> *what each one is individually. However, hard aspects to Jupiter*
> *can show excessive sexual appetites and a certain Don-Juan-*
> *like constant need for new experience in this area. On the other*
> *hand, I have seen difficult aspects to Jupiter in the 8th reveal a*
> *person who has trouble reconciling his or her philosophical and*
> *religious beliefs with the sexual drive. Jupiter in this house may*
> *also have such high expectations of what sex should be that they*
> *are disappointed if bells don't ring and mountains don't move*
> *every time they make love.*

In other words, for those with Jupiter in the eighth, sexuality must be seen within a larger context of broader meaning, not simply as a physical instinct; and there is often a certain emotional turbulence experienced as the individual seeks to understand these powerful, but often warring, urges.

We cannot leave the discussion of the eighth house without also mentioning its correlation with business and investment, another expression of seeking security through accruing behind-the-scenes power and/or wealth. Moore and Douglas use the keywords "finan-cial finesse" for this position, which aptly describes the abilities of many who have this placement. They describe such a person as a "shrewd operator" who "can salvage and turn to profit the waste which other people discard." These people recognize value where most people don't see it, and they often have strongly-felt intuitions about where current trends will lead in the future. These "gut-feelings" often turn out to be strikingly accurate, which is one of the keys to the investment success of people who have Jupiter here.

We should briefly mention some other well-known people with this chart factor: scientist Louis Pasteur, whose research improved the health of millions; TV commentator and director Bill Moyers, who has explored the deeper aspects of many issues in a simple, direct way that the general public can understand and whose *The Power of Myth* series and book reached tens of millions of people, making them think about symbols, religion, and ancient traditions in an entirely new way; and author Norman Mailer, whose first hit novel was about the turbulence of warfare and who later published a book with the appropriate eighth house title *The Prisoner of Sex*. Quite a few actors who have played rough, rebellious, or evil characters (the eighth house symbolizes the underworld, taboo behavior, and the dark side of human character) have Jupiter in the eighth: James Dean, Clint Eastwood, Henry Winkler, Vincent Price, and Rip Torn. And finally, we must mention Paramhansa Yogananda, who was instrumental in teaching thousands of people how to *elevate their emotions* (Jupiter in the watery eighth) in order to find inner peace.

Jupiter in the Ninth House
Keywords: **LEARNING ON THE LEVEL OF IDENTITY**

The above keywords are meant to convey the idea that an emphasis on this house often, at one level or another, impels the individual to seek to discover *who he or she really is*, beyond the level of surface personality. In other words, with what ideal, force, goal, philosophy, or truth will I identify myself and enthusiastically dedicate myself to? And, of course, the outcome of that search has a continual and profound impact on each person's attitude toward life itself. One might also call this house a sector of "self-discovery" or the field of experience wherein one searches for meaning for its own sake. Perhaps this is why many Vedic astrology traditions consider the ninth house, one of the fiery houses of *dharma*, to be the second most important house in a chart, after the first house. The ninth house has much to do with what some Eastern teachings call *right action*, and this seems confirmed by Charles Carter describing this as the "house of conscience." In other words, if the higher mind is developed and disciplined, a person can focus on a more profound discerning of right from wrong and on dedicating oneself to constant self-improvement. If the higher mind is not developed, planets in this house can be expressed as wildly and carelessly as the negative manifestations of Sagittarius described in earlier chapters. (For example, James Earl Ray, who murdered Martin Luther King, Jr., has Jupiter in this house, and while in itself it does not account for his criminal activity, Jupiter in Aries in the ninth house–conjunct Uranus in Aries–shows the possibility of acting upon his own "version" of the law without reference to objective morality.)

When Jupiter is in its own house, naturally all the tendencies of Jupiter–both constructive and wasteful or excessive–are augmented.

Hence, moderation is almost invariably needed when this placement is found. Since this entire book is concerned with all the various manifestations of Jupiter's energies and potentials, it seems redundant to go over that again here. Let us, therefore just summarize briefly as we discuss some well-known people as examples of this position.

Aspirations, dreams of the future, and ideals play a great part in the lives of those with Jupiter in the ninth. There tends to be a broad, philosophical, optimistic outlook on life, and the person often has a playful, humorous nature. An example of this would be Albert Einstein, who in addition to his scientific inventiveness was known to cultivate deep philosophical reflections about the meaning of life and science and who in fact was profoundly religious; he was also known for a beguiling sense of humor. TV pioneer and song-writer Steve Allen made his mark as a wildly funny humorist and conversationalist, but in his later years he has been extremely active publicizing all sorts of philosophical and cultural ideas through both TV and numerous books.

British mathematician, philosopher, and social theorist Bertrand Russell also had Jupiter in the ninth, as did astrological author Isabelle Pagan whose *Signs of the Zodiac Analysed* presented a profound explanation for the general reader of the deeper religious and philosophical meanings of astrology. Robert Redford, whose chart is examined in detail in Chapter 9, has Jupiter in Sagittarius in the ninth house—a triple Jupiterian vibration! Particularly in his later work as a producer and director, he has been involved with creating some of the most idealistic and morally-persuasive films of his generation. Promoting ideas or ideals comes naturally to those with Jupiter here, whether through cinema, writing, speaking, teaching, or simply using their lives as examples of their idealism.

This placement has long been known for favoring dealings with foreigners and/or living in foreign countries. This seems to be borne out by many examples in my experience. Often, those with an emphasis on the ninth house feel much more authentically "themselves" when outside of the borders and the psychic boundaries of their native land. A good example here would be British actress Vivien Leigh, who gained instant worldwide fame by not only starring in an American movie but also playing the role of down-to-earth American Scarlett O'Hara in *Gone with the Wind*. Another

Franklin D. Roosevelt

It would be hard to imagine a more perfect example of Jupiter in its own house than Franklin D. Roosevelt, President of the USA for twelve years of tremendous challenge during both an economic depression and a vast world war. One might characterize Roosevelt as a preacher of and a believer in *faith in the future*. As British philosopher Isaiah Berlin wrote, "He was one of the few statesmen ...who seemed to have no fear of the future." Of course, Roosevelt's most famous line from his hundreds of public speeches is: "The only thing we have to fear (pause) is fear itself."

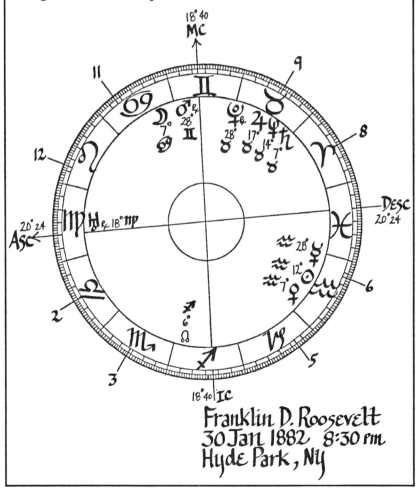

Franklin D. Roosevelt
30 Jan 1882   8:30 pm
Hyde Park, NY

Roosevelt focused on the "big picture," and its implications for the future, even if many immediate problems would cause most people to doubt the ultimate successful goal for free peoples worldwide. As Doris Kearns Goodwin wrote in *No Ordinary Time* (a book from which all the Roosevelt quotations in this book are taken), Roosevelt would "provide the framework, the opportunity, and the inspiration, [all ninth house factors] and the people would do the rest."

Roosevelt was far more aware of the importance of international affairs (Jupiter and ninth house) than were the majority of his isolationist countrymen. In fact, his intuitive rapport with Sagittarian Churchill formed the cornerstone of the international alliance which finally secured victory. And his focus on human rights and freedoms for all human beings on earth, encouraged and promoted by his wife Eleanor (see Chapter 9 for her chart and biography), is yet another manifestation of his powerful Jupiter. In a sense, he was a channel for the *national conscience* (again, supported and even pushed by his wife), or *dharma* (in the sense of the Vedic notion of *right action*), in relation to both domestic social changes and the necessity of responding to fascism abroad.

(See also comments on Roosevelt's chart in the Jupiter in Taurus section and in Chapter 10 in four different sections. The chart is based on FDR's mother's statement about the time of birth, as rectified by Dane Rudhyar.)

example of this position's connection with international affairs is Erich Maria Remarque, author of *All Quiet on the Western Front*, a book that explores the profound realities of international conflict, and who left his native Germany to become a U.S. citizen.

Jupiter in the Tenth House

Keywords: ACTION ON THE MATERIAL LEVEL

With Jupiter in a worldly, ambitious house known traditionally for status, reputation, and authority, it is no wonder that there is no shortage of well-known people to discuss in this section. As Margaret Hone wrote in her superb *Modern Textbook of Astrology*, Jupiter here is an "excellent indication for success in affairs of the world, in business, profession, political or social life." This is the traditional view, and it is fairly well founded; however, because this is a

Saturnian house, which implies fulfilling an impersonal role, those with this placement may not always experience "fame," in the sense of a cult of personality. In fact, in many cases they will put more value on reputation, respect, and real authority than on ephemeral fame and popularity.

Fame of course does accrue to those with Jupiter here, since Jupiter lends itself toward grand expressions and social involvement. For example, boxer Muhammed Ali has this position and was always well known for his assertion, "I am the greatest!" (a sentiment also bolstered by his Leo Ascendant). Another individual with Jupiter here, the Duke of Wellington, was the most famous and heroic figure of his era, at least in the UK and Commonwealth. But let us probe beneath the surface of this placement a bit.

Those with Jupiter in the tenth live energetically in the arena of worldly achievement. Status and authority are important to them, sometimes for the idealistic reason that this enables them to accomplish their goals more easily, and sometimes simply for ego-aggrandizement. Those with Jupiter here tend to have long-range ideals that they strive for with sustained determination and committed ambition. They often have an optimism and confidence that in some cases derives from an inner sense of a "calling." Carter points out the sense of responsibility the tenth house placements express, and Moore and Douglas elaborate on this idea nicely in relation to Jupiter in this house:

> *An ingrained sense of responsibility and a capacity for far-sighted planning combine to raise this individual to a position of prominence.*

These people often have broad talents for organizing and managing substantial projects or enterprises. Accomplishment and tangible results matter to most of them, whereas in some other cases status (and recognition) seems to be an end in itself. For example, it was not enough for Leo Jupiter-in-the-tenth Nelson Rockefeller to be extraordinarily rich and the governor of New York; he still wanted to be President of the entire U.S.A., although he seemed to have very little vision of what he would do if ever elected.

There is a large number of famous and great painters with Jupiter here: for example, Renoir, Courbet, and Seurat. And if we extend this category to include sculptors, we can also add Auguste Rodin, who is well known throughout the Western world and to whom an entire Paris museum is now dedicated. Writers and musicians include Honoré de Balzac, Victor Hugo, and Franz Schubert. Film-maker and actor Orson Welles also had Jupiter in the tenth (in Pisces, sextile his Taurus Sun and Mercury), and at an early age he was regarded as a groundbreaking filmmaker who loved to tackle the biggest issues without shirking from controversy. The fact that his Moon was conjunct Uranus in Aquarius *in the ninth house* no doubt added to the extraordinary cultural impact his work had and to his ability to promote it effectively on an international stage.

Thinking of Orson Welles brings to mind Jupiter-in-the-tenth people who project an image "bigger than life" or who are in the public mind associated with something extraordinarily large and powerful. Consider the following (and I am sure that Jupiter would not mind the humorous aspect of this comparison): Herman Melville, whose greatest work *Moby Dick* has come to represent an epic *quest*, is thus associated in the public mind with a huge white whale; actor Christopher Reeve attained fame through his portrayal of the larger-than-life Superman; and cowboy actor Roy Rogers whose co-star in over ninety movies was a large Jupiterian animal, his horse "Trigger." Another remarkable figure whose "larger than life" image pervaded the Roman empire for centuries after his death is Augustus Caesar–Emperor during Rome's "Golden Age." A historian of the times, Seutonius, gives a birth time that places Jupiter in his tenth house.

Another tenth house Jupiter person who, like Orson Welles, attained recognition in his chosen calling at a very young age is historian Arthur Schlesinger, Jr., whose Jupiter in Gemini in the tenth (trine both Mercury and the Moon in Libra) earned him considerable respect through his scholarship and writings. (See Chapter 10 for more on his chart.) Former First Lady Betty Ford broke the silence about addiction, fearlessly courting controversy, as is so often the case with Jupiter, when her outspoken Jupiter in Gemini in the tenth propelled her to speak her mind bluntly. Indira Gandhi also had Jupiter in the tenth (opposite Mercury in Sagittarius), and her poor judgment in deciding to approve an attack on the holiest shrine of the Sikh religion may have indeed led to her assassination. In contrast, famed astrological researcher and statistician Michel Gauquelin had Jupiter in the tenth in Taurus, opposite a Scorpio Mercury in the fourth house–an apt symbol for his multi-year, patient, persistent gathering of data and investigation of astrology's validity.

Jupiter in the Eleventh House

Keywords: **SOCIAL & INTELLECTUAL SECURITY**

Those with this placement tend to be idealists, dreamers, and vast schemers, often with a strongly optimistic motivation. With future-oriented Jupiter in the future-oriented eleventh house, the person is often overflowing with plans, goals, and a multitude of vast objectives. (Note that traditionally the eleventh is the house of "hopes and wishes," and that Jupiter here is usually considered a benefic influence for attaining one's objectives.) A planet of considerable social involvement, Jupiter naturally functions freely and enthusiastically in the house that represents the larger human community; there is often an emphasis on dealing with society at large or with social or international issues. Quite often there is a need to be involved with social change or social improvement schemes, and so these people are often found in politics, organizations, foundations, and professional associations that share a common—usually a humanitarian or progressive—goal.

The keywords point to the fact that these individuals seek security in merging their energies with a large group or movement, which gives them a feeling of prosperity and well-being. With a generous planet in a generous house, they are usually liberal with the time and resources that they will devote to a greater cause. Moore and Douglas state that these folks are natural planners and organizers of group activities, although Sasportas rightly points out that sometimes this placement results in an over-involvement in social activities, to the point of wasting their energies and spreading themselves too thinly.

The other aspect of the above keywords reveals how these people also seek intellectual security and thus are attracted to vast systems of thought. They often want to be with people who share their concepts and world view; sometimes they create *entirely original mental worlds*. Some examples are Karl Marx, who envisioned a future society of total security for everyone (Jupiter in Capricorn trine a second house Sun and Moon in Taurus!); poet W.B. Yeats, who created his own poetic imagery out of his imaginary perfect society of "Byzantium" and who was also involved in Irish politics (Sagittarius Jupiter opposite Sun and Uranus in the fifth); and priest-scientist Teilhard de Chardin, whose books attempt to reconcile science with a deeply mystical Christian devotion (Jupiter closely conjunct Saturn in Taurus).

Another such innovator, conceptually and socially, was Maria
Montessori*, whose Gemini Jupiter in the eleventh revolutionized
educational theory and whose discoveries are still making a positive
impact on society today, decades after her original writings were
published. The first woman in Italy to receive a medical degree (in
1894), Maria Montessori developed her own entirely original concep-
tual system regarding education, which she outlined in her book *The
Montessori Method*. Not only is her Jupiter in Gemini (a planet
having to do with education in a sign of learning), but also it is almost
exactly opposite her fifth house in Saturn in Sagittarius (a symbol of
creating an educational system having to do with children). Her
fiercely independent Mars-Uranus conjunction is tied into that
opposition, in close semi-sextile to Jupiter and quincunx Saturn; and
in fact her respect for the child's individual freedom is one of the
hallmarks of the method. Self-discipline, she felt, emerged spontaneously from an independent learning environment. Reputedly
influenced by astrology, she saw self-discipline as something that
emerges as a result of natural law, an emanation of the cosmic order
that governs the movements of stars and planets.

Jupiter in the Twelfth House

Keywords: LEARNING ON THE EMOTIONAL & SOUL LEVEL

Jupiter in a house that has both a Jupiterian and a Neptunian
coloration is usually expressed as an active fantasy life, full of
imagination, dreams of the future, and/or yearnings toward a spiritual or idealistic goal. There is usually an inner generosity of spirit,
sometimes manifesting as charitable or philanthropic activity or as
work in the helping professions or healing arts. In the deepest region
of their heart, these people usually trust in life (or God) and feel that
they will be taken care of; hence, they are eager to treat others with
similar protection and abundant giving. The experience of solitude,
or even of loneliness, is not an oppressive condition for these folks but
rather a profound inner need, to enable themselves to search within
and to explore their inner world and higher goals.

---

*Born August 31, 1870; Chiaravelle, Italy; 3:30 AM LMT; died 1952.

The Catholic Trappist monk Thomas Merton*, whose religious and social writings have had a wide influence, had Jupiter conjunct Mercury in the twelfth house. His biographer Monica Furlong wrote, "It was as if the solitude were a form of essential nutrition for him." She quotes Merton as saying, "Solitude is not found so much by looking outside the boundaries of your dwelling, as by staying within." And she adds, "In solitude, Merton said, he could find love and reverence for others. Above all, in solitude he could find God, who can only be found in solitude, because [to quote Merton] 'His solitude is His being.'"

As life goes by, these people learn subtle but very essential life lessons on a profound level, sometimes at a level so deep that it is impossible to express in words; it may even be completely unconscious. These individuals need to grow beyond the constraints of the past by exploring old emotional patterns and transcending them. Tuning in with a positive attitude toward spiritual truths helps them to overcome the feeling of confinement that the twelfth house often symbolizes. In fact, those with Jupiter here will often find fulfillment and enjoy working in places of confinement (hospitals, prisons, special schools, etc.) or in charitable or educational institutions. A tendency toward seclusion is usually apparent, although less so than with most other twelfth house placements, since Jupiter represents a rather enthusiastic and outgoing energy. However, even those with Jupiter in the twelfth are usually not particularly ambitious (unless other powerful chart factors indicate it) because their need for growth and social involvement is often expressed in less "worldly" fields of activity. And so, while Jupiter here is comparatively rare in prominent people, we can still find a wide variety of expressions of this principle.

As one might expect with Jupiter in a somewhat Jupiterian house, there are a large number of successful athletes in this group, including football player Larry Csonka, tennis champ Pancho Gonzales, skier Jean-Claude Killy, and baseball great Warren Spahn. There are many more–too numerous to list here–including many Olympic champions. We might inquire, however, why this is so, for this is not a Mars factor, the astrological symbol traditionally associated with athletics. In addition to the rulership of the outdoors

---

*Born January 31, 1915; Prades, France; 9:00 AM GMT; died 1968.

by Jupiter, physical activity of this type gives one a sense of expansiveness, room to breathe, and a sense of exhilaration. Also, the team games constitute their own fantasy world, an appropriate twelfth house domain, in which the individual can try to accomplish the impossible or at least can realistically experience the satisfaction of constantly improving his or her own performance. In addition, most athletic training requires a solitary focus, separate from the rest of the outer world. And finally, a sense of deep faith is required to sustain oneself during the times of inevitable defeat, frustration, and personal failure. In many ways, one needs to transcend, at least temporarily, one's ego-self in order to perform at one's peak in many athletic endeavors.

The tremendous life of the imagination mentioned earlier is often expressed through the arts. Charismatic actress Greta Garbo had a Gemini Jupiter in the twelfth and finally declared, "I want to be alone," and, as Lois Rodden writes, "She went into reclusive retirement in 1941 at the peak of her career." Singer Dionne Warwick expressed her twelfth house Taurus Jupiter in an amazingly rich voice and then went on to conduct psychic talk shows on TV. Actor Paul Newman has enjoyed continuous popularity for four decades and eventually started a line of food products, from which all the profits go to charity. Painter Paul Cezanne developed slowly as an artist in a solitary life and had his first one-man show at the age of 56. Some writers with this placement exaggerate and mythologize their own experience in their work, making themselves seem larger than life and more romantic or exciting than was the reality; Henry Miller and Lord Byron both expressed this flair for expanded fantasies about their own lives. Two other writers devoted themselves to fantasy in a different way: H.G. Wells achieved great popularity with his fantastic imaginings of seemingly impossible adventures, whereas Hans Christian Andersen focused on fairy tales with which people worldwide could identify. Those simple tales have been translated into more languages than any other book except the *Bible*. Andersen's *Sagittarius* Jupiter in the twelfth house was trine his Mars, Sun and Mercury. In addition, he had Sagittarius rising.

Although there is some debate over the accurate chart of Abraham Lincoln*, I believe that his psychology and temperament, not to mention his empathy for the powerless slaves that he eventually

---

*Born February 12, 1809; Hodgenville, Kentucky, USA; "about sun-up"; died 1865.

freed, most closely reflect a chart that places Jupiter in the twelfth house. Not only did he sacrifice his life for higher principles (he even believed in a type of karmic law, as his second inaugural address proves), but he was also visited by prophetic dreams on numerous occasions. Certainly Lincoln's craggy, rough appearance, the decisiveness of his actions, and directness of his verbal expression seem appropriate for an Aries Ascendant, placing Jupiter in the twelfth. In any case, Jupiter was in Pisces, giving some of the same orientation as Jupiter in the twelfth.

Psychologist R. D. Laing also took action on behalf of those in need by developing innovative half-way houses for the mentally disturbed. His Jupiter in Pisces (in the twelfth but close to the Ascendant) is conjunct Uranus in the first, and his book *The Divided Self* presented revolutionary insights into our understanding of the interaction between the conscious and unconscious mind.

We cannot leave the subject without acknowledging that individuals with Jupiter in the twelfth can be extravagant, irresponsible, and so unrealistic that they can become caught up in big schemes that lead them toward destructive behavior. One particularly negative example of Jupiter in the twelfth is Susan Atkins, a follower and murderous accomplice of Charles Manson. In contrast, the highly moral dimension of Jupiter can be seen in Simon Wiesenthal, the most prominent "Nazi hunter" in the world, who is seeking to bring to justice all surviving Nazi officials, and who also has Jupiter in the twelfth house.

Margaret Mead & Emily Dickinson*

The lives of Margaret Mead and Emily Dickinson, while radically dissimilar outwardly, clearly demonstrate Sagittarian/ Jupiterian motivations. Both birth charts feature an emphasis on Sagittarius, and in both, Jupiter is placed in Capricorn. Mead, with a Mercury-Uranus-Sun conjunction in Sagittarius, was a world-renowned, pioneering explorer of foreign cultures, such as Samoa, New Guinea, and Bali. Dickinson, the reclusive nineteenth century New England poet, not only did not travel, but virtually never left her parents' house during the last twenty years of her life. However, she too has three planets conjunct in Sagittarius. With aesthetic Venus and verbal Mercury conjunct the Sun, her poetry

---

*Ed. note: This dual biography illustrates how house placement modifies the manifestation of similar sign and planet chart factors (in this case, Sagittarian emphases and Jupiter in Capricorn).

later became her "letter to the World/That never wrote to Me." Unlike Mead, Dickinson achieved fame posthumously, and is now celebrated as "one of the finest lyric poets in the English language." (quoted from Richard M. Ludwig) It is fascinating to see how the contrasting house positions of their planetary placements helped to direct the lives of Mead and Dickinson onto such different paths.

Margaret Mead's *eleventh house* Sagittarius planets drew her into a lifelong exploration of the patterns of human community, as lived out in different cultures. With the dauntless courage of a Jupiter-Mars conjunction (exactly on the Ascendant!), she braved challenging, and at times dangerous, conditions in her fieldwork. In her twenties, she immersed herself for a year in the observation of the lives of adolescent Samoan girls, which led to her acclaimed–though now controversial–book *Coming of Age in Samoa*. This "immersion" in foreign cultures is resonant with her Sagittarian Sun near the cusp of the *twelfth* house. For ethnographic work, one has to relinquish the narrowness of one's own cultural identity in order to be open enough to comprehend completely different social patterns. Another twelfth house manifestation that incorporated her eleventh house interests was Mead's position for over forty years as a curator of ethnology for the American Museum of Natural History. Museums are traditionally associated with the twelfth house; for Mead, her hidden-away office in the tower of the museum provided a sanctuary from her intense public life.

Between her ethnographic journeys, Mead translated her discoveries (with the intellectual speed and brilliance of the eleventh house Mercury-Uranus conjunction in Sagittarius) into forty books and hundreds of essays and lectures. The inventiveness of this planetary combination, as well as the cutting edge quality of the eleventh house, is evident in Mead's ability to develop new techniques for fieldwork. James I. Robertson, Jr. writes that her work in Bali in the late 1930s marked "a major innovation in the recording and presentation of ethnological data and may prove in the long run to be one of her most significant contributions to the science of anthropology." A family friend (quoted by Mary Catherine Bateson in *With a Daughter's Eye*), who was commenting on Mead's mental style, revealed the Sagittarian essence of Mead as well: "Margaret is always shooting thousands of ideas out in all directions."

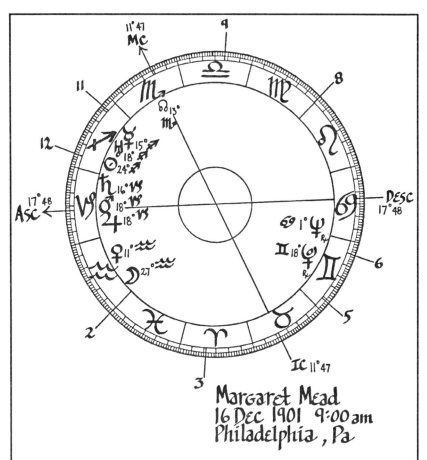

Margaret Mead
16 Dec 1901 9:00 am
Philadelphia, Pa

Mead's life was a whirlwind of Sun-Uranus frenetic activity, full of robust Sagittarian enthusiasm for her eleventh house web of social networks. Her indefatigable community-oriented nature was noted humorously by a fellow anthropologist speculating about the future: "None of us knows what really lies ahead, not even Margaret Mead. But I assure you, if there is a committee in charge, she will be on it." (quoted by Robert Cassidy in *Margaret Mead: A Voice for the Century*) This expansive social life included three marriages, two of which were with men who were partners in her anthropological fieldwork. With a characteristically Jupiterian spin, she declared, "All my marriages were a great success."

Later in her life, Mead naturally evolved into the role of

outspoken commentator on a variety of eleventh house humanitarian concerns (note also Moon and Venus in Aquarius), including over-population, race relations, and education–always seeking ways to improve conditions in society. Robert Cassidy described this eleventh house-Sagittarian interplay: "Her concern for human welfare carried religious and moral connotations that emanated from her deep ethical beliefs and that prompted her leadership in such groups as the World Council of Churches." It is a fitting tribute that Mead's epitaph reads: "To Cherish The Life Of The World."

While Margaret Mead's eleventh house Sagittarian energy was expressed in a *centrifugal* way, dispersing her vitally dynamic self out into the world, "all over the map" in every sense, Emily Dickinson's Sagittarian nature had a *centripetal*, inward-focusing orientation in its expression through the *fourth house*, which, to quote Howard Sasportas, is associated with "the home, the soul, and the roots of the being." Dickinson, who was vividly aware of her vocation as a poet of visionary experience, withdrew from the distractions of an active outer life, and concentrated her creative forces on an *interior* Sagittarian quest. Unlike Mead, whose keen ear was attuned to world events, Dickinson listened to other messages. In one poem she writes: "The only news I know/Is bulletins all day/From immortality." Her poetry explores death, God, nature, and experiences of loss and love. (Even though reclusive, she formed intense relationships, primarily through letter-writing.)

Scholars have interpreted her decision to remain in her parents' house (and in later years, almost never to emerge from it) in various ways–including agoraphobia. However, while Dickinson was a genuinely shy person, the clustering of planets in the fourth and fifth houses in her birth chart affirms her choice of a life centered on a deep plumbing of the personal psyche and the distilling of her experiences into art. (Interestingly, the poet Rilke, who also wrote poetry of profound internal experience, likewise had both the Sun and Venus in the fourth house in Sagittarius.) Judith Farr, in *The Passion of Emily Dickinson*, notes that Dickinson found support for her path from one of the most renowned poetic voices of her century: "Emerson's conviction that great art is made in isolation and silence undoubtedly helped to convince Emily Dickinson in a way of life to which she was personally drawn....And

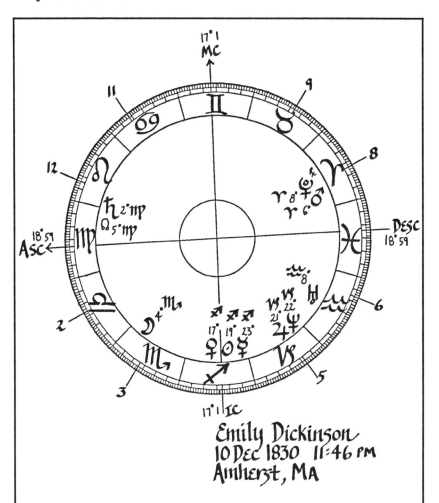

Emily Dickinson
10 Dec 1830 11:46 PM
Amherst, MA

she adhered to a plan of self-reliance in working our her destiny as artist." One of her poems evokes the inward depth to which she felt called and the wider life that she discovered through this exploration. It also comments wryly on those who (like some twentieth century scholars!) fail to grasp the significance of her life:

> *A hallowed thing–to drop a life*
> *Into the mystic well–*
> *Too plummetless–that it come back–*
> *Eternity until–*
> *....*

And then—the size of this "small" life—
The sages—call it small—
Swelled—like Horizons—in my vest—
And I sneered—softly—"small"!

The same Sagittarian *largeness* of spirit that infused Margaret Mead's efforts to build bridges of understanding between cultures, motivated Dickinson's choice of a life separate from her own society—it allowed her to pursue the creation of her astonishingly original poetry. Her writing expanded boundaries in both style and content, and some scholars have said that it was fifty years ahead of its time—another example of the Jupiterian propensity to be future-oriented. While uniquely visionary in content, her poetry has a condensed, sometimes cryptic, shorthand style: Sagittarian vision is channeled into the world through a Virgo Ascendant's economy and precision of expression. This paradoxical combination is noted by Bettina Knapp: "Within each line and stanza exists the vastness of a universe, explored through the poet's direct and acute observation of the world." Displaying a Mercury in Sagittarius fecundity that mirrored Mead's, Dickinson produced almost 1800 poems, most of which were extensively refined and polished with her Virgo rising sense of craftsmanship.

The expansiveness of Dickinson's Sagittarian planets, expressed through the fourth house—and augmented by the Jupiter-Neptune conjunction—can be seen in this quote from Dickinson scholar Joan Kirkby: "Everything she did was calculated to serve the largest need of the mind and soul; she had various words for it—'Prospective,' 'Immensity,' 'Boundlessness,' 'Expanse,' 'Possibility'—but essentially her commitment to the unknown led her to turn her back on 'the times, customs, graces, politics, or opinions of men' in favour of what she called the 'Finite infinity' of 'A soul admitted to itself' (Poem 1695)." Howard Sasportas writes that "the 4th house represents where we go when we settle back into ourselves—the inner centre where our 'I' returns to rest. As opposed to our public face [tenth house], the 4th house describes what we are like deep down inside." This definition certainly resonates with the phrase: "A soul admitted to itself"! And Dickinson's uncompromising focus on a quest for the "inner center" is described in this quote from Helen McNeil: "Her physical world was bounded by the walls and hedges of home. That, she felt, was as wide a horizon as she could encompass without losing something of her search for the essential."

The impetus for this search was propelled by Dickinson's fiery nature, indicated not only by the Sagittarian planets, but also by an Aries conjunction of Mars-Pluto and a Moon in the "fiery" water sign Scorpio. She was, in fact, a power house of passionate intensity. Bettina Knapp describes Dickinson's use of "strong, savage, brutal words, along with warm and gentler ones...to penetrate the inner corridors of the mind, the heart, and the vital organs." And Knapp also notes: "Images such as lightning, fire, red, lava, crater are part of Dickinson's volcanic vocabulary." It is a testimony to the strength of the Ascendant in shaping the persona that her image, in general, is associated with the demure and modest qualities of Virgo. Dickinson's obituary aptly portrayed her as "a soul of fire in a shell of pearl."

Emily Dickinson and Margaret Mead were both supported in their endeavors by the placement of Jupiter in Capricorn. Each of them showed extraordinary discipline. (Jane Howard quotes an anthropologist friend of Mead's as saying "she may have been the busiest, hardest-working incarnation of the Protestant ethic since Calvin.") Both women displayed a powerful sense of Capricornian personal authority. Mead, with Jupiter on the Ascendant, met the world through this authority as a natural expression of her persona (and it was readily accorded to her). For Dickinson, with Jupiter near the cusp of the fifth house of creative self-expression, trust in her own authority was crucial to her survival as a poet. Experiencing incomprehension from editors to whom she sent her poems, she resolutely chose to adhere to her own aesthetic perception. Jupiter in Capricorn gave them both the ability to endure hardship in the present, while maintaining faith in their long-term goals.

In her autobiography *Blackberry Winter*, Mead wrote, "I didn't find out about being a Sagittarian–someone who goes as far as anyone else and shoots a little farther–until I was sixteen, when we learned about astrology from the physicist husband of one of my mother's college friends." Both Margaret Mead and Emily Dickinson–two Sagittarian archers–"shot a little farther" than others. But their bows were aimed at different horizons.

—B.McE.

CHAPTER 9

Ruled by Jupiter: Sagittarius & Pisces Rising

Don't be scared to take big steps—
you can't cross a chasm in two small jumps.
—David Lloyd George

Although Jupiter is naturally powerful in the lives of all who have major placements in Sagittarius or Pisces–and this is certainly so for those with the Sun or Moon in those signs–there should be special attention paid to Jupiter's birth chart placement when one is "ruled by Jupiter," in other words, when one has either of the Jupiter signs rising. Although at first glance one might wonder how two such different signs can be treated together and considered in any way to express similar qualities and abilities, in this chapter we will explore the remarkable similarities between these two ascendants, whose natures sometimes tend to run parallel.

I do not want to force this comparison, for these signs are very different, as their square relationship within the zodiac attests. But we should remember the ancient idea (before Neptune was discovered and eventually allocated to Pisces as a co-ruler) that Sagittarius is the active expression of Jupiter, while Pisces is the passive expression. In more modern terms, Sagittarius is the extroverted, self-expressive mode, whereas Pisces is the introverted, self-repressive or self-sacrificing mode.

---

* Because in Northern latitudes Pisces is one of the quickest signs to rise over the horizon (being a "sign of short ascension" in contrast to Sagittarius' being a "sign of long ascension"), there is a statistical reason to some extent why Sagittarius rising prominent people are so much more numerous than those with Pisces rising. But still, I do not think that the fact that there are simply fewer people with Pisces rising accounts for the entirety of my findings. The nature of Pisces is such that the general observations made in this chapter seem to hold, no matter what statistics say. Further, it is much easier to find notable examples of well-known people who have the other signs of short ascension rising than it is to find such examples with Pisces rising.

In fact, in assembling the research for this chapter, it became apparent that there are remarkably few famous people with Pisces rising, and that–if they are well known–it is because of their achievements rather than because of their personalities (such as inventor Alexander Graham Bell and Pierre Curie, co-discoverer of radium). On the other hand, there are dozens and dozens of Sagittarius rising notable individuals whom I could have selected for special treatment in this chapter.* This discovery absolutely confirms the notion and my expectation that, indeed, whereas Pisces rising individuals hold themselves back from the limelight and rarely seek credit or approbation for their achievements, Sagittarius rising folks naturally seek prominence and recognition. They are often natural leaders and inspirers of major undertakings or large enterprises, whereas those with Pisces rising generally reserve their inspirational effectiveness to a more private sphere, and often in behind-the-scenes roles.

It may come as no surprise to experienced students of astrology that more Presidents of the U.S.A. have had Sagittarius rising than any other Ascendant; Madison, Van Buren, Taylor, Fillmore, and Theodore Roosevelt have published charts with that rising sign (it is notable that Theodore Roosevelt was an avid outdoorsman and an early conservationist, which clearly reflects the love of the outdoors and nature which Sagittarius rising–and Pisces rising also to some extent–usually expresses). The public prominence of Sagittarius rising compared to Pisces rising also parallels our finding that Jupiter's twelfth house position likewise diminishes the likelihood and the desire for public fame and notice.

Before going into the details of these rising signs' characteristics, it is important to mention a few salient facts about the Ascendant. Although representing an instinctive orientation and a prominent tone in the varied colorings of the individual's personality, the rising sign by itself (i.e., exclusive of planets in that sign) does not always signify qualities and capabilities that are *under the person's command and mastery*. Indeed, often they are not even conscious in the individual. These energies spring up spontaneously, as a sort of natural instinct; and sometimes they are not consciously developed much at all by the persón (or they become consciously known and utilizable only as the person gets older). It is as if nature or fate or God or a cosmic intelligence supplies each person with the Ascendant that will goad him or her into life and the appropriate experiences needed by that soul, even if he or she doesn't have any conscious desire for such a mode of expression. Yet, the Ascendant is in many ways the *outward* "image of the personality," and other people tend to believe what they see, even if in reality the Ascendant does not accurately reflect the *inner* person. We do sometimes find Virgo risings who cannot spell or master details, Aries risings with no leadership talents, and Leo risings with little sense of humor or self-confidence. One really has to look at the entire chart, especially whether other planets are in the rising sign, whether there are close aspects to the Ascendant, and the placement and aspects of the ruling planet.

In some traditions, the ruling planet of the rising sign is in fact called the "ruler of the chart," so dominantly does its placement "rule" over the person's interests, consciousness, and active efforts at self-expression. If you were born with a Jupiter sign rising, it is especially important that you understand the varied meanings and potentials of your Jupiter's placement, since tuning into that field of experience (house) and energy (sign–modified somewhat by the aspects) will enable you to feel more *alive*, more motivated to express yourself, and more inwardly confident and optimistic. In fact, since most people with Sagittarius rising are quite optimistic anyhow, it is perhaps more important that those with Pisces rising consciously work to tune in to their Jupiter's potential; because it will help them to go beyond the self-doubt or self-pity that often afflicts them. Jupiter's sign will reveal a primary motivating energy in one's actions and self-expression for anyone ruled by Jupiter. And of course, Jupiter's house for these people invariably shows a field of experience where much of one's life-energy and effort manifest and where one will encounter issues and self-improvement opportunities that cannot be ignored. One simply *must* be active in this area of life in order to express many of one's essential abilities and to stimulate those upbeat, core energies which enhance buoyancy and increase one's capacity for living enthusiastically.

Parallels in the Expression of Jupiter's Rising Signs

Your worrying shows that you have no faith in the goodness of God or even in God Himself. Let Him accomplish things in His own way rather than in the way that you desire. Try to adjust yourself to all that He does and you will never be unhappy.
—Sardar Bahadur Jagat Singh
(Professor of Chemistry and spiritual teacher)

The above quotation is an example of the philosophical attitude that both of these Ascendants display when they are functioning optimally and positively. At best, both Ascendants instinctively want to make people feel better, to inspire them, and to support those who need help. They don't want to worry themselves, and they don't want to see others enmeshed in worry or fear. They always want to improve and uplift others. Neither can stand the boredom of the here-and-now status quo. Both are dynamic, mutable signs—always eager to learn *and generously to share* their learning, their inspirations, and their faith. They both have an awareness of being part of something far greater than the isolated individual self. They both want to focus on the *vision of life* that they have perceived as possible, even if it is in the far distant future. In fact, both signs are known for being prophetic, intuitive, psychic, and living a life based on some kind of faith or devotion to a cause or ideal. This philosophical attitude toward life's real meaning is common to both signs, and is also why it can often be said of these far-sighted visionaries: "A philosopher is one who is ahead of his time and behind on his rent."

Both Sagittarius and Pisces rising are quite gullible, as discussed in Chapter 1. Since both like to see and believe the best in everyone, they rarely doubt or analyze the possibility of their being overly optimistic. At best, both these rising signs are also irrepressible! Their buoyancy is amazing to others, especially in the face of adversity. However, since both prefer to believe what they want to believe, in spite of facts that may be obvious to everyone else but them, both of them have a definite need to continually communicate with and listen to trusted, practically-oriented advisors. Even though both of these signs are known for giving helpful advice to others, when it comes to clarifying their own situations and the implications of decisions they are about to make, they are relatively helpless; for these two signs lack *discrimination*, as can be seen in their natural opposition and square to the analytical, skeptical signs of Virgo and Gemini.

Both Pisces and Sagittarius rising people have a perpetual desire to be on the move, to experience new things, to travel, to encounter a wide variety of people, places, and things. They are both interested in broad, over-arching moral, social, philosophical, and religious issues. And also, except for those Pisces risings who are especially shy, they both can be rather talkative! This is not to say necessarily *communicative*, for often they get lost in their own mental outpourings and become oblivious to whoever is or is not listening to them. In other words, they can wander through their own vast, personal mental realms endlessly if they are not *grounded* or *focused* in the here-and-now. Once again, one must look to the entire chart but especially to the position of natal Jupiter. Jupiter in an air or fire sign, for example, is far more likely to be talkative and sometimes simultaneously rambling and undisciplined than is Jupiter in, for example, Virgo, Cancer, Capricorn or Scorpio.

Sagittarius Rising

So much has already been discussed at length earlier in this book that directly applies to those with Sagittarius Ascendant (for example, much of Chapter 3) that there is no need to repeat those generalizations, especially since this chapter contains numerous additional examples of Sagittarius rising individuals. It is worth commenting briefly, however, on a few specific Sagittarius rising characteristics. These folks are almost always enthusiastic, sometimes to an extreme. And in spite of their impersonal attitude toward other people, it is difficult not to like them since they are almost always tolerant and obviously well-intentioned. But cultivating close relationships may not be easy for them. As Esther Leinbach wrote in her book, *Sun Ascendant Rulerships*:

> They will give the shirt off their back to a friend, and friends are numerous. They find it easier to make new friends than to settle down to working on a relationship. Their families usually feel neglected by them because of their many outside interests....They are wonderful administrators for their ability to draw things together into meaningful workable wholes. They are detached in their attitude towards people, never playing favorites and harboring "pets." They love everybody and are frank and outspoken to the point of alienating people except that they are so innocent about meaning to hurt anyone's feelings that you look pretty silly trying to hold a grudge against them.

One thing I noticed early in my studies of astrology, through my many associations with Sagittarius rising friends, was that their handwriting will usually have some "bigness" about it and that the slant of it will tend to go up on the page, as if the person cannot contain his or her upbeat optimism (naturally, this is more evident if the writing is being done on unlined paper!).

Sagittarius rising people almost always love the outdoors; rarely are they purely mental types like Sagittarius Sun can be. They are physically restless and are more prone toward definite *action* based on their inspirations and aspirations than is Sagittarius Sun and more so also than Pisces rising. As Howard Sasportas writes in *The Twelve Houses*, "Another image associated with Sagittarius is that of the Seeker–there is always further to go, always something else to chase after and pursue." And it is this impulse toward continual expansion that can drive them to living beyond their means and also failing to ground their grand visions in the reality right in front of them.

Since so many earlier comments about the sign Sagittarius were focused on general principles and often on those individuals with that Sun sign, it is also worth quoting here from my book *Chart Interpretation Handbook* to reveal the contrast between Sagittarius rising and Sagittarius Sun:

> The optimism, buoyancy, enthusiasm, and broad-mindedness that are often, but not always, seen in Sagittarius Sun people are almost uniformly expressed by those who have Sagittarius ASC. Virtually every Sagittarius ASC person I have

ever seen could be described as perpetually "up beat," even in the face of continued disappointments or obstacles. Although the tendency toward forcefully preaching one's personal beliefs as universal truth is present in Sagittarius ASC as well as Sagittarius Sun, the ASC expression of this tendency is usually more tolerant and inspiring, while the preaching of a Sagittarius Sun person is often experienced as being hit over the head with "the Truth." In other words, self-righteousness seems considerably more flagrant in those with Sun in Sagittarius. Also, Sagittarius ASC people almost never show the aimless, drifting discontent that is so often seen in those with Sagittarius Sun. Sagittarius Rising seems more inclined toward definite action in line with an ideal, whereas Sagittarius Sun is sometimes limited to mental or theoretical activity alone.

As Paul Wright wrote, it is remarkable how often those with Sagittarius rising become "larger than life," often idolized or eventually becoming a cultural icon. Two of the most glorified figures in history–Leonardo da Vinci and Michelangelo–were both born with Sagittarius rising, according to birth records. In more recent times, Elvis Presley, Bob Dylan, and Charles Lindbergh are obvious examples. On a level of perhaps slightly less extreme adulation, Fred Astaire and George Gershwin both had Sagittarius Ascendants, as do Shirley Temple Black, Mickey Rooney, and singer Eartha Kitt. Fred Astaire's Ascendant is especially interesting since he had Uranus conjunct the Ascendant on the twelfth house side, while Saturn was in Sagittarius 10° below the Ascendant. Certainly, Astaire's dancing and screen persona were known for their lively, happy, upbeat tone, as he was able to put into an artistic form (Saturn) his innovative, creative high-stepping Uranus in Sagittarius. He was also a noted aficionado of horse racing!

Other Sagittarius rising notables include: actor Hal Holbrook, whose most famous role was as Mark Twain, a Sagittarian; baseball player Ernie Banks, probably the most likable, upbeat player in modern times (and for years the most popular man in Chicago, where he played for twenty years), who always expressed great love for the game and for the outdoors; and Ted Turner, the media mogul and owner of professional sports teams. Numerous great athletes have had Sagittarius rising: Roger Maris, who broke Babe Ruth's single-year home run record; star football player Roger Staubach; tennis star Tracy Austin; and Bob Mathias, who was an Olympic champion in the decathlon and then went on to be elected to Congress. One also finds spokesmen and spokeswomen for various causes: Brando propagandized Native Americans' rights; Dylan of course is well known for his championing of the downtrodden; Jesse Helms, the right-wing U.S. Senator who never hesitates to take on controversial issues; Betty Friedan, the noted feminist writer and pioneer; and Mary Baker Eddy, who founded the positive-thinking religion of Christian Science (see Chapter 10 for details of her chart).

Although Jupiter aspects will be explored in Chapter 10, we should mention in passing that many of the characteristics discussed above will also be found in those who have natal Jupiter closely aspecting their Ascendants. Jupiterian concerns and themes are likely to be prominent in the person's life. Also, the optimism and expansiveness are usually apparent, but these people may not necessarily exhibit the same flamboyance and spontaneity as Sagittarius rising individuals. The sign quality of Jupiter will color its expression and may sometimes tone down the Jupiterian uplifting flame. A good example would be Ralph Waldo Emerson, whose Jupiter in Virgo conjunct the Ascendant made for a more deliberate, analytical–but yet still optimistic–philosophy of life, which caught the American public's fancy for decades (see the Jupiter in Virgo section of Chapter 5 for a detailed discussion of Emerson).

Eleanor Roosevelt

In October 1948, *Time* Magazine wrote: "At sixty-four, Anna Eleanor Roosevelt has become perhaps the best known woman in the world." Enjoying both the enormous popularity that is common for Sagittarius rising (many polls in the 1940s showed her to be the "most admired woman living today in any part of the world"), Eleanor also experienced the controversy that this Ascendant both generates and seldom shrinks from. During the twelve years of Franklin Roosevelt's Presidency, Eleanor Roosevelt took the role of "First Lady" into entirely unprecedented territory–at a time when there was far less support than today for women acting independently in public life.

Eleanor Roosevelt's life is remarkable for the intensity of her support for humanitarian causes, and for her effective use of every available means to promote those concerns. Jupiter, the chart ruler, is in Leo at the cusp of the ninth house: Her generous and

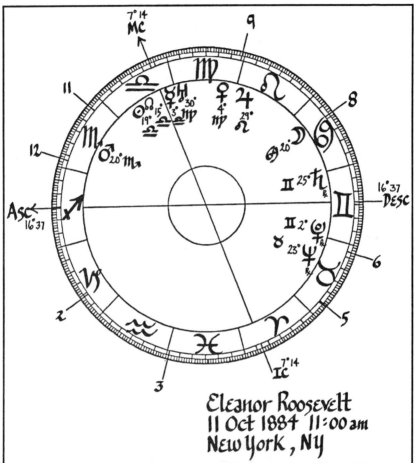

Eleanor Roosevelt
11 Oct 1884   11:00 am
New York, NY

warm personality opened doors to forums that allowed her to
publicize her message. And her bountiful vitality–expressive of
this fiery emphasis–was legendary. Her biographer, Blanche Wiesen
Cook (who met her several times during Eleanor's last years)
observed, "The room simply changed when she walked into it–one
felt the air fill with her vibrancy." And Doris Kearns Goodwin, in
her August 1994 *New Yorker* article on the Roosevelts, notes: "It
was said jokingly in Washington that Franklin Roosevelt had a
nightly prayer: 'Dear God, please make Eleanor a little tired.'"

Shortly after moving into the White House, Eleanor began to
hold her own press conferences for women journalists, something
no other First Lady had ever done. Demonstrating the heightened

mental activity of Mercury conjunct Uranus in the ninth house, she wrote a daily syndicated newspaper column, did regular radio commentaries, lectured throughout the country, and wrote twelve books and numerous magazine articles. Sagittarius is never faulted for reticence, as this quote from Goodwin shows: "She also wrote memos–scores of memos which she sent not only to her husband but to various Administration officials, describing what she had seen and what needed to be done. So voluminous was her correspondence with the War Department that General George Marshall assigned a separate officer just to deal with it. 'Oh, my God, here's another one,' officials would lament when yet a sixth or seventh missive from Mrs. Roosevelt reached them." Although she communicated prodigiously during the presidential years, the *frankness* of Sagittarius emerged even more strongly after Eleanor left the White House: "For the first time in my life I can say just what I want. For your information it is wonderful to be free." (quoted by Cook)

Eleanor's humanitarian concerns were evident early in life: she was occupied with social work as a young woman. Later, as the wife of a President whose mobility was limited by paralysis from polio, she willingly stepped into the role of traveling envoy to observe social conditions and to gather the information that FDR sought as he shaped his New Deal policies. He freely acknowledged her great influence on his programs. Some of the social reforms that she advocated were: protective legislation for women workers; civil rights for blacks; abolition of child labor; and establishment of the minimum wage.

To seek fulfillment through an active public life was natural to a Sun in the tenth house individual such as Eleanor Roosevelt. And with the Sun's placement in Libra, the opportunity for prominence opened up through her marriage. To quote Goodwin, "Franklin was the instrument through which her own unusual qualities were able to find their widest stage." But Franklin clearly was indebted to her as well. A White House advisor (quoted by Goodwin) acknowledged, "He would never have become the kind of president he was without her." Theirs was a vitally interdependent working (although not, in later years, romantic) relationship, reflective of Eleanor's Venus in *Virgo* conjunct Jupiter in Leo.

Sagittarius, of course, is known as the sign of the traveler, and by 1940 Eleanor Roosevelt had covered over 280,000 miles crisscrossing the country (according to the 1949 *Current Biography*). Goodwin writes, "So often was she out of Washington that the Washington *Star* once printed the humorous headline 'MRS. ROOSEVELT SPENDS NIGHT AT WHITE HOUSE!'" During World War II this mileage vastly increased as she visited Allied armed forces around the world to help build morale (a Sagittarian forte!) among the servicemen.

It is fitting that after the death of Franklin Roosevelt, President Truman appointed Eleanor as delegate to that most Sagittarian of institutions–the United Nations. For seven years she served as chairman of the U.N. Commission on Human Rights and, in response to the Holocaust, helped to draft the Universal Declaration of Human Rights. According to Cook, "It was adopted on 10 December 1948 largely as a result of the vision, stamina, and personal diplomacy of Eleanor Roosevelt." In this work, Eleanor Roosevelt's great Sagittarian spirit ultimately found a global scope.

—B.McE.

Bob Dylan

Born Robert Zimmerman on May 24, 1941, the songwriter-troubadour best known as Bob Dylan is a great example of Sagittarius rising in numerous ways. And, in Dylan's case, he is an especially Jupiterian type since his ruling planet Jupiter is conjunct his Sun as well (Jupiter is also conjunct Uranus–revolutionary originality–and even widely conjunct the Moon). Few songwriters have ever been so prolific and so widely recorded by other artists. His works include literally dozens of generational and internationally popular "classics," most of which are still as vibrant and relevant today as when they were written. Among the features of his songs which reflect Sagittarius rising (and the strong Jupiter influence) are:

a) Moral and ethical issues and themes have always been important to him, from the "civil rights" songs of the 1960s to songs written over 25 years later.

b) A philosophical acceptance of life pervades many of his works, such as "Don't Think Twice, It's All Right," which reflects the perpetual buoyancy of Sagittarius Rising, no matter how clearly

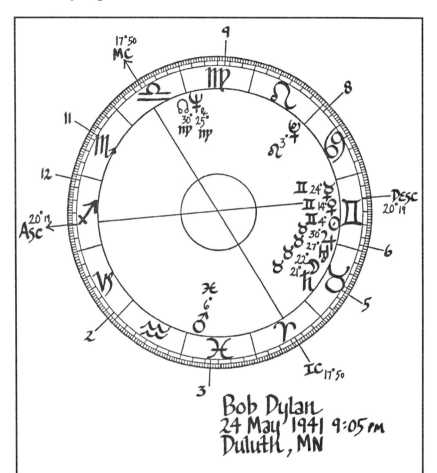

Bob Dylan
24 May 1941 9:05 pm
Duluth, MN

Dylan saw the problems and pains and injustices of life.

c) Religious and philosophical concerns have also dominated his personal life-quest, incorporating not only Christian devotional songs and feelings, social justice, and Zen-like word-spinning until the mind reels in cosmic comedy, but also serious philosophical questionings that transcend all traditional religions, as expressed, for example, in one of his most original but little appreciated albums, *John Wesley Harding*.

d) The idealism of Sagittarius rising is apparent throughout his work, as is his profound attunement to the future ("The Times, They are a Changin") and indeed, a prophetic and even archetypal method of expression that recalls virtually a Biblical tone.

We should also mention that Neptune (the planet of vision, music and imagination) is in the 9th house and that his Mars is in Pisces, the sign co-ruled by Neptune and Jupiter–an apt symbol of how he asserted himself in spite of his natural shyness.

In addition, the placement of his Jupiter in Taurus, I feel, is profoundly significant, for that groundedness enabled him to give concreteness, depth, and detail to his imaginative imagery, as well as to be rhythmically attuned to the ebbs and flows and cycles of nature.   —S.A.

Hermann Hesse

In his late fifties, Hermann Hesse, the acclaimed German novelist and poet, observed: "Writing is every time a mad, exciting business, a voyage in a tiny craft on the high seas, a solitary flight through the universe." Through his writing, the Sagittarius-rising Hesse distilled meaning from turbulent personal experience and affirmed faith during dark times. With Jupiter also placed in Sagittarius, near the Ascendant and opposite Mercury in Gemini, Hesse was a born writer: "From my thirteenth year on, it was clear to me that I wanted to be either a poet or nothing at all." Hesse's attainment of international literary recognition was closely aligned astrologically with the Ascendant and Jupiter in Sagittarius. The overnight success of his first novel *Peter Camenzind* in 1904, as well as the award of the Nobel Prize for literature forty-two years later, correlated with Uranus transits to the Jupiter-Mercury opposition and to the Ascendant-Descendant axis. But the Sagittarian influence can be traced also in Hesse's childhood, in the themes that engaged him, and in his role as a spiritual guide to readers, who, like Hesse, were profoundly concerned with seeking meaning during times of personal and social crisis.

Born in Calw, Germany, Hesse grew up in a household that was permeated by the multi-cultural spirit commonly associated with Sagittarius. His parents and his maternal grandfather had been missionaries in India, where his mother was born. Hesse's grandfather, who also lived with the family, ran the missionary publishing house in Calw. For Sun-in-Cancer Hesse, childhood memories

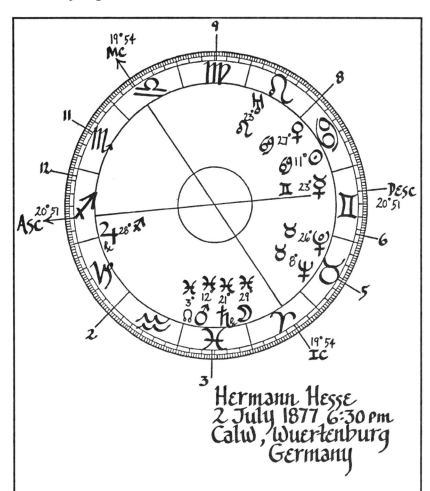

Hermann Hesse
2 July 1877 6:30 pm
Calw, Wuertenburg
Germany

were crucial, and in his *Autobiographical Writings* he vividly sketches the Sagittarian ambiance of his family's home (note the Sagittarian Jupiter square to the Moon in Pisces):

> Many worlds, many quarters of the earth, extended arms, sent forth rays which met and intersected in our house....Here people prayed and read the Bible, here they studied and practiced Hindu philology...here there was knowledge of Buddha and Lao-tse, guests came from many countries with the breath of strangeness and foreignness on their clothes, with odd trunks of leather and of woven bark and the sound of strange tongues....

Ernst Rose, in *Faith from the Abyss*, commented on the profusion of languages in Hesse's home: "He heard his grandfather converse in English, French, Italian, and East Indian and Malayan dialects." This multi-lingual tradition would take another Sagittarian globe-spanning form in Hesse's life: his books have been translated into thirty-five different languages, including nine major dialects in India. In Japan he has been the most popular of all German writers. Almost fifteen million copies of his English translations sold in the USA in the decade from the mid-sixties to the mid-seventies, "a literary phenomenon without precedent in America," according to biographer Joseph Mileck. Hesse, the Sun-in-Cancer son of missionaries, remained rooted in Europe while still having a powerful impact in countries throughout the world.

While Hesse's childhood home was a vortex of Sagittarian intersections, it was also pervaded by his parents' deep, but severely ascetic and repressive, spirituality—symbolized by Saturn-Moon in Pisces. Hesse rejected this narrow, orthodox form of religion, and struggled with the emotional scars it left on him. However, he remained committed to a search for ways "to enter that 'timeless realm of the spirit' where Hesse felt most at home and which he has mapped out as his most characteristic literary province." (quoted from Theodore Ziolkowski in the "Introduction" to Hesse's *Autobiographical Writings*) The Sagittarian Jupiter challenged conservative Saturn-Moon by seeking wider spiritual horizons. In turn, the third house Saturn in imaginative Pisces helped Hesse give *shape* in writing to his Jupiterian explorations.

One expression of Hesse's spiritual search was his lifelong affinity with Eastern philosophies (again consonant with his blend of Sagittarian-Piscean influences). This interest was first ignited in his grandfather's library of thousands of books, which, Hesse recalled, "contained not only learned works on theology and oriental philology, but also translations of the sacred books of the East." Over the years Hesse developed a deep appreciation for Hinduism, Buddhism, and most especially Taoism and Chinese philosophy in general. (Richard Wilhelm's 1924 translation of the *I Ching* had a particularly strong influence on Hesse's perspective.) Some of Hesse's novels, such as *Siddhartha* and *Journey to the East,* directly express his absorption of Eastern wisdom. Hesse's wide-ranging, multi-cultural spirituality is evident in his description (in *Autobiographical Writings*) of "the dancing idol from India which stood in my grandfather's fabulous glass cabinet." Hesse writes:

> *Behind his form, behind his face and image, lived God, the Infinite lurked*
> *there, which at that time as a boy, without knowing its name, I recognized*
> *and revered not less than in later days when I called it Shiva, Vishnu,*
> *named it God, Life, Brahman, Atman, Tao, or Eternal Mother. It was*
> *father, was mother, it was woman and man, sun and moon.*

While the Sagittarian/Jupiterian influence drew Hesse beyond any Cancerian tendencies towards provincialism, he did maintain his roots in his own culture and traditions. As Ralph Freedman notes (in *Hermann Hesse: Pilgrim of Crisis*): "A missionary in the best sense, Hesse could approach another world, another identity, and make it his own while also maintaining his Christian and Western self." He had a "dual self, both German and romantic and Taoist and Buddhist, living simultaneously in two seemingly opposite interior worlds." This bridging of worlds was part of the universal appeal of novels which were, in essence, highly autobiographical. (Hesse called them "biographies of the soul.") Ernst Rose describes the reaction of a scholar in India to *Siddhartha*: "He was amazed to find a European who had actually understood the spirit of the country." Hesse himself acknowledged this Eastern/Western "dual self" in his *Autobiographical Writings*. The following quote also includes a reference to his Sagittarian Ascendant. (One of Hesse's close friends, Josef Englert, was an astrologer and possibly introduced Hesse to the subject.) Hesse writes again about the deities in his grandfather's collection:

> *Long before I could read and write they so filled me with age-old*
> *Eastern images and ideas that later, whenever I met a Hindu or*
> *Chinese sage, it was like a reunion, a homecoming. And yet I am a*
> *European, was in fact, born with the sign of the Archer on the*
> *ascendant, and all my life have zealously practiced the Western virtues*
> *of impetuosity, greed and unquenchable curiosity.* [One suspects a
> possible tinge of irony in Hesse's use of the word "virtues" here!]

Hesse's frank acknowledgment–that his life often did not attain the Eastern ideals of serenity and detachment which attracted him–was accurate. His fervent spiritual quest was fueled by the internal conflicts signified by the mutable sign T-square–with the third house Pisces Saturn-Moon at the apex. Hesse wrestled with depression, suicidal impulses, alcoholism, and strong urges for escape. This struggle with the shadow side of life is also shown by the Sun exactly semi-square Pluto (and semi-square Uranus in the *eighth house*). Psycho-analysis with an analyst trained by Carl Jung was one way that Hesse found healing. Hesse drew upon this experience in writing his novel *Demian*, which includes the compelling dream images to which his Piscean side was naturally attuned.

In his mid-forties Hesse entered a time of especially deep crisis when transiting Pluto conjuncted natal Sun in the seventh house. The conflict between the spiritual and the sensual sides of his nature powerfully erupted, and he suffered through a short-lived, explosive marriage. (Not long after this transit, Hesse found his "life companion Ninon," with whom he formed a warm and supportive marriage.) Hesse's writing of the novel *Steppenwolf* at the end of this Pluto transit shows how he used the craft of writing (Mercury in Gemini) to transmute and create meaning from intense emotional upheaval. As Ernst Rose notes, "The clarity of Hesse's language was meant as a defense against chaos." (Mercury in Gemini square to Pisces planets!) Astrologers will recognize the classic Plutonian dark journey in Ernst Rose's comments on this novel: "*Steppenwolf* literally signifies a walk through hell–through the inferno of the modern soul–with the will to overcome it....It was the first German novel to include a descent into the cellars of the subconscious in its search for spiritual integration." This Plutonian novel became a kind of "bible" for Americans during the turbulent years of the mid-1960s, when the transiting Uranus-Pluto conjunction unleashed widespread radical, transformative forces. This was a very different "bible" from the one Hesse's missionary parents carried; but perhaps not altogether so: for Hesse called the New Testament the "repository of the most precious and the most dangerous wisdom."

Sagittarius represents not only the Journeyer, but also the Guide–the one who has *been there* and becomes a way-shower to others. With Jupiter in Sagittarius near the Ascendant, Hesse became, in Ralph Freedman's words, "a mythic *persona*, a pilgrim whose voice reads as a sacred script," which "rendered him a powerful influence on several generations" as the "Sage of the Interior Journey." Young people in particular sought out Hesse for guidance and deluged him with letters. But the larger-than-life dimension of Sagittarius rising took on truly dramatic proportions in the USA after Hesse's death in 1962. Ralph Freedman observes: "In his American incarnation he became a myth–a mixture of Jesus and Buddha in no way tied to contemporary time schedules or geography. In this ahistorical role, Hesse enjoyed posthumously an explosion of acclaim considerably greater than anything he had enjoyed during his lifetime."

Freedman points out that although Hesse's popularity has continually waxed and waned both before and since the 1960s crest, it often surges during times of social crisis, because Hesse depicted the emergence of faith and meaning amidst personal and social breakdown. And, like another first house Jupiter writer, Emerson, he maintained "an unwavering belief in the ultimate value of the individual–even when it ran counter to the social values around him." (quoted from Freedman)

Hesse's last novel, *The Glass Bead Game*, written when he was in his mid-fifties to mid-sixties, was the culmination of a life of seeking a unifying vision to resolve the tension of life's polarities. This quote from Hesse's poem "Stages" (which is included in the novel) expresses Hesse's affirmative Sagittarian philosophy of life as a *journey*:

> *Serenely let us move to distant places*
> *And let no sentiments of home detain us.*
> *The Cosmic Spirit seeks not to restrain us*
> *But lifts us stage by stage to wider spaces.*
> *If we accept a home of our own making,*
> *Familiar habit makes for indolence.*
> *We must prepare for parting and leave-taking*
> *Or else remain the slaves of permanence.*
>
> *Even the hour of our death may send*
> *Us speeding on to fresh and newer spaces,*
> *And life may summon us to newer races.*
> *So be it, heart: bid farewell without end.*

—B.McE.

Pisces Rising

Having already mentioned earlier in this chapter some of the qualities that Pisces rising shares with Sagittarius rising, it is now time to clarify exactly in what way Pisces rising is unique. I pointed out earlier that those with this Ascendant tend to stay in the background, preferring to have their actions speak for them more than their words, and devoting their energies to supporting and encouraging others. As Carolyn Dodson wrote in her self-published book, *Rising Signs*:

> *Pisceans barely whisper their own ideas in fear of backlash*

or rejection; yet, they seem to know more about the universe and its workings than any of the rest of us will ever fully comprehend. They were born to soften and to beautify your life and to guide you toward the invisible, unexplainable forces that you may not comprehend; yet, you know these forces are there.

Indeed, those with Pisces rising so often lead such a private life that many people do not know them or at least do not know them very deeply. They need substantial privacy, and they have a love of nature somewhat reminiscent of Sagittarius, but of a much more delicate and wistful type. Artistic expression, in fact, is one way that these people may express their sensitive emotions, and sometimes this takes the form of nature photography, drawing, or painting. Invariably, these people need *emotional expression*, and quite often music plays a key role in their daily lives, whether they perform it or merely listen to it. (Note that internationally acclaimed orchestra conductors Leopold Stokowski and Zubin Mehta both have Pisces rising. Two other extremely popular musicians are bandleader Lawrence Welk and Beatle Ringo Starr.) Dodson also points out that persons with Pisces rising may have an affinity for being around water or water activities. Almost always, as she writes, they are "more sensitive than we to sights, sounds, smells, and the vibrations of our universe."

Although Pisces rising often *appears* to be in a somewhat melancholy mood, they often simultaneously have an inner happiness which, like that of Sagittarius rising, can be contagious and inspiring to others, although admittedly less flamboyant. Their sensitivity to others is remarkable, and they may well have natural gifts in the healing arts. As Esther Leinbach points out,

...Pisces people are cherished for their sympathy and listening ability. A Pisces is not likely to dig in and help you complete a work project as a Capricorn is likely to do. But it is a source of dismay and frustration to the Capricorn that he does not attract the close relationships that Pisces soaks in with seemingly no effort. Pisces will listen attentively longer than any other sign.

As many people in the healing arts come to realize, it is not only specific knowledge, science, and technique which contribute to therapeutic effectiveness, but also the sympathy and ability to listen of the doctor, healer, or therapist. This innate capacity gives Pisces Ascendant people the ability to serve others effectively in the most subtle of ways; sometimes they themselves do not realize how helpful they are being. But in any case, there is a need to be useful and of service to others, or to an ideal, for this person to feel inwardly happy. Their Jupiterian generosity must be actively engaged in life. A notable example of Piscean service can be seen in the life of astrologer Evangeline Adams, who was very prominent in the first half of the 20th century. She had not only Pisces rising, but also Mercury, Jupiter, and Venus in Pisces, and during her lifetime gave consultations to over 100,000 persons.

In addition, there is a need for a Pisces rising person to have an inner life of some kind in order that the individual can contact her or his inner light. They have a natural inclination toward the transphysical, metaphysical, or mystical; and if it is not fulfilled, there can be a tendency to take other roads to escape from the humdrum mundane realities of uninspiring life, which can lead to self-destructive habits. They are often quite dependent on others as it is, and getting further lost in escapist paths will make them even more liable to being victimized by others, thus fulfilling their sometimes subconscious need to be a martyr. As Howard Sasportas wrote,

A keynote for Pisces rising is the sacrifice of the personal will. However, if taken to an extreme, those with this Ascendant

Neptune's Co-rulership of Pisces Rising makes
this Ascendant far more otherworldly than
Sagittarius Rising.

may repeatedly set up situations through which others take advantage of them.

In fact, Sasportas classifies three types of Pisces rising people: the victim, the artist, and the healer/ savior. He further points out that a person with this Ascendant is "overwhelmed by his or her sensitivity and openness." Hence, we can conclude that, while learning how to serve others by using this sensitivity, the individual must simultaneously learn how to protect his or her own self!

It is not mentioned often enough in the literature of astrology how much inner strength these people do have. In fact, their apparent malleability and easy-going demeanor belie their great strength of character. Their philosophical outlook is not flaunted as it so often is with Sagittarius rising people, but it is usually there nonetheless, as is an excellent sense of humor that likewise enables them to rise above petty troubles. Accurately described by *Sagittarius rising* author Isabel Hickey as "sympathetic, supersensitive, affectionate, sentimental, and romantic," they often seem out of place in this material world. And in fact, they must be careful that they do not, as Hickey wrote, "dream through life rather than living it."

In spite of the Jupiter co-rulership of this rising sign, some of these people do get lost in self-pity or allow themselves to be held back by vague fears (perhaps this is a manifestation of the Neptune co-rulership of Pisces). They often "hide their light under a bushel basket," never revealing or even using great innate abilities. I find it quite interesting that the Pisces symbol of the two fish in many medieval representations was shown with the fish tied together at the mouths. And, according to one legend, one fish is dead and the live fish cannot get anywhere until it cuts itself loose! *Cutting loose of the past* was always emphasized by Dane Rudhyar (who had *Sagittarius* rising) as a key necessity in the twelfth phase of any cycle, such as the zodiac signs or the houses of a birth chart. And to do so takes faith (Jupiter) but also courage. As psychologist Rollo May wrote, "Courage means the power to LET GO of the familiar and the secure." Those with Pisces rising do worry far more than those with Sagittarius ascending, and perhaps one

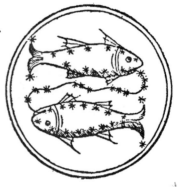

of my favorite quotations is pertinent here, since it applies so well to that negative mental habit, one which afflicts so many people, and especially those who have squares or oppositions between mutable signs. Sardar Bahadur Jagat Singh, a professor of chemistry who late in life became a great spiritual master, wrote:

> *Did worry ever help to solve any problem? It is born of confused thinking. Form the habit of clear thinking always and laugh away your troubles and sorrows. Even the devil himself can do nothing to a man so long as he can laugh. Does a laugh cost anything? It is as easy to laugh as to worry and fret. Only a little effort is required in the beginning. It becomes a habit after a time.*

In researching well-known people with Pisces rising, one thing jumped out at me which applied to the majority of them: very often, they are self-deprecating and have a rather low-key demeanor, making them extraordinarily likable. Such diverse people as Senator and Presidential candidate Walter Mondale; the star of the long-running TV hit *Gunsmoke* James Arness; baseball player and "philosopher" Yogi Berra; dancer Gwen Verdon; comedian Richard Pryor; and Olympic champion figure skater Dorothy Hamill all have Pisces rising. In addition to Mondale, Senator Robert Byrd and German Chancellor Konrad Adenauer round out a group of socially influential politicians. One finds actors such as Robert Redford (who has produced socially-conscious movies) and Robert Duvall, who has starred in many controversial films, as well as David Carradine, whose most famous role, in *Kung Fu*, helped popularize Eastern philosophy as well as martial arts. One finds many stage and screen personalities with Pisces rising, such as Carol Burnett and Raquel Welch, which makes sense, since Neptune traditionally rules the world of movies. And there is a large number of accomplished athletes with this Ascendant, such as high-jump champion Dwight Stones; baseball Hall of Fame infielder Eddie Mathews; the all-time most base hits batting champion Pete Rose; and Olympic champion swimmer John Nabor.

Robert Redford

Early in his acting career, through movies such as *Butch Cassidy and the Sundance Kid, The Candidate,* and *The Way We Were,* Robert Redford acquired the glamorous "golden-boy" image that reflects his Sun in Leo trine a Sagittarius Midheaven (and Mars in Leo in the fifth house). However, the prominence of his Pisces Ascendant is evident in Redford's ambivalence with the effects of his own celebrity, as well as in the concerns that animate his creative work.

Rather than glorying in his fame, Redford questions its consequences. The placement of Saturn in Pisces–in the twelfth house, eight degrees from the Ascendant–emphasizes this serious soul-searching approach to his life. *Current Biography* states that Redford has "always disdained the circus-like atmosphere on which some film celebrities thrive." Redford explored this theme in an October 1994 *Rolling Stone* interview, by discussing his interest in "what celebrity can do to someone, the threats of celebrity on your soul. The temptations that come your way...Are you going to continue on this path, where things are irresistibly tied to wealth and fame and privilege? Or can you stop, reorient yourself and redirect yourself for the sake of your own soul?"

The philosophical outlook of Redford's Pisces Ascendant is amplified (and given a socially oriented focus) by the placement of the chart's co-ruler, Jupiter, in Sagittarius in the ninth house. Jupiter is a focal planet located at the apex of a T-square to Saturn in Pisces and to a stellium of Venus, Neptune, Mercury, and the Moon in Virgo. Redford seeks to highlight his social concerns and various moral issues in both his acting roles and in the films he directs. *All the President's Men* depicted the exposé of the Nixon administration's Watergate scandal. *Brubaker* focused on prison reform. In many of his films, the Piscean themes of disillusionment and loss of innocence in American society have been particularly important, as reflected in *The Candidate, The Natural, A River Runs Through It,* and *The Quiz Show.*

But true to the low-key approach of his Pisces Ascendant (in contrast to fiery Sagittarius rising), Redford prefers not to bludgeon his audience with his point of view. In the *Rolling Stone* interview, he says, "I've never believed in agitprop because I don't think it works. People don't like to be preached to, treated like

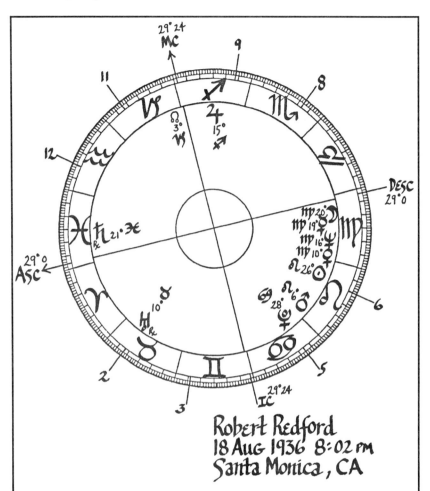

Robert Redford
18 Aug 1936 8:02 pm
Santa Monica, CA

children. I do believe in working politically in film, but I also believe that it has to be entertaining, because that's your medium." This concern for entertainment value, as well as the great artistry of Redford's films, reflect the skillful creativity of his Leo Sun in the sixth house.

Robert Redford is actively involved with environmental issues and nature conservation, and is enthusiastic about most outdoor activities, such as fishing, skiing, and horseback riding (all of which show the Jupiter influence). This love of nature is expressed in such films as *A River Runs Through It* and also in *The Milagro Beanfield War*, which depicts the struggle of small farmers who challenge developers' disregard for the natural environment. Redford knows such battles firsthand, through his efforts to preserve the environment around his 7,000 acre Sundance Ski Resort near Provo, Utah. He has also founded the Institute for Resource Management to promote research on environmental protection.

Redford's birth chart is an excellent example of the creative blend of vision and practical realism. The Pisces Ascendant and ninth house Jupiter in Sagittarius are grounded through the T-square to Saturn and to the Virgo stellium in the sixth house. Redford's Jupiter in Sagittarius moral convictions are given *form* through the square to Saturn in Pisces (a sign that has particular affinity with film-making). The squares from Jupiter to the Virgo/sixth house planets challenge Redford to deal with the myriad nitty-gritty details of bringing his visions into the world. "By the time you finish with the budget, the lawyers, the agents, the managers, the publicists, the funding mechanisms and the partnership deals, you're so exhausted and overwhelmed that you almost don't have the energy to make the picture." (quoted in *Architectural Digest*) Projects such as Sundance Institute, which fosters independent film-making and playwriting, show Redford's desire to use his resources in service to society and to foster the creative work of others. This service orientation is evident in the sixth house placement of Neptune, which is part of the T-square to Jupiter and Saturn.

Behind all his activities is Robert Redford's panoramic Piscean perspective, which is movingly expressed in this quote from an article in *Architectural Digest*: "Sometimes I'm an activist with a great sense of urgency, and sometimes I'm a fatalist who takes a very long and dark–a geological–view of time. At those moments I remind myself that nothing is meant to last: These mountains will be worn down; that lake will evaporate like a drop of water; we'll probably extinguish ourselves as a species. But then something new will happen. The sediment at the bottom of the Grand Canyon is five hundred and seventy million years old. When I'm feeling the weight of my problems, I go down and take a look at it. It improves your perspective."

—B.McE.

Ringo Starr

Born Richard Starkey in a working-class neighborhood in Liverpool, England, the future drummer for the Beatles quit school at age fourteen, and within ten years had attained international renown as a member of the world's most popular band. In many ways, Ringo is a perfect example of a Pisces rising person: self-effacing, likable, obviously vulnerable and sympathetic (emphasized even more by his Cancer Sun), and quite content to stay in the background. And yet, many people would agree with the observation that he was the main *unifying* energy of the Beatles, although he remained in the background, rarely had a drum solo, and only

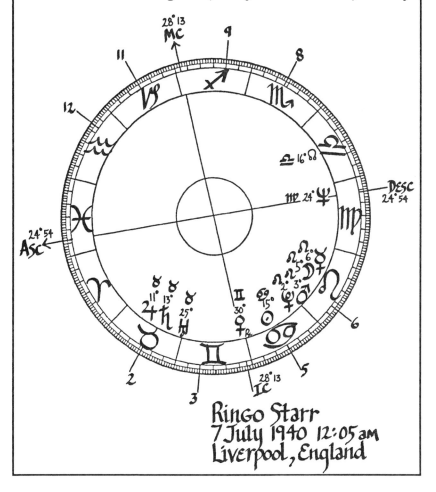

Ringo Starr
7 July 1940 12:05 am
Liverpool, England

had a few vocal solos (some of which bordered on being self-deprecating and comic in tone, such as "Yellow Submarine"—what a perfect image for a Cancer Sun with Pisces rising!). He retained an engaging simplicity in his style, never overriding the vocals or George Harrison's guitar innovations, but yet effortlessly expressing a playful, *fluid*, engaging rhythm in a tremendously wide variety of songs. These rhythms provided by Ringo helped to forge the characteristic Beatles' sound—innovative while still retaining a certain simplicity.

The powerful Jupiter (the chart's co-ruler along with Neptune), in the sign Taurus and sextile the Sun, enabled him to project a simple, earthy buoyancy and a perpetually upbeat and playful energy that spoke, without words, of pure enjoyment. Ringo Starr, in other words, is typical of Pisces rising in that he allowed a bigger force, group, ideal, or artistic expression to be expressed through him, without his ego getting in the way.

In addition, it is worth noting that, with his packed fifth house (including a strong fifth house Sun, since it is conjunct the 5th house cusp) and his Cancer/Leo combinations, he has acted in a number of movies and has also been quite active in children's shows on TV. His Gemini Venus also adds to the ability to relate to younger people with ease.

—S.A.

Walter Mondale & Konrad Adenauer

In researching well-known people with Pisces rising, some rather remarkable parallels were evident in these two prominent political figures. Mondale was a social-activist, liberal U.S. Senator, then Vice-President under President Jimmy Carter, then a Presidential nominee of the Democratic Party who lost to Ronald Reagan, and eventually the U.S. Ambassador to Japan. Adenauer was the Mayor of Cologne, Germany from 1917 until 1933, was forced from office and occasionally imprisoned by the Nazis, and then became the first post-war Chancellor of West Germany, a position he held for a remarkably long time—from 1949 until 1963.

In Piscean fashion, both men had authority thrust upon them by being in the right place at the right time, rather than by overtly

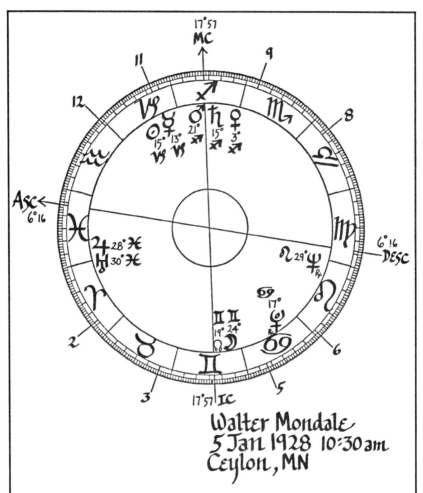

Walter Mondale
5 Jan 1928 10:30am
Ceylon, MN

seeking power. Mondale was appointed Minnesota State Attorney General after his predecessor's resignation; and then he was later appointed (rather than elected) to the U.S. Senate to complete Senator Hubert Humphrey's unexpired term, which promoted him into the national arena and into the center of the most social-activist Congress in the history of the U.S.A. Adenauer was one of those leaders of proven administrative ability who, at the end of World War II, did not have any taint of Nazi involvement or sympathy attached to him, making him acceptable to the Allies as a new governmental structure of West Germany was taking shape.

Astrologically, not only do both men have Pisces rising, but both also have the ruling Jupiter in water signs, an indication of the subtle strategic maneuvering that made them so successful. In addition, both were born on January 5th and have the Sun in 14° of Capricorn in the politically-oriented eleventh house. Each has a dynamic, extroverted planet in Pisces in the first house, perhaps accounting for why they were both more prominent and self-assertive than are most Pisces rising people; Mondale has Jupiter in Pisces and Adenauer has Mars there. Adenauer's Mars is also trine to Jupiter, making it doubly colored by Jupiter's expansiveness and prosperous glow. In Mondale's chart, Jupiter is not only conjunct Uranus (a superb symbol of a visionary of radical social change with a possible attunement to the desires of the masses, especially with the conjunction in Pisces), but it is also at the apex of a T-square configuration involving Mars (in Sagittarius!) and the Moon.

Mondale's chart is so Jupiterian that it is no wonder that he was known for his tolerant, liberal views, his sense of ethics, his legal expertise, and his willingness to spend endlessly on social programs, even if the funds were not available! In addition to the Pisces emphasis already mentioned, the Sagittarius Mars is conjunct a Sagittarius Saturn at the Midheaven, and Venus is also found in Sagittarius *in the ninth house*. His Capricorn attunement, as well as the fact that Saturn was in Sagittarius to bring those distant visions down to earth to some extent, help explain why he was involved in the field of politics and the daily struggles of the "real world" rather than just being perhaps a speaker or commentator on the sidelines.

Adenauer likewise seems to have been a practical idealist, with his Saturn in Aquarius (the sign *par excellence* of social activism) and almost exactly squaring his Jupiter. Rather than this square holding him back, as some astrological traditions would maintain, it made him an extremely determined and disciplined worker, as it does in so many people's lives, persistently trying to *make real* one's visions for the future. What makes Adenauer a notable figure? One reason is that he nurtured a new democratic spirit into full growth and prosperity in a severely devastated country. In addition, as the *Times* of London stated in his obituary,

In the early days of the Federal Republic, it had been Dr. Adenauer's great virtue that he possessed absolute confidence in himself and the

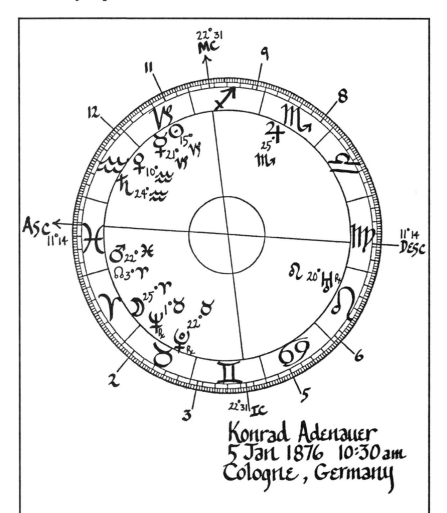

Konrad Adenauer
5 Jan 1876 10:30 am
Cologne, Germany

unshakable conviction that West Germany must be welded firmly into Europe and the Atlantic community. For the German people, perhaps his greatest contribution was that he restored their self-respect, brought them friends, and gave them a role to play in the world. A towering figure at the height of his powers, he possessed the air of inevitability that marks a man who seems destined for a particular moment in history.

In many ways, Konrad Adenauer was the father of the new Germany, fostering economic growth and democratic institutions and sentiments that evoked the surprise and the admiration of the world.

Although from a young age Mondale had an extremely involved

life in local politics, just as Adenauer did, we only have room here to touch on a few of his characteristics and achievements on the national scene. Throughout his life, Mondale demonstrated a continuing commitment to the powerless "underclasses" of society, as one might expect from the tremendous emphasis on Pisces. He was extremely active in promoting the entire range of civil rights and "Great Society" legislation that was put forth in the mid-1960's. He did notable work regarding both the problems of the aged and the nutritional needs of children being raised in poverty. No doubt Mondale was aided in achieving these goals by his Piscean style, which, as *Current Biography* notes, included a "self-deprecating sense of humor" and a "low-keyed and homespun approach to politicking."

After being elected Vice-President under Carter, Mondale became probably the most activist Vice President in history, not only involved in domestic policies but also undertaking thirteen different foreign assignments, including numerous sensitive missions. Later, when running for President, in a Jupiter-Uranus break with tradition, he selected Geraldine Ferraro, the first female Vice-Presidential candidate on a major Party ticket, as his running mate. Mondale's other achievements include an important book critical of abuses of Presidential power (*The Accountability of Power; Toward a Responsible Presidency*, 1975); tax reform initiatives; and a confrontation with abuses within the FBI and CIA.
—S.A.

CHAPTER 10

Jupiter's Aspects in the Birth Chart

I am a Christian, a Quaker, a Moslem, a Buddhist, a Shintoist, a Confucian, and maybe a Catholic pantheist or a Joan of Arc who hears voices–I am all of these and more.

—Carl Sandburg
(born with Jupiter conjunct
the Sun within one degree)

Since I have dealt extensively with the theory of aspects in other books (see especially Chapter 6 of *Astrology, Karma & Transformation*), in this chapter I will initially mention only some general observations that pertain specifically to Jupiter aspects and then systematically go through various Jupiter interchanges with other planets and their interpretive guidelines. These guidelines are meant to encourage understanding of the basic principles involved in each aspect and to provoke independent thought in applying these principles to people's real life situations. This is the main reason why the planetary interchanges that follow do not generally distinguish between the challenging and the harmonious angles. These planetary interactions (or "blendings" of their energies) are usually judged too rigidly as "good" or "bad," "easy" or "difficult." However, by its fruit shall ye judge the quality of a tree, to paraphrase the *Bible*; and the examples of well-known people mentioned in this chapter give convincing proof of the creative potential of "stressful" aspects, as well as those usually regarded as flowing or harmonious. I should also mention that "easy" aspects of Jupiter at times incline to wastefulness, laziness, or too much reliance on luck, unless there are some energizing factors in the chart–such as some "hard" aspects.

The following quotation from my book *Chart Interpretation Handbook* summarizes the general impact of Jupiter in any aspect:

Any aspect involving Jupiter bears examination since Jupiter expands whatever it touches. Jupiter can show where you try to improve things and develop them to their maximum potential, as well as to express those energies to their fullest, possibly at a very high level. Jupiter's expansiveness and pervasive optimism can, however, also lead to over-extending oneself in the areas indicated by aspect, signs, and houses, if moderation is not regularly observed. The generosity and positive attitude and broad, philosophical approach often shown by Jupiter can, at best, lend an aura of nobility and masterful accomplishment to those areas of life supported by Jupiter's upbeat energies.

Any planet closely aspected by Jupiter is colored and energized with an urge to seek *new* experiences, to expand the scope of its expression—even though it may require taking substantial risks. Whatever dimension of experience Jupiter influences is where we need to open doors and walk through, perhaps cautiously, but nevertheless courageously—facing things honestly in the increased daylight of broader understanding. Many authors have connected Jupiter with "opportunity," and this seems in general to be accurate; but of course many opportunities—indicated by both challenging and harmonious aspects—require effort for them to come into manifestation. Grant Lewi adds another facet to our understanding when he says that, if other planets are in the same sign as Jupiter or in harmonious aspects to Jupiter, one can make use of those energies to one's benefit relatively easily. This may also be true if more challenging aspects are involved, but it may require significantly more effort.

It is appropriate that the largest planet (and the chief deity in some mythologies) often seems to be little influenced by the other planets. It is as if Jupiter stands "aloof" from the smaller planets, pulling them into *its* energy field rather than adapting to the other planet's energy field. Jupiter always holds its own; it expands and amplifies anything it touches. Only Saturn seems to hold it down somewhat, but even then Jupiter still simultaneously expands the Saturnian urges and ambitions.

Ordinarily, I am a proponent of using quite tight orbs in interpreting aspects, but with Jupiter one must make allowances for its tremendous aura of influence! For example, if Jupiter is in one's Sun or Moon or rising sign, even if separated many degrees from the luminary or the Ascendant, the upbeat Jupiterian energy will usually show clearly in the person's nature and psychology. In addition, if a person is particularly Jupiterian, by virtue of having significant factors in Sagittarius or Pisces, Jupiter's orb will be greater since its energy is more active in that person and thus particularly *big* and vital. The Jupiter energy then, as it were, *grabs on to the other planets' energies* with which it is in aspect and amplifies them noticeably.

There are some general comments that can be made in relation to the overall personality and attitude of people who have strong Jupiter aspects. For convenience and clarity, we can contrast the positive with the negative expressions of this planet's energy, but one should not assume that the positive manifestations are always inherent in the harmonious aspects, nor are the less constructive expressions invariably attributable to the stressful, challenging aspects. It should candidly be admitted that there is a tendency for this correlation to exist in individuals, but by no means should it be assumed to be a reliable interpretive *fact*; rather, it may be a *tendency*, depending on the rest of the chart and also upon the person's life experience and level of consciousness.

Charles Carter mentions in *The Principles of Astrology* that "The action of the planet [Jupiter], when well placed, is that of orderly and healthy growth and increase." He goes on to say that the positive expression can manifest as persons who are fortunate beyond the average, especially if they possess common sense and a sense of moderation. Otherwise, he writes, they tempt their fortunes too far. Jupiter positively can indicate a healthy optimism and good vitality, whereas negatively it can mean over-optimism, poor judgment, and perhaps excessive or scattered energy. Generosity on one hand can deteriorate into extravagance or making excessive promises on the other. Idealism can degenerate into self-righteous judgmentalism. Nobility can become inflated into egocentricity. Faith in life can leave one open to gullibility if not tempered by realism. Excessive Jupiter energy or a poorly integrated Jupiterian attunement can result in a person always overstepping the immediate situation that exists in the present and wildly scattering energy into activities that will only be relevant in the distant future. For example, a would-be author who makes lists of book titles when not one book is yet written; or a person who does hundreds of hours of investment research when he has no funds to invest, instead of working to earn more money!

Vedic astrology expert Chakrapani has pointed out that Jupiter, expressed negatively, can be a sense of superiority, and this often manifests in those with stressful aspects to Sagittarius planets as well as in those with various Jupiter aspects. It can be expressed as arrogance, snideness, and superciliousness. In other words, the lively pride of the fire element, as is also so often seen in the sign Leo, and the optimism and confidence of Jupiter must be disciplined and channeled for it to be useful and encouraging to others. Perhaps the most notable manifestation of this negative Jupiterian expression is *indignation*, resulting from one's pride and dignity being offended, whereupon a surprisingly fierce anger sometimes erupts from a normally good-natured, broad-minded personality.

 **Jupiter-Sun Interchanges**

The need to be recognized interacts with the urge to expand beyond the self, to become one with something bigger than self

Sense of individuality incorporates faith and openness to grace

[All Sun-Jupiter aspects show a great need for ego gratification by doing something big, something that will make others take notice. A very common blending in those involved with stage work, big business, etc.]

It should not be surprising that many of the famous people we have already mentioned in this book have a close Jupiter-Sun aspect, for it does often lead to recognition, worldly success, and advancement in society. It is also a tremendously *vital* interchange, and nothing can be achieved without the health and energy to do it. It is likewise a profoundly creative and—usually—optimistic indication. How can one be anything other than optimistic when the Sun and Jupiter work together? The urge to expand into larger arenas of power and influence is also present, as is often the arrogance that goes with it. Wastefulness and pretentiousness are commonly seen in these people, although by no means in all cases. In contrast, notorious cheapskate John D. Rockefeller had Jupiter square the Sun. He did eventually establish huge charitable organizations, but he and his family derived huge tax savings from them.

There is often an aura of nobility about these individuals. Sometimes it is real, as in the cases of George Washington (the quincunx), Paramhansa Yogananda (the square), the Dalai Lama (the trine), and Saint Teresa of Avila (the sextile). In other cases, there is the assumption of a noble bearing, but much of it is pretense, such as in the cases of Francisco Franco (trine) or Ronald Reagan (square). It cannot be denied that Jupiter-Sun interchanges can be obnoxious and ostentatious. At worst, there is a keen desire for self-aggrandizement. I have even seen that most rare of creatures–an arrogant Virgo–who had Jupiter in his Virgo Sun sign.

Naturally, fame and the fate of becoming an icon often goes with the territory if one is born with this interchange. Elvis Presley (square), Bob Dylan (conjunction), Mick Jagger (conjunction), and Marlon Brando (trine) all have a close Sun-Jupiter aspect. So also do such creative forces as Leonardo da Vinci (sextile), W.B. Yeats (opposition), Joseph Campbell (conjunction), T. S. Eliot (sextile), and Herman Melville (opposition). Show business is also the scene of self-expression for many who are born with this blending: movie producer David Selznick (square), actors Gregory Peck (conjunction) and Vivien Leigh (sextile), and singers Harry Belafonte (conjunction) and Richie Valens (conjunction).

John Lennon

Although John Lennon is not a particularly Jupiterian person, the closest major aspect to his Sun is the quincunx with his Jupiter/Saturn conjunction in Taurus. This configuration is an indication of how extensively he identified with the new cycle of social change that always begins at each Jupiter/Saturn conjunction, as well as how he poured his creative energy into building a practical faith. His Jupiter/Saturn conjunction's placement in Taurus is also significant as a symbol of how down-to-earth he was and how deeply he appreciated both the aesthetic elements of daily life (see the section on Jupiter in Taurus for more on this subject) and the earthy rhythms of rock and roll music.

There are other reasons for including Lennon's chart here as

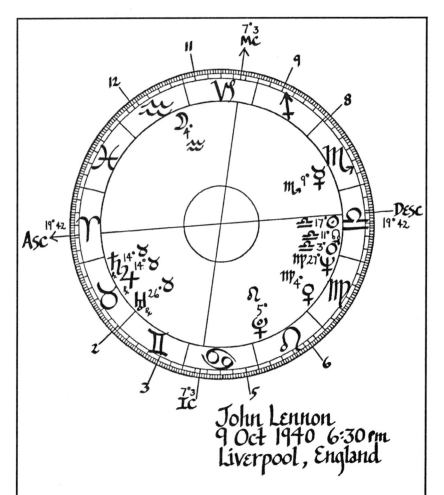

John Lennon
9 Oct 1940 6:30 pm
Liverpool, England

well. As I will discuss, numerous aspects and aspect structures are intriguing and give us insight into one of the primary creative and culturally influential forces of recent times. And, for a person who was so significant not only in the world of the arts but also in his impact on social change worldwide, I feel the most accurate chart available for him should be broadly published. There have been at least three birth charts so far published for Lennon. This chart, with Aries rising, is not only based on a birth time given by Pauline Stone, his step-mother, quoting Lennon's father, but it seems to me infinitely more descriptive than the others of John Lennon's talents, personality, and his life.

First of all, this chart gives him an early Aquarius Moon, which certainly fits his socially-conscious orientation more than does the Capricorn Moon found in other charts. In addition, an early Aquarius Moon makes for a tremendously dynamic artistic chart configuration (see below), as well as symbolizing the originality and rebelliousness which marked everything Lennon did from an early age. Furthermore, his partnership with Yoko Ono (an Aquarian Sun) and the importance he attributed to that relationship fits perfectly with this chart, for this map also places the Sun conjunct the seventh cusp and Mercury in the seventh house. These factors sharply symbolize one for whom a close working partnership is supremely important (don't forget the amazing partnership with Paul McCartney also!), as well as a person for whom a mentally compatible partnership was crucial–something he felt he had found with Yoko Ono.

The sense of what the masses of people are feeling and what social changes they yearn for is also aptly symbolized by the Aquarian Moon, a placement that often gives an attunement to the popular sentiments and intellectual trends of the times. Just as George Gershwin (Sun Libra/Moon Aquarius–see Chapter 6) had his finger on the pulse of his times and attained unrivaled widespread popularity, so Lennon and the Beatles held the same position during their careers. [It might be noted that spy novelist John LeCarré has Sun in Libra and Moon in Aquarius also, and he may well be regarded as the most internationally popular and revered writer in his genre during a period encompassing over thirty years.]

It is my belief that Lennon was, more than anyone else, responsible for keeping the Beatles' music "at the cutting edge" of artistic, social, and even psychological transformation.* His chart in fact might be said to symbolize a living "cutting edge"–there is such *sharpness* to his nature and his insight. Mercury's placement and aspects reveal a deep intelligence, probing widely and deeply, and then expressing ideas artistically but also often quite bluntly. His Mercury is not only in Scorpio but also closely square Pluto, a double indication of reflecting upon and investigating the inner

---

* Only two weeks after I wrote this, I heard a TV interview with musician Elton John, who had known and worked with Lennon. I was startled to hear him say that John Lennon was always at "the cutting edge."

workings of life, even if they are taboo areas of experience. Mercury is also sextile the Virgo Venus, adding both an aesthetic quality and a sharpness of wit and analysis. And further, Mercury is in a moderately wide opposition to the Jupiter/Saturn conjunction, attuning his mental explorations to the unfolding social changes of his time.

Another factor that seems to validate this chart, as well as indicating why Lennon was always at the cutting edge in every field of activity he engaged in, is the appropriateness of an Aries Ascendant. He was known from a young age for playing the tough guy–the leather jacket rebel with an abrasive personality. And this assertiveness and abrasiveness is further symbolized by the Mars placement in his Sun sign. But Mars also represents directness of manner, and Aries is also known for pioneering into new areas of activity continually, never being content with repetition, tradition, or restriction. This quality seems to have been expressed in John Lennon as his always being driven to try new musical modes as well as new kinds of lifestyles–a forcefulness and creative restlessness at the heart of why every Beatles album broke new artistic ground.

In fact, there are numerous interactions between Mars and Venus factors in his chart, often an indication of artistic creativity. Not only the opposition of the Aries Ascendant with a Libra Sun indicates this, but also Mars and Venus are in a close semi-sextile–an important aspect when so exact. Furthermore, Mars is in the Venus-ruled sign of Libra; and Mercury, the dispositor of Venus (ruler of his Sun sign), is in Scorpio, ruled by Mars/Pluto.

In summary, a deep intelligence and intuition applied to artistic creativity–through which he made great art and was working on making an artful lifestyle when he was murdered–can be shown by a complex chart configuration incorporating *six major chart factors*. If the reader will draw lines on his chart connecting the Moon, Pluto, Venus, and Mars, he or she will see a triangular structure of great dynamic intensity–so close are all the aspects. But then, in addition, if one adds Mercury's squares to both Moon and Pluto and Mercury's sextiles to both the MC and Venus, as well as the MC's trine to Venus, there emerges a six-factor cosmic design, all the components of which interact with each other energetically. A full public life of great intensity is thereby symbolized. And no doubt, when John Lennon experienced a strong transit of one of these factors, it must have impacted his entire life profoundly for a considerable period of time. And the MC's intricate relationship with this configuration seems especially apt for someone whose life was not only very public but which took on widespread public symbolism.

—S.A.

♃ / ☽ Jupiter-Moon Interchanges

Great sensitivity toward connection with a larger order, with going beyond the self–very tolerant of others' behavior but not always of their ideas if too caught up in own subjectivity

A subconscious predisposition toward optimistic expansion and enthusiastic emotional reactions

These aspects tend toward generosity, popularity, and rather good fortune in many areas of life. There tend to be noble inclinations and a concern for "social betterment," as Reinhold Ebertin put it. There is a feeling that "things will get better" which sustains the person through the ups and downs of life–an inner faith that is not always orthodox but is usually of a broad religious character. For example, Joseph Campbell (the trine) showed in his writings on myth how universal religious truths are still vital in the modern era.

Wastefulness can be apparent in this group of people, but they also often seem intent upon using their assets to help others, sometimes carrying out their ideals on a large scale. In general, they feel that life has *meaning*, and this keeps them fully engaged in living wholeheartedly. There is at times too much concern about looking "noble," to the point of vanity and self-consciousness about the impression they are making on others.

The theme of social betterment is clearly evident in a large number of well-known people who were born with this interchange. Jules Verne was born with the conjunction, and we discussed his idealism in Chapter 8. Walter Mondale, whom we discussed in Chapter 9, was born with the square (some might say he went to excesses of liberalism and socialistic generosity). On the other side of the political spectrum, Ronald Reagan was born with the opposition between his Scorpio Jupiter and his Taurus Moon; and–although Jupiter seems to have provided him the aloofness and protection that gave him the title of the "teflon president"–he personally was extraordinarily cheap, giving very little to charity while simultaneously urging the citizens to do so. Robert F. Kennedy was born with the conjunction, and John F. Kennedy was born with the trine; and both were actively involved in promoting social reform policies. Even Marlon Brando, who has the trine, has been active in championing Native Americans' rights. Prince Charles, who also has the trine, has been more involved in social issues than any previous Prince of Wales. And Karl Marx, who also had the trine, was of course obsessed with changing society in a way that he viewed as more generous to those in need.

The easy access to and expression of the emotions that these people have, especially if the aspect is harmonious, explains why quite a few popular actors have this aspect. Both Dustin Hoffman and Jack Nicholson have the trine, and both Omar Sharif and Warren Beatty have the sextile. All four are also known for a particular popularity with women. Tenor Mario Lanza also had the sextile, which manifested through the power and grace with which he expressed emotional nuances in his singing, not to mention his worldwide popularity with the opposite sex.

Discovery and invention also seem to be common manifestations of this interchange, perhaps because it can give a person an intuitive glimpse into the future. Jules Verne, Copernicus, and da Vinci all had the conjunction, while Nikola Tesla had the opposition.

Arthur Schlesinger, Jr.

Arthur Schlesinger is not only a renowned historian and prolific author of gracefully written prose, but also unique among scholars in that he has been so politically active and influential in actual policy formulation and in the public explanation of those policies. A precocious student, he graduated *cum laude* from Harvard at age 20 and was already awarded a Pulitzer Prize for his book *The Age of Jackson* before his thirtieth birthday. He was later awarded another Pulitzer Prize for his 1965 work *A Thousand Days: John F. Kennedy in the White House*, a subject he knew from the inside since he was a special assistant and speech writer for Kennedy.

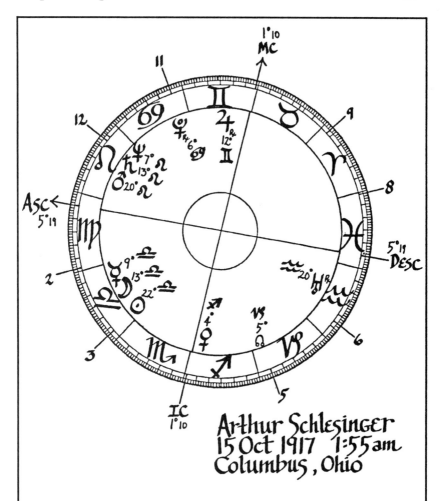

Arthur Schlesinger
15 Oct 1917 1:55 am
Columbus, Ohio

In between those two awards, he wrote many other books and reviews of other historians' works, and he was an active promoter of liberal Democratic candidates. With his Sun and Moon both in the humane sign of Libra, as well as his elevated Jupiter in Gemini, it is not at all surprising that his sentiments were instinctively toward people's real needs and how society and government were responding to those needs. In fact, if one allows wide orbs, one could say that Schlesinger has a grand trine in the air element (people and social/intellectual concerns), encompassing the social activist planet Uranus (in Aquarius!) with the Libra and Gemini factors.

Not only is his Gemini Jupiter prominent in the tenth house (and he certainly did win early respect for his intellectual brilliance), but also the dispositor of his Sun, Moon, and Mercury (Venus) is placed in Sagittarius. In other words, he has what I call a powerful Sagittarian subtone to his Sun, Moon, and Mercury. This, combined with his strong Jupiter and its powerful aspects, reveals why he fought for idealistic causes, crusaded for "morally right" goals, and was known to be strongly opinionated, backing up those views with an eloquence and clarity that was difficult to refute.

There are numerous striking aspects in his chart, such as the close trine of Uranus with the Sun (a perfect symbol for someone who is an agent of social change), and Pluto exactly sextile his Virgo Ascendant (a precise image of someone who is known for exhaustive research and comprehensive attention to detail). However, I will focus on those aspects which relate to Jupiterian qualities. The trine of his Sagittarius Venus to Neptune, for example, accounts for some of the visionary idealism that infused his life and made him sensitive to the needs of the underprivileged.

The most significant aspect structure in his chart is the triangular formation of Jupiter sextile to Saturn as well as trine to both Moon and Mercury, while Saturn is also sextile the latter two planets. A far-seeing but practical mind is thereby indicated, one for whom ideas and verbal expression (Mercury in an air sign) are naturally and instinctively the channels for his personal feelings about life (Moon).

No doubt he expressed his inner intimations and his soaring ideals with such ease that many could well envy his facility with language and concepts. Jupiter's close trine with the Moon can symbolize a certain nobility of the instinctive feeling nature, and Jupiter's trine with Mercury reveals a comprehensive understanding of his chosen field of study. Schlesinger is yet another successful writer with a Mercury/Jupiter interchange. Many others are mentioned in this chapter.

—S.A.

♃/☿ Jupiter-Mercury Interchanges

*The mode of communication and the way of thinking
are deeply colored by a sense of breadth, expansion,
and optimism—a wide-ranging, philosophical
intellect, with overflowing curiosity*

*Needs to explore broad interests and establish
connections with others based on trust, a common
faith in the future, and philosophical agreement*

All forms of verbal expression and intellectual exploration are symbolized by this interchange. We find a wide variety of types of expression under this heading: the screen plays, short stories, and jokes of Woody Allen (the conjunction); the eloquent oratory as well as the spontaneous quips of John F. Kennedy (the conjunction); the wide-ranging insights into a new level of astrological understanding reached by author Charles Carter (Scorpio Jupiter square Mercury and Sun in Aquarius); the philosophical searching of Emerson (square) and Hermann Hesse (opposition); the poetry of William Blake (conjunction), Tennyson (square), Rimbaud (sextile), and Whitman (square); the screen-writing and vocal power of Orson Welles (sextile); the theoretical works of Ruskin (conjunction), Margaret Mead (semi-sextile), and Freud (sextile); and the novels of André Gide (opposition), Henry Miller (sextile), and H. G. Wells (trine). The inventive verbal play of both Muhammed Ali (trine) and John Lennon (opposition), in addition to Lennon's song-writing skills, are further expressions of this verbal/mental attunement. Lennon is also a good example of another trait often seen in those with this interchange—namely, the urge toward such truthfulness that they are sometimes known for being excessively blunt and tactless.

No matter what field of study or area of interest these people pursue, they do so with tremendous enthusiasm and a wide-ranging interest that can enable them—at best—to display a comprehensive understanding of their field of endeavor. Tycoons J. Paul Getty and Andrew Carnegie both had Jupiter trine Mercury; so this aspect is by no means limited to the arts or writing. An active, optimistic, adventurous mind characterizes these individuals; their interests are so broad, in fact, that it often leads them to one of the more problematical manifestations of this blending; having too many interests or ideas and scattering their mental energies too widely for them to focus properly on one subject or task. Such mental tension is more likely to be found in the challenging aspects, but the conjunction sometimes displays this tendency as well.

In addition, all the aspects of these two planets are sometimes guilty of exaggeration, so much do they like to go on and on, expanding (and expounding) upon their ideas. Absent-mindedness also afflicts some of these folks, since their minds are so easily directed into new interests. At worst, this blending can be an indication of bad judgment and opinionated intellectual arrogance. At best, a person with this interchange exhibits a comprehensive understanding and expresses his views and decisions philosophically, tolerantly, and, in some cases, even in an *inspired* manner. For example, mythologist Joseph Campbell (conjunction), monk and prolific writer Thomas Merton (conjunction), and Saint Teresa of Avila (sextile) whose 16th Century devotional writings are still read today, all helped their readers to live lives more infused with meaning and religious significance.

William Blake

If the doors of perception were cleansed everything would appear to man as it is, infinite. For man has closed himself up, till he sees all things through narrow chinks of his cavern.

The works of William Blake, Jupiterian poet, painter, and engraver, invite us to widen the "narrow chinks" that limit our outlook, to unlock our "mind-forg'd manacles." Ever expansive, Blake channeled the prodigious creativity of the Mercury-Jupiter-Sun conjunction in the fifth house into works that celebrate life, denounce tyranny, and affirm the sacred: "For everything that lives is holy, life delights in life." The Cancerian/Sagittarian Blake was "a gentle, yet fiery-hearted mystic" according to biographer Mona Wilson, and with fifth house Sagittarian planets, visionary experience and art were intertwined. (The Sun near the sixth house cusp correlates with Blake's renowned technical skill in the craft of engraving.) His poetry and paintings expressed his quest for meaning, his experience of the divine. Kay and Roger Easson note: "William Blake is a spiritual teacher, a prophet who, having

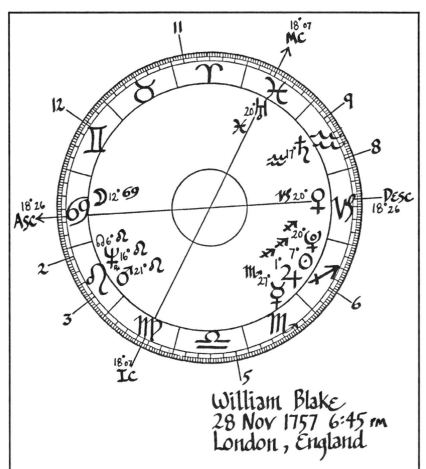

William Blake
28 Nov 1757 6:45 pm
London, England

'discover'd the infinite in every thing,' is committed to 'raising other men into a perception of the infinite.'" (quoted from the Eassons' "Commentary" on *The Book of Urizen*)

Blake was a master myth-maker. His highly complex, multi-layered mythical poems express the grand vision of Jupiter in Sagittarius coupled with the penetrating insight of Mercury in Scorpio. These poems, about struggles between god-like beings, depict both the vast powers of the cosmos and the internal forces at work in the human psyche. "All deities reside in the human breast," Blake reminds us. The blending of Mercury in Scorpio and Jupiter in Sagittarius is apparent in this quote by Michael Davis about Blake's epic poems:

His allegorical scheme shows astonishingly advanced insight into human urges, conflicts, repressions, tensions and eruptions. More than a century before Freud and Jung, Blake found the mind of Universal Man not only in the Bible, the alchemists and Neoplatonists, but in himself, and recreated it in poetic allegory.

Another Jupiter-Mercury theme in Blake's work is the enlarged perception that can transform one's view of ordinary reality. This visionary seeing was central to Blake: "Imagination is My World," he asserts. Bernard Nesfield-Cookson (in *William Blake: Prophet of Universal Brotherhood*) writes that for Blake, "Life reveals itself to Imaginative Vision, not to the corporeal eye. An expansion of consciousness is called for, a change in ourselves." Visionary experience was a matter-of-fact part of Blake's life, starting in childhood when, according to biographer Alexander Gilchrist, he saw "a tree filled with angels, bright angelic wings bespangling every bough like stars." While mystical Neptune conjunct Mars in Leo contributed to such epiphanies, the widened mind of Jupiter-Mercury set the stage. This Jupiter-Mercury perception shines in Blake's famous lines:

> *To see a World in a Grain of Sand*
> *And a Heaven in a Wild Flower,*
> *Hold Infinity in the palm of your hand*
> *And Eternity in an hour.*

David Punter writes that Blake had "a pronounced capacity for seeing the wonderful in life, be it in birdsong or in the bricks and stones of the city." The qualities of joy and delight, the magical world of childhood innocence, were essential to Blake, and he celebrated them in his *Songs of Innocence.* With Jupiter conjunct the Sun in the fifth house, expansive joy was creative fuel.

Above all else, Jupiter-Sun in Sagittarius needs freedom and amplitude of being. Consequently, Blake found oppression in any form abhorrent. (Uranus at the Midheaven heightened his rejection of tyranny.) Blake condemned social injustices, particularly involving children—consistent with his fifth house emphasis and Leo planets. Some of his poems are stinging Mercury-in-Scorpio indictments of the child labor practices of his time. Blake also denounced the repressiveness of conventional morality and in *The Marriage of Heaven and Hell* turned traditional views of good and evil inside out. Praising the fiery energy of "hell," in contrast to the passive "good" of "restrained desires," Blake wrote such Sagittarian proverbs as: "The road of excess leads to the palace of wisdom." "If the fool would persist in his folly, he would become wise."

For Blake, whose sense of morality was resonant with a fifth house Sagittarian Jupiter, what mattered was "truth to one's own spirit, the courage to acknowledge and act upon one's own distinctive vision." (quoted from David Punter) Blake insisted that we be "just & true to our own Imaginations" rather than remain "in the chains of the mind Lock'd up." Blake was misunderstood by most of his contemporaries, but held true to his visions. His work, according to modern assessments, was far ahead of its time. Even at the time of his death, Blake continued to see far through the "narrow chinks of the cavern." One of Blake's students records it this way: "Just before he died His countenance became fair–His eyes Brighten'd and He Burst out in Singing of the things he saw in Heaven."

—B.McE.

♃ / ♀ Jupiter-Venus Interchanges

Love is expressed in an open, generous, and expansive manner, and a sense of beauty is often dominant in the character

A liking for adventure and a concern for self-improvement color one's approach to relationships; can be excessive sensuality and extravagance with money or emotional expression

Any blending of the two "benefics" has the potential to develop an aesthetic mode of expression that is extraordinarily broad and active. A sense of form, harmony, and beauty is important to these people, and they pour their emotional energies into expressing it. Although at worst their tastes may run to vulgarity and excessive displays of ostentatiousness, even the more challenging aspects by no means have to manifest in this way. For example, the following artists all have a Venus-Jupiter square within less than four degrees of exact: Van Gogh, Edgar Degas (whose delicate paintings of ballet scenes can hardly be called vulgar), and Gustave Courbet (whose art often radiated a glowing simplicity and subtle use of light). I think the sign placements of these planets, as well as other chart factors, must be taken into consideration before pronouncing any sort of negative interpretation of the two benefic planets' blendings. The delicate, refined music of Maurice Ravel, whose Jupiter and Venus were almost exactly square, as well as part of a T-square with Neptune, is another example of this phenomenon. One could say that rock star Elton John, who also has the square, does go to excess in his public performances, wearing all sorts of costumes that are excessively flamboyant, but he cannot be accused of lacking musical talent!

There is usually a certain grace of expression evident in many of those with this combination, even if they are not active in the arts. This gives them an appealing quality which seems to draw other people to them easily, and they often have a rather sympathetic social nature. Sometimes this sympathy for people will be extraordinarily broad, as for example in the case of Robert Kennedy (Jupiter conjunct Venus), who in his last years developed an especially strong affection for the underprivileged in American society and was wildly popular with them. Arthur Conan Doyle had a close sextile and was not only tremendously popular but keenly sympathetic to a wide range of humanitarian and religious issues. On the other hand, Mussolini was also popular with the masses for quite a while, and his Jupiter-Venus conjunction certainly was expressed with considerable flamboyance. The exaggerated emotions that he displayed are often seen in those with Venus-Jupiter interchanges, especially when in challenging aspects. This is what Ebertin called "excessive expression of feeling." They may also expressively crave attention or expressions of affection from others, even to the point of becoming insatiable! Mussolini also exemplifies the vanity quite often found in this combination.

Generosity and an abundance of kindness, as well as money, are sometimes indicated in this blending. Much depends on Venus' sign placement. Robert Kennedy was obviously born into one of America's wealthiest families, and Henry Ford II was also well situated socially. Ford was born with Venus trine Jupiter, as well as a close Jupiter-Sun square. The negative side of the Jupiter-Venus interaction's association with wealth is the tendency toward greed and wastefulness.

Understanding and tolerance of human nature sometimes characterizes these individuals, and can be expressed in such diverse ways as Paramhansa Yogananda (trine), Emerson (quincunx), and

Goethe (opposition). Composer Claude Debussy, who was often compared with Ravel in the style of music he wrote, had almost as close an aspect between Venus and Jupiter as did Ravel, although it was a sextile rather than a square. Puccini (opposition) and Schubert (sextile) also had this blending within less than three degrees of exact, as did master violinist Yehudi Menuhin (sextile), who also was outspoken in various humanitarian causes. Pianist Van Cliburn likewise has this combination (a trine). Poets as diverse as Verlaine and Tennyson (sextile) and Baudelaire (conjunction) also exemplify the artistic dimension of this cosmic blending.

Jupiter-Mars Interchanges

An expansive need for physical, sexual, or pioneering excitement, and an urge for adventurous action and accomplishment

Desire and initiative focused toward improvement of self and toward broad, inspiring goals for improving life for others (often leadership in one's chosen field)

If there is any Jupiter combination that can rival that of Jupiter and the Sun for creativity, leadership, and liking for power, it is the interaction of Jupiter with Mars. Always strong willed, these people constantly strive to expand the scope of their activities and influence. They are so physically restless that they require constant action and become easily discontented if they do not have an outlet for their assertive urges. This is true for worldly achievement as well as for sexual expression. Enthusiastically tackling all sorts of challenges comes naturally to them, and they are rarely lacking in self-confidence once they have become conscious of their inner strength—which can take some time if there are challenging aspects to one or both of these planets, or if Mars is weak by sign placement.

Courage is rarely lacking in those with this blend of energies, as we can detect in a wide variety of examples: Martin Luther (conjunction), who took on the might of the Roman Catholic church, disgusted with seeing so many compromises with the ideals that the teachings of Jesus represented; Amelia Earhart (conjunction) and John Glenn (sextile), whose courageous breakthroughs were described in their mini-biography in Chapter 5; anti-war activist Philip Berrigan (sextile), who opposed his government's policies as well as defying the orders of the Catholic church while he was a priest; his brother Daniel Berrigan (square), who was also put on trial with Philip for his dramatic anti-war protests; Upton Sinclair (trine), whose reforming initiatives in literature and politics are described earlier in this volume; scientist Rachel Carson (opposition), whose book *Silent Spring* brought about a major change in the use of pesticides; Sigmund Freud (opposition), who dared to break the silence about the importance of sexuality in human life; Konrad Adenauer (trine), whose achievements are detailed in Chapter 9; and baseball great Jackie Robinson (trine) and tennis champion Arthur Ashe (square), who both challenged the racial barriers in their respective sports, as well as excelling in their athletic achievements. Ashe and Robinson are also excellent examples of how *competitive* Jupiter-Mars aspects are.

Astrological author Charles Carter had Jupiter in Scorpio trine his Pisces Mars; and his work reflects not only extensive research achievements and the courage to object to many pointless, old-fashioned astrological traditions, but also is a good example of how intuitive those with this combination can be. In other words, their adventurous thrusts into the future are often guided by a sense of where current trends will lead. This may be another reason why these folks so often achieve their expansive goals. It is certainly no coincidence that the following group of wealthy and powerful men all have this interchange in their birth charts: J. P. Morgan, Sr. (Jupiter conjunct Mars in Leo, square Saturn); Walt Disney (Mars, Jupiter and Saturn conjunct in Capricorn); Howard Hughes (Jupiter in Taurus square a Mars-Saturn conjunction in Aquarius); John D. Rockefeller (Jupiter conjunct Mars in Libra, sextile Saturn); Joseph P. Kennedy, father of JFK and RFK (Jupiter conjunct Mars in Scorpio, sextile Venus); and John F. Kennedy (Jupiter conjunct Mars and Mercury in Taurus, square Uranus). The Mars-Jupiter blending, however, can also take the form of intellectual leadership, as in such examples as Bertrand Russell (sextile), C. G. Jung (sextile), and Margaret Mead (conjunction), or religious leadership such as we find in the life of Saint Teresa of Avila (conjunction), who founded a new order of nuns and established sixteen convents throughout Spain.

In summary, one should never underestimate the potential achievement in any field of those with this combination. Even in the field of the arts, although one might think that somewhat rough and assertive Mars-Jupiter contacts might not be appropriate, the energy and drive and persistence this blending generates can lead to substantial accomplishments. Witness, for example, Shelley (conjunction, with Neptune also); Toulouse-Lautrec and Mario Lanza (opposition); Proust, Van Gogh, Gershwin, Seurat, and Carl Sandburg (all the square); and Raphael, Menuhin, Henry Miller, and Gregory Peck (all the trine). Surely, such an abundance of cases proves that the phrase chosen by Reinhold Ebertin for this principle is supremely accurate: "successful creative activity." Although it can manifest as impatience, rebelliousness, and a tendency to go to excess in many areas of action, if well disciplined this energy can signify a major talent and creative power, harnessing a strong will together with an expansive vision, resulting in an enterprising spirit that can decisively cut through life's obstacles in order to achieve one's ambitions.

Francisco Franco

Just as the challenging aspects of Jupiter do not by any means imply "bad" or negative results or personality qualities, so also the flowing, harmonious aspects of Jupiter do not invariably indicate that noble personal qualities and beneficent attitudes will be expressed in the individual's life, as the chart and life of Spanish dictator Francisco Franco amply demonstrate. His birth time is based on records recorded in his parish church and therefore is probably reliable.

If one draws aspect lines on his chart linking Saturn, Sun, Jupiter, and the Moon/Neptune/Pluto stellium, one will find an almost perfect rectangle, with both Saturn and Jupiter in a trine or a sextile to the other factors in the configuration. Jupiter and Saturn are also opposite each other, in addition to the Sun being in opposition to the Gemini stellium. On the surface level, one could say that Franco was "successful" in attaining his ambitions. He became the youngest general in the history of the Spanish army and ultimately ruled Spain with an iron hand for almost forty years. During that time, one might say that he succeeded in "saving" Spain from communism and other liberal or left-wing influences, aligning himself with the Catholic church in a repressive regime disguised as a holy crusade. But what a price Spain had to pay! Estimates are that over 600,000 people died during the 1930s civil war, during which time Franco developed an alliance

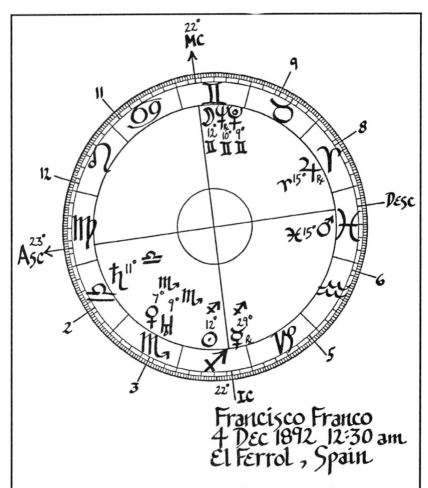

Francisco Franco
4 Dec 1892 12:30 am
El Ferrol , Spain

with both Hitler and Mussolini and allowed the Spanish people to
be targets for Hitler's new serial bombing tactics. In addition, over
two million people fled or were imprisoned.

Franco's chart is extraordinarily Jupiterian. His Sagittarius
Sun is trine Jupiter in Aries (conjunct the eighth cusp). His ruling
planet Mercury is also in Sagittarius, although retrograde and
unintegrated with the rest of the chart—perhaps an indication of his
complete lack of logic or capacity for self-analysis. Jupiter is also
sextile his Moon and in an opposition with the exalted Saturn in
Libra in the first house. All the World War II dictators (including
Stalin) had a strong Saturnian quality, and certainly a first house

exalted Saturn could be expressed as an extraordinarily heavy-handed authoritarianism. And in Franco's case, Jupiter's opposition seems to have expanded this Saturnian tendency even more.

Franco's chart also contains a T-square configuration with a Pisces Mars at the apex, tying in and energizing the entire rectangular configuration described above. Mars is closely square both Sun and Moon, but it is also doubly Neptunian since not only is it in Pisces but also square Neptune—a clear symbol of his self-delusion. Franco was convinced that he was chosen by God to rule and save Spain from evil. This self-righteous tendency ties in with many other factors in his chart. His Mars is also doubly colored by Jupiter (the "righteous crusader," one might say), since it is not only in a sign co-ruled by Jupiter but it is *exactly* semi-sextile to Jupiter. Even in Pisces, Mars can be quite assertive in such aspect relationships; it is merely more sly and sneaky than a more brash Mars sign would be.

The self-righteousness and feeling of being morally superior, even while slaughtering thousands, pervades Franco's chart. The most activated house in his chart is the ninth, which contains the powerful stellium of the Moon with the two outermost planets, Neptune and Pluto, a signal of his tremendous involvement with the mass movements of his time. This ninth house emphasis further proves the reliability of the traditional resonance of the ninth house with Jupiter, which some modern astrological commentators have tried to deny.

Finally, it should be noted that this chart is very *impersonal*, so much so that one has to wonder if Franco ever realized that he was torturing real living human beings. Not only do Saturn and the Virgo Ascendant put a chill over his entire chart, but the usually friendly Gemini Moon was evidently undermined by Neptune and Pluto. And Venus, the planet of personal relationships, has its closest aspects with impersonal Uranus (the conjunction) and with Pluto (the quincunx), a potentially impersonal and obsessive combination. Seemingly, Franco lost touch with his human feelings and allowed cold efficiency and maintaining order to dominate his social concerns.

—S.A.

> Note on Jupiter's aspects with Saturn, Uranus, Neptune and Pluto: These interchanges must be interpreted in relation to how they are integrated with the more personal factors in the chart. Interpreting them in isolation will often be misleading.

♃/♄ Jupiter-Saturn Interchanges

(Especially important if Jupiter or Saturn rules a sign emphasized in the birth chart.)

Urge toward a larger order is brought down to earth and stabilized–expands the ambitions

One's urge to expand constantly interacts with one's need to retain the existing structure for safety

[Whether Saturn or Jupiter is stronger in a chart will have much to say about these energies' expression. The challenging aspects of Jupiter and Saturn are sometimes quite problematical in complicating the person's ability to work out his or her ambitions and long-range goals. Whereas the conjunction tends to be fairly harmonious and stimulates strong ambition in a focused way, the other dynamic aspects often manifest as a deep-down feeling that there is not enough work, money, or opportunity until one has over-extended oneself and finds that one in fact has too much to handle. Either feeling, that of having too much or too little, leaves the person frustrated. There is a profound need to learn contentment with working with what is at hand in the present.]

At the outset, I must state how completely useless I have found many authors' attempts to interpret this interchange. Perhaps the most misleading, and baffling, phrase used to describe some of these more challenging aspects is Marc E. Jones' indication that it signifies a "last chance lifetime," a dubious statement that unfortunately many other authors have repeated. I wonder on whose authority Mr. Jones came to that conclusion? Even Charles Carter, who usually is more cautious and reliable in his conclusions, treats the "inharmonious" aspects between Jupiter and Saturn in an inordinately negative way, concluding that they rarely thrive in a worldly way. And yet, immediately thereafter he mentions as examples of the inharmonious blendings such successful individuals as Edison (square), Robert Louis Stevenson (square), G.B. Shaw (square), and George Washington (opposition). I can add to this list Woody Allen, Konrad Adenauer, Sidney Poitier, Sigmund Freud, Gregory Peck, and Judge Hugo Black, all of whom have the square aspect, and Jacques Cousteau, who has the quincunx.

The conjunction of these planets has also received quite a lot of negative comment, or at least poorly understood analyses of this powerful union of profound energies. Isabel Hickey states, for example, that it indicates an easy life! Tell that to two lads from Liverpool's rough working class neighborhoods named Lennon and (Ringo) Starkey. John Lennon had quite a disturbed home life with considerable instability, and Ringo had to leave school and start working at a very young age. A man I know was born one of the youngest of nine children and grew up in a poor southern family; his father died when he was seven. And yet this man, through tremendous hard work, started his own company at the transit of Saturn over this conjunction and became a multimillionaire (and a happy one!) within twenty years. Galileo also had this conjunction in his chart and had to struggle against the narrow-minded authorities of his time for years. Charles Carter is much more accurate in his comments about the conjunction than those on the inharmonious aspects; he states, "It is distinctly a sign of great possibilities to be realised by hard work. It favours great singleness of purpose and endless patience." Other examples of such hard-working, single-minded people are John Glenn, Margaret Mead, Clara Barton, and Mary Baker Eddy–all of whose birth charts appear in this book.

Neither does the opposition deny worldly success, as J. Paul Getty, Bertrand Russell, and Maria Montessori prove. I think it is fair to say, as I explored extensively in Chapter 2, that there always needs to be a balance of Jupiter and Saturn *in a person's consciousness* in order to systematically and steadily build worldly success. The more challenging aspects may well demand that the individual pay close attention to *developing* that balance if he or she wishes to succeed in many areas of life; learning the lesson may involve some frustration and failure, but it can be learned. Those with the harmonious blendings of these planets undoubtedly have that balance more naturally established within themselves and readily put it to use more smoothly. Admittedly, if I had to choose to be born with one of these interchanges in my chart, I would choose the trine or sextile, but I have seen no reason to disparage the other angles between these great planets. With the challenging aspects, the individual simply has to learn how to live in a new way with an adjusted attitude, and usually with more faith and patience.

If Saturn is stronger, one may hold oneself back through fear, unproven assumptions, or negative attitudes. There may be an unwillingness to pay the price of hard work or self-denial in the challenging Jupiter-Saturn interchanges. One needs to evaluate what one's real long-term plans and priorities are. If Jupiter is stronger, its soaring dreams may motivate one to go to excesses of action or experiment in ways that are not supported by Saturnian preparation and practical facts. More research and realistic appraisal may be needed to build a foundation for supporting one's ideals and aspirations.

A lack of self-confidence characterizes many people who have Jupiter-Saturn challenging aspects; it is as if they have to *earn* that sense of well-being and expansiveness that Jupiter represents. And they often do that by taking on some kind of work or duty that may even entail risk or obvious chance of failure, as well as by learning to moderate their pessimism and tendency toward negative thoughts or self-doubt. Developing a religious faith or a sustaining philosophy of life can also contribute to their building inner strength. I believe Ebertin sums up this interchange accurately when he declared its essential principle to be: "Patience (achieving success through perseverance)."

Clara Barton & Mary Baker Eddy

In 1821, the year of two important planetary conjunctions (Uranus-Neptune in Capricorn and Jupiter-Saturn in Aries), two remarkable women were born in New England, less than five months apart. With the Uranus-Neptune conjunction at the Midheaven of Clara Barton's birth chart, and near the Ascendant of Mary Baker Eddy's, both women's lives were dedicated to giving Capricornian form to an unprecedented vision. Each of them displayed Aries initiative in launching, single-handedly, organizations (Saturn) with global outreach (Jupiter) that continue to thrive more than a hundred years later. The ways in which their lives and work embodied their Jupiter-Saturn beliefs demonstrate similar—as well as contrasting—factors in their birth charts.

Clara Barton, founder of the American Red Cross, had Aries rising with the Jupiter-Saturn-in-Aries conjunction in the first

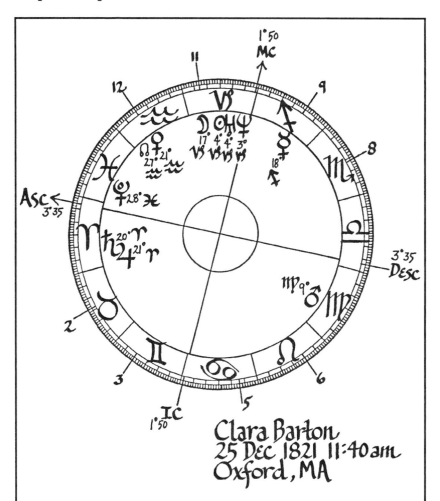

Clara Barton
25 Dec 1821 11:40 am
Oxford, MA

house. She was impelled to *act* upon her convictions—in unusually daring ways. When the Civil War began, she overcame all obstacles in order to minister to soldiers in the battlefields. Refusing to remain safely on the sidelines, she was often the first on the scene after a bloody battle. She nursed and comforted the wounded, sometimes with bullets still zinging around her. These heroic deeds earned her the title "Angel of the Battlefield." Later, after observing the International Red Cross in Europe, she resolved to create a similar relief organization in the United States. Using the same Capricornian savvy and Aries daring that had served her well in the Civil War, she fought her way to victory in the battlefields of Congress (no small feat!).

As founder and president of the American Red Cross, Barton spent the rest of her life fostering its growth, and in later years, wrestling with the challenges to her autocratic rule of the organization. She never lost her Aries rising/first house Jupiter-Saturn craving to be on the frontlines of the action in disaster scenes. She directly attended to the victims of such catastrophes as the 1889 Johnstown flood, in which the town was virtually destroyed, and three thousand people lost their lives.

In Barton's view, the Red Cross had an international scope—a perspective expressive of her Mercury in Sagittarius in the *ninth house* trine to Jupiter-Saturn. She led Red Cross relief efforts in both the 1892 Russian famine and the 1896 Armenian massacre (when she was seventy-four years old!). Clara Barton died in 1912 at age ninety, just eight years after she considered moving to Mexico to start a Mexican Red Cross. Her global humanitarianism was honored in this 1912 tribute in the *New York Globe* (quoted by David H. Burton in *Clara Barton: In the Service of Humanity*): "Her religion ran to the whole of mankind....She not only preached but practiced the new internationalism....Give the world enough Clara Bartons and the brotherhood of man will be ushered in."

For Sun-in-Cancer Mary Baker Eddy, it was the struggle with *personal* crisis that eventually led to her creation of what became a world-wide church. From childhood she was restricted, and often bed-ridden, with illness. As an adult she sought out the alternative healing options available at that time. At the age of forty she experienced dramatic improvement through treatment by a mental healer, Phineas Quimby, but continued to have intermittent relapses. Eddy's breakthrough to the reality of spiritual healing occurred during the winter of 1866, with transiting Uranus opposing the natal Uranus-Neptune conjunction. After a fall on an icy street, which resulted in severe injuries according to the doctors who attended her, Eddy experienced through prayer a sudden spiritual awakening that induced a spontaneous recovery.

Transformed by this breakthrough, Eddy began to heal others and to give talks about her discoveries. To undertake this public speaking, Eddy tapped into her Jupiter-Saturn-in-Aries daring. As her biographer Robert Peel points out, in the 1860s "it was still

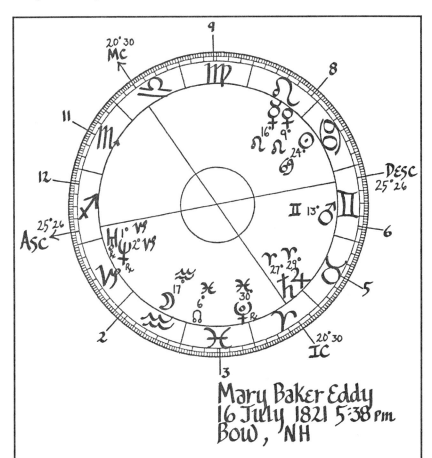

Mary Baker Eddy
16 July 1821 5:38 pm
Bow, NH

considered a scandalous thing that a woman should give a speech in public." Eddy continued to develop her philosophy of Christian Science, and in 1875 her 456 page book, *Science and Health*, was published. Her popularity grew; with Sagittarius rising and first house Uranus-Neptune, Eddy had a charismatic influence on her followers. (She is yet another example of a Sagittarius-rising individual who evolved a "larger than life" persona.) Her early students recorded that she began to say, "Someday I shall have a church of my own!" Robert Peel observes: "They thought...of a small Lynn [Massachusetts] church with a settled congregation; she thought in terms of a Church embracing the world." Eddy founded "The Church of Christ, Scientist" in 1879, and her prediction came true: There are now over 3,200 branches of the church in at least fifty countries, and her book is still in print and avidly read and discussed by church members. In the case of both Eddy and Barton, the Jupiter-Saturn conjunction resulted in amplifying Saturn's ambition, rather than restricting Jupiter's expansiveness.

With practical idealism, Clara Barton and Mary Baker Eddy both founded organizations (Saturn) that embodied their beliefs and values (Jupiter). Interestingly, in both birth charts, Mars, the dispositor of the Saturn-Jupiter-in-Aries conjunction, is in the *sixth house* of health and service. This was the central focus for each of them, although in different ways. Barton's Mars is in *Virgo* trine to her tenth house Capricorn planets, and she excelled in attending to the practical needs of wounded soldiers and of disaster victims. In whatever chaotic situation she entered, she brought superb skills of organization and the ability to create order. Eddy's sixth house Mars is in *Gemini* sextile the eighth house Mercury. She was concerned with the *mind's* role in healing, with how intangibles, such as one's beliefs, have an impact on the outcome of disease processes. She developed techniques of spiritual healing, and both healed others and taught them her methods. Her work anticipated by a hundred years the movement towards "holistic health" and "mind-body" medical alternatives.

It is fascinating to learn that, despite the different arenas of these two women, they were friends. Barton mourned the loss of Eddy, when she passed away, a little over a year before Barton herself. According to David Burton: "Barton felt a strong attraction to the teachings of Christian Science as expounded by Mary Baker Eddy in her book *Science and Health*....She termed Mrs. Eddy 'the greatest living American woman.'"

For both Barton and Eddy, the Jupiter-Saturn in Aries conjunction is evident in their conviction that beliefs must be *acted* upon in concrete ways. David Burton writes of Barton: "For her, Christianity was not a profession of beliefs but action taken toward all mankind based on those beliefs." Eddy proclaimed the same view, as these quotes of hers (from Robert Peel's book) show: "The error of the ages is preaching without practice." "The essential language of Christian Science is deeds rather than words." Not that *words*—considering her 456 page book—weren't important to this Mars in Gemini woman! In fact, in 1908 Eddy also founded a newspaper, *The Christian Science Monitor*, which became a success and is still highly respected today.

Both Barton and Eddy were controversial figures, whose power was sometimes challenged. How could it *not* be so for two nineteenth century women who assumed such pioneering leadership roles? From the perspective of over a century later, just after another Uranus-Neptune conjunction in Capricorn, it is clear that the Uranus-Neptune lives of Clara Barton and Mary Baker Eddy embodied a renewed vision of universal humanitarian compassion. In Eddy's words: "True prayer is not asking God for love; it is learning to love, and to include all mankind in one affection."

—B.McE.

♃/♅ Jupiter-Uranus Interchanges

(Especially important if Jupiter or Uranus rules a sign emphasized in the birth chart.)

Faith and large-scale future plans are electrified and expressed in an individualistic and unconventional way

The need for change, experimentation, and excitement is expansive and pervasive

Originality and creativity, as well as often a marked interest in politics or social change, can be indicated by these aspects, although much depends upon how they are integrated into the entire chart and attuned with the personal factors of the birth map. There is very often rebelliousness, although often manifesting more smoothly as a healthy urge for personal freedom of expression in the trine and sextile. Scientific inventiveness may also be shown, as is a general craving for new kinds of knowledge, especially if these discoveries or new ways of thinking depart radically from traditional ideas. For example, Einstein (see chart in Chapter 6) and Margaret Mead (close semi-sextile) have this interchange.

This is an intuitive combination known for sudden revelations that can give a person an *immediate* understanding, without going through a systematic logical procedure to arrive at a conclusion. Of course, the intuitive leaps do not always result in accurate perceptions; for Uranus is erratic, and Jupiter is known for a fondness for generalizations that overlook the specific factual details. Fighting energetically for a cause may be apparent, as is often an understanding of other people's need for freedom of expression. We certainly see this in Washington's chart, as Uranus and Jupiter harmonize (see Chapter 3). We also see it in Maria Montessori's educational theories; her Jupiter is semi-sextile her Uranus-Mars conjunction. In Fidel Castro's chart, we can see the powerful urge for freedom and revolution, but in relation to Cuban citizens, his regime has not tolerated the freedom of expression that Castro would want for himself! Castro's chart incorporates a fiery grand trine: Jupiter is exactly conjunct Uranus in Aries (he sets his own rules!), and trine both a Sagittarian Saturn and a Leo Mercury.

In Franklin D. Roosevelt's chart, the Jupiter-Uranus aspect (a trine) is not only almost exact, but also it ties in with his Ascendant. The resultant capacity to *project* his intuitive faith in freedom and in humanity's greater qualities to a vast, international public gave FDR a remarkable charisma and the ability to provide a desperately needed leadership for the free world. By clearly enunciating his vision of humanity's inherent right to have various freedoms, he laid the groundwork for all of the "human rights" dialogues and improvements worldwide since World War II. When Roosevelt died, even the normally staid *New York Times* could not hold back its editorial praise:

> *It was his hand, more than that of any other single man, that built the great coalition of the United Nations....It was his leadership which inspired free men in every part of the world to fight with greater hope and courage. Gone, now, is this talent and skill....Gone is the fresh and spontaneous interest which this man took, as naturally as he breathed air, in the troubles and the hardships and the disappointments and the hopes of little men and humble people.*

Another summing up of his unique Jupiter/Uranus personality was expressed by Isaiah Berlin, who wrote: "He was one of the few statesmen in the twentieth century, or any century, who seemed to have no fear of the future." [See Chapter 8 in the Jupiter in the ninth house section for FDR's complete chart.]

Many other advocates of radical social change also have this blending; for example, Franklin D. Roosevelt had a very close trine, John F. Kennedy had the square, and Prince Charles has the opposition. As Richard Tarnas points out in his pioneering book on Uranus (see Chapter 11 for more details), those with Jupiter-Uranus aspects may be keenly attuned to the vast cultural, social, or scientific changes of their times. A man whose long life embodied an attunement to all those types of changes is Bertrand Russell, who was born with a close Jupiter-Uranus conjunction in Cancer, in the ninth house.*That conjunction was also closely sextile his Sun-Mars conjunction in Taurus, in the socially-conscious seventh house. Russell's active life for over ninety years included significant achievements in mathematics, philosophy, education, social commentary, anti-war activism, and daring questioning of traditional norms related to family, marriage, and sex. He spent most of his life fighting for various causes, and he had an intuitive understanding of other people's needs for freedom of expression. During World War I, for example, he lost his university teaching job due to his outspoken defense of the rights of a conscientious objector. Always controversial, his international speaking tours and over forty books resulted in his being awarded the 1950 Nobel Prize for literature, honoring his dedication to the rights of humanity and freedom of thought–an appropriate description of a Jupiter-Uranus blending of energies.

Henry Ford, who was quite politically active and also experimented with numerous revolutionary methods of paying his workers, in addition to providing automobiles for the masses through a new kind of mass production, had these two planets in trine. Astrological author Grant Lewi, whose contributions toward making intelligent, practical astrology accessible to the masses through his books *Astrology for the Millions* and *Heaven Knows What*, was born with Jupiter in Aquarius, sextile Uranus–a doubly Uranian Jupiter! And author of *The Little Prince*, Antoine de Saint-Exupéry, expressed his Jupiter conjunct Uranus in Sagittarius not only through his famous allegorical story but also in numerous writings in the field of aviation, not to mention his many adventures in foreign countries, including a wartime mission that led to his death. He was professionally regarded as a chief influence in the developing literature of aviation.

---

*Born May 18, 1872, Trelleck, Wales; 5:45 P.M.

2+/ΨΨ   Jupiter-Neptune
         Interchanges

**(Especially important if Jupiter or Neptune
rules a sign emphasized in the birth chart.)**

*A pervasive need to experience oneness with something
larger than one's own individual self and petty
personal concerns*

*One believes in the reality of the intangible realm of
experience, sometimes leading to an overactive
imagination and a constant urge to escape or to a
sense of meaningful inspiration*

It is difficult to be much more specific about the potential
manifestations of this interchange than is stated in the above
guidelines, so varied are the ways that individuals have put this
inspiration and psychic sensitivity to use. Naturally, when the two
most idealistic planets are combined, the result is a soaring idealism,
a broad sense of the infinite possibilities which life can provide. This
can lead one to become a practical idealist, such as Churchill
(opposition), Bertrand Russell (square), or Albert Schweitzer (opposition), an idealistic or imaginative artist such as Percy Shelley or
Laurence Olivier (both the conjunction), or an escapist, such as the
Duke of Windsor (conjunction), who abdicated the English throne.
Another practical idealist, Franklin D. Roosevelt, expressed a broad
imagination focused on solving practical problems (Jupiter conjunct
Neptune in Taurus).

There is often a profound fantasy life, but one must look at all
the other factors involved in the chart as well. For example, Joseph
P. Kennedy always dreamed of power and of being President, and
eventually of having his son become U.S. President; but his Jupiter
is opposite not only Neptune but also *Pluto*, which shows this
obsessive drive for power (and Jupiter was conjunct Mars in Scorpio, too). Jules Verne's soaring imagination was well represented by
his Jupiter-Neptune sextile, and he was not only fond of sailing all
over Europe and Africa (Neptune is associated with the sea), but
also his *20,000 Leagues Under the Sea* has become one of his most
enduring creations. It is curious that another watery performer,
Olympian Mark Spitz, was born with Jupiter trine a Neptune-Mars
conjunction.

This combination can also indicate considerable intuition, a talent which Joseph Campbell*used to vastly expand our knowledge of literature, mythology, and the personal quest for meaning and transcendence. His Jupiter (conjunct Sun and Mercury) square Neptune was thus poured into such works as *Hero with a Thousand Faces* and *The Masks of God* decades before Jungian studies became broadly accepted. Poet T. S. Eliot,** who also contributed significantly to revitalizing modern interest in mythology, had an exact opposition of Jupiter to Neptune in his chart. Poet and translator Robert Bly likewise was born with the opposition.

At worst, these aspects can indicate personal delusion and self-deception, as was lived out by Mussolini and Albert Speer, for example, both of whom had the sextile. But at best, they can manifest as a compassionate love of humanity (e.g., Dr. Albert Schweitzer–see biography in this chapter) and an appreciation of metaphysical and artistic subtleties. Another perfect example of this higher manifestation of the Jupiter-Neptune blending is the monk and writer Thomas Merton , whose exact Jupiter-Neptune quincunx manifested as inspired writings that thousands found uplifting.

Albert Schweitzer

Albert Schweitzer–medical missionary, theologian, master organist, and music scholar–lived an exemplary life of rare dedication. In his birth chart, Jupiter is in opposition to a Neptune-Moon conjunction. These planets form a T-Square to the Sun-Mercury conjunction in Capricorn. This configuration challenged Schweitzer to devote himself to purposes beyond the sphere of narrow personal achievement. During a remarkable life's journey, Schweitzer developed and acted upon a Jupiterian ethic that reflects the compassion of Neptune. In Schweitzer's words, "The ethic of Reverence for Life is the ethic of Love widened into universality."

Neptune's capacity to identify with the pain of others, combined with the moral awareness of Jupiter, was at the heart of Schweitzer's desire to serve. In his autobiography (*Out of My Life and Thought*), he reveals this central motivation:

> *I could not but feel with a sympathy full of regret all the pain that I saw around me, not only that of men but that of the whole creation. From this community of suffering I have never tried to withdraw myself. It seemed to me a matter of course that we should all take our share of the*

*Born March 26, 1904; New York, NY; 7:25 P.M. EST.
**Born September 26, 1888; St. Louis, Missouri, USA; 7:45 A.M. CST; died 1965.

burden of pain which lies upon the world.

Even during his boyhood, Schweitzer was haunted by this awareness of suffering and by his Neptunian sense of obligation. Describing his early years, he wrote: "It struck me as incomprehensible that I should be allowed to lead such a happy life, while I saw so many people around me wrestling with care and suffering." In this quote we can see the polarity between Schweitzer's first house Jupiter and his seventh house Neptune-Moon. At the age of twenty-one these feelings took shape as a remarkable decision:

> *There came to me, as I awoke, the thought that I must not accept this happiness as a matter of course, but must give something in return for it....I settled with myself before I got up, that I would consider myself justified in living till I was thirty for science and art, in order to devote myself from that time forward to the direct service of humanity.*

With this pledge to himself, Schweitzer satisfied the needs of both his Capricorn Sun *and* Jupiter-Neptune. At this time (late spring 1896) transiting Jupiter in the tenth house had just squared natal Jupiter; and transiting Saturn, conjunct natal Mars, formed the last quarter square to natal Saturn. Schweitzer, with Jupiterian prescience, already understood the form his life would take.

In the years leading up to his first Saturn return, Schweitzer compressed a lifetime's worth of Capricornian achievement. He pursued his scholarly ambitions at the University of Strasbourg and earned *three* Ph.D. degrees: in philosophy in 1899; in theology in 1901; and in music in 1905. Schweitzer also served as principal of a theological college, preached regularly at a church, and became both a master organist and an expert on organ construction. He wrote an authoritative study of Bach and also the renowned and controversial book *The Quest of the Historical Jesus.*

With Jupiter in the first house, Schweitzer expanded eagerly into many areas–all of which had a Neptunian dimension. For instance, biographer James Bentley writes that "music was for him as much a spiritual as an intellectual vocation." And he quotes Schweitzer: "'In short, to plunge your whole soul in Bach is exactly the same as doing theology.'"

Schweitzer remained committed to the promise he had made at age twenty-one. Nearing his thirtieth birthday, he considered possible forms of humanitarian service. During his Saturn return, Schweitzer's destiny came into focus. In October 1904, as transiting Saturn made a station exactly conjunct natal Saturn in Aquarius, he casually glanced at a magazine published by the Paris Missionary Society. Schweitzer writes: "As I did so, my eye caught the title of an article: *Les besoins de la Mission du Congo* ('The needs of the Congo Mission')....My search was over....The result was that I resolved to realize my plan of direct human service in Equatorial Africa." Schweitzer's choice of a foreign country as the context for fulfilling his compassionate desire to serve was a fitting alliance of Jupiter and Neptune. (Interestingly, Mother Teresa, who was born with Jupiter square Neptune, left her native Yugoslavia to minister to the dying in the streets of faraway India. And Father Damien, the nineteenth century Belgian priest who worked for many years with lepers in the Hawaiian Islands, was born with Jupiter square to a Neptune-Mars conjunction.)

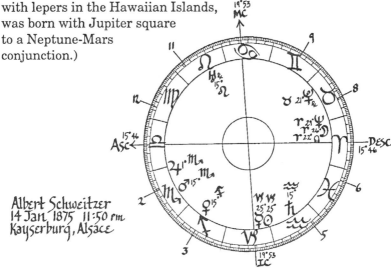

Albert Schweitzer
14 Jan. 1875 11:50 PM
Kayserburg, Alsace

Schweitzer, the brilliant scholar, became also a pragmatic man of action: "My new occupation would be not to talk about the gospel of love, but to put it into practice." Significantly, the dispositor of both Neptune in Aries and Jupiter in Scorpio is *Mars*. Schweitzer felt impelled to *act* upon his ideals. After completing seven years of medical school, including special training in tropical diseases, Schweitzer traveled in 1913 to French Equatorial Africa with his wife Hélène, a nurse. In their first year they treated over 2,000 people under highly primitive conditions: Schweitzer's operating room was in a chicken coop! With Mars in *Scorpio*—opposite Pluto in the eighth house—Schweitzer's skill and courage as a doctor were both challenged and fostered by these difficulties.

Schweitzer's "truly extraordinary will-power" (in biographer Werner Picht's words) was called upon in building, often with his own hands, the hospital compound at Lambaréné. This will-power was generated by Mars in Scorpio in a fixed sign Grand Square. Bil Tierney (in *Dynamics of Aspect Analysis*) writes that "the Fixed Grand Square suggests powerful inner fortitude, awesome determination, and masterful planning ability"–words that fit Schweitzer perfectly. Tierney, though, also cautions about "dictatorial behavior" if Mars, Uranus, or Pluto are part of the configuration. All three planets (plus authoritarian Saturn!) form Schweitzer's Grand Square. That side of his nature is evident in James Bentley's description of the "iron rule [Schweitzer] was to exercise in the unique jungle hospital he created." Another biographer (Gerald McKnight) saw Lambaréné "as a place that permitted Schweitzer absolute dominion and control." But author Norman Cousins, who spent time in Africa with Schweitzer, summed it up this way: "At Lambaréné I learned that a man does not have to be an angel to be a saint."

True to the Jupiter-Neptune influence in Schweitzer's life, many of his most crucial insights came in unexpected, revelatory ways. In September 1915, while transiting Neptune in Leo was squaring natal Jupiter and transiting Jupiter in Pisces was exactly sextile the natal Sun-Mercury conjunction, Schweitzer was riding a barge slowly up a river in Africa:

> *Late on the third day, at the very moment when, at sunset, we were making our way through a herd of hippopotamuses, there flashed upon my mind, unforeseen and unsought, the phrase, "Reverence for Life." The iron door had yielded: the path in the thicket had become visible. Now I had found my way to the idea in which affirmation of the world and ethics are contained side by side!*

To formulate an ethic that included "affirmation of the world" (a Jupiterian concept) had special meaning for Schweitzer at that time: World War I was raging in Europe, and Schweitzer and his wife, as German citizens in French territory, had been taken prisoners of war. (They returned to Africa in 1924 and continued their work at the hospital for many decades.) The significance of Schweitzer's affirmation, during this dark time, is conveyed by Werner Picht: "It was a revelation at a moment when men were seized with horror at the tangible results of the failure of humanness. It was the word of a prophet in a historical moment of appalling danger." Schweitzer emphasized that Reverence for Life extended to *all* life. Clearly the universalism of Neptune embraced not only the human, but all other creatures and plants.

Schweitzer, with Jupiter in the first house, retained the buoyancy characteristic of that placement—even though his life was immersed in the reality of suffering. Norman Cousins describes the wry sense of humor with which Schweitzer broke the tension at the hospital: "His use of humor, in fact, was so artistic that one had the feeling he almost regarded it as a musical instrument." (Venus in Sagittarius in the third house trine Uranus contributed to this talent too.) The optimism of the first house Jupiter, tempered by the unflinching realism of the Scorpio sign placement, infused Schweitzer's outlook—as the following quote from his autobiography shows:

Because I have confidence in the power of truth and of the spirit, I believe in the future of mankind. Ethical acceptance of the world contains within itself an optimistic willing and hoping which can never be lost. It is, therefore, never afraid to face the dismal reality, and to see it as it really is.

Schweitzer, who lived to be ninety, received many honors during his lifetime—most notably the Nobel Peace Prize in 1952. (He used the prize money to establish a leper colony near his hospital.) In the following tribute by Norman Cousins, Albert Schweitzer's living out of the Jupiter-Neptune aspect is apparent:

His main achievement is a simple one. He has been willing to make an ultimate sacrifice for a moral principle. Because he has been able to make the supreme identification with other human beings, he has exerted a greater force than millions of armed men on the march.
—B.McE.

♃/♇ Jupiter-Pluto Interchanges

(Especially important if Jupiter or Pluto rules a sign emphasized in the birth chart.)

A need to experience total rebirth stimulates the search for faith in a greater order in the universe

Seeks to improve oneself through the power of transformative methods and pursuits

This blending often propels the person to seek and to employ power on some level–spiritual, mental, occult, financial, political, etc. There is often an extraordinarily willful streak in the personality, which can repel others because of its obvious ruthlessness (for example, Margaret Thatcher–with a very close opposition). These individuals need to be alert to the danger of becoming obsessed with their own personal goals, to the exclusion of concern for other people who may be affected. At worst, they can be exploitive, manipulative, or obsessed with the dark side of life. At best, they can express a tremendous, unconquerable courage and a dedication to the reform of self or society, even if it requires self-sacrifice. The lives of Gandhi and Ram Dass exemplify this positive manifestation; both have the conjunction.

There may be leadership talents and a certain charisma, as well as innate abilities to determine the underlying reasons for things or the motivations for people's behavior. There can be wide occult interests, curiosity about psychological matters, or a fascination with large-scale social, corporate, or governmental functioning. C. G. Jung and Margaret Mead both had a close quincunx between Jupiter and Pluto, and both are known for achieving breakthroughs in understanding human behavior through their in-depth research.

The ideals guiding the use of this substantial will power are absolutely crucial in determining how such energy will be expressed. Other examples are Albert Einstein (square), whose research and insight unlocked profound knowledge but also frighteningly deadly power; actor Jack Nicholson (opposition), whose projection of the dark side of human nature adds a compelling quality to the characters he portrays; and George Gershwin (close trine), whose instinctive understanding of deeper human feelings enabled him to infuse even his apparently light songs with memorable poignancy.

Mohandas Gandhi

Mohandas Gandhi, social reformer and catalyst for India's independence movement, is often regarded as a "modern saint." During his lifetime, such notables as the Nobel prize-winning Indian poet Rabindranath Tagore bestowed on Gandhi the title "Mahatma," which means "Great Soul." But Gandhi, with a Libran Sun in the twelfth house, wished to elude such honorifics. In fact, this man, who was so often at odds with government policies, playfully exclaimed: "Though a non-cooperator I shall gladly subscribe to a bill to make it criminal for anybody to call me a Mahatma." Gandhi *did* live an extraordinary life, in which the Jupiterian principle played a significant role—especially through its conjunction with Pluto. Jupiter, in fact, is heavily aspected in Gandhi's birth chart as part of a fixed sign T-Square in angular houses. Gandhi's philosophy and ethical concerns, his search for "Truth," which he equated with God, pervaded all dimensions of his life.

The Jupiter-Pluto conjunction, with its dynamic aspects, amplified Gandhi's power to effect change. As an agent of social transformation, he inspired the masses of India to challenge several centuries of subjugation under the British Empire. Gandhi blended Jupiterian moral ideals with a Plutonian magnetic hold over others, as described in this tribute by Einstein (quoted from Howard Gardner's *Creating Minds*): "Gandhi had demonstrated that a powerful human following can be assembled...through the cogent example of a morally superior conduct of life. In our time of utter moral decadence, he was the only true statesman to stand for a higher human relationship in the political sphere."

Gandhi's concern for human relationship, and his role from childhood as a peace-maker, are reflected in the placements of Sun and Ascendant in Libra. The interplay between justice-seeking Libra and the intensity and drive of the Jupiter-Pluto T-Square, can be seen in this statement by biographer Gerald Gold: "Affronts to [Gandhi's] sense of law and fair play seemed to touch off an explosion that almost automatically led to action." Another writer on Gandhi, Martin Green, notes that we can sense "volcanic emotion, in controlled and refined form, behind his reflections on nonviolence, which strike us as going as far as the human mind can go in the direction of peace and truth." During Gandhi's twenty years as a young lawyer in South Africa, he successfully mediated compromises between opponents in legal disputes—using his skillful Libran awareness of human relationships. He also fought intensively for the political rights of Indians living in South Africa. Through such experiences, he developed his philosophy of nonviolent social activism. With the crusading courage of the Jupiter-Pluto opposition to Mars, Gandhi's challenges of injustice became over time more daring and of greater scope—and each challenge reflected his core philosophy of *satyagraha*.

Satyagraha was Gandhi's term for confronting social wrongs through a method of nonviolent resistance that emphasized re-

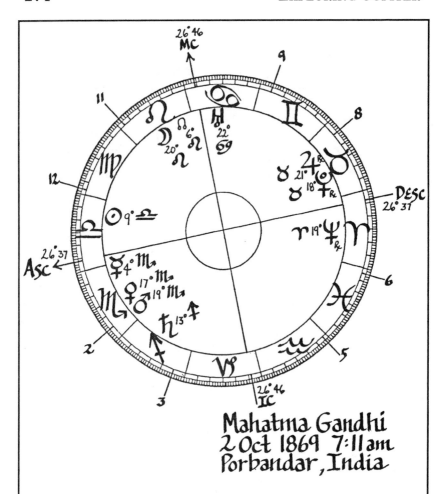

Mahatma Gandhi
2 Oct 1869 7:11am
Porbandar, India

maining respectful, even loving, of the opponent. The Libran Sun
and Ascendant qualities are evident again here. Also Jupiter-Pluto
in the *seventh house* (with Jupiter close to the eighth house cusp)
prompted Gandhi to explore the constructive potential of transformation within relationships. Gandhi's aim was a conversion of an
adversary's perspective through the willingness of the followers of
satyagraha to undergo the suffering that results from resistance.
Literally translated, *satyagraha* means "the force of truth and
love"–almost keywords for Gandhi's Mars-Pluto-Jupiter-Venus
aspect configuration. Gandhi honed the principles of Venusian love
and Jupiterian truth-seeking into a Mars-Pluto force for confront-

ing and healing injustice. This dynamic is described by Manmohan Choudhuri in *Exploring Gandhi*:

> *Though Gandhi equated love with nonviolence, his nonviolence was a synthesis of love and the warrior spirit [Venus conjunct Mars in Scorpio!]. He used it as a scalpel, and not only in respect to political or social causes. Love was a principle that he believed should suffuse the whole of life, all the activities and relations of a person.*

The seventh house Jupiter-Pluto conjunction is in a *Venusian* sign, Taurus, in opposition to their dispositor, Venus in Scorpio (which is also the chart ruler). This Venusian emphasis underscores the importance of love in Gandhi's philosophy. Gandhi wrote: "To see the universal and all-pervading Spirit of Truth face to face one must be able to love the meanest creatures as oneself." (quoted by Gold from Gandhi's *Autobiography*) Gandhi painfully experienced racism in South Africa when a white passenger objected to his presence on the first class coach of a train; Gandhi was ejected for refusing to give up his seat. (Later, Gandhi would prefer riding third class to show solidarity with the impoverished people of India.) Gandhi's cold night in the train station was a turning point. From then on, he fought relentlessly, and with great compassion, for the rights of society's most neglected and needy people.

One expression of Pluto's symbolism may be seen as society's rejected underclass–those "meanest creatures," in Gandhi's words, whom the more fortunate often despise and fear. In India the "Untouchables," virtual outcasts on the lowest rung of society, were in this position. Gerald Gold writes: "Acceptance of untouchability was almost universal even among the Untouchables, but Gandhi saw this as one of the principle blights of Hinduism and of India, and beginning at the *ashram* he fought against it throughout his life." Gandhi used the reforming zeal of the Pluto-Jupiter conjunction to expose the plight of the Untouchables, whom he called "*Harijans*," "children of God." He insisted, despite objections–even from his wife, on allowing Untouchables to live at his *ashram*, the community where Gandhi and his closest followers practiced the simple lifestyle he espoused. Catherine Bush writes that he also "traveled the country, staying in the homes of Untouchables in order to break the taboo against them by his example." Gandhi's stance was a direct expression of his spiritual views: "The entire universe has been created out of a single divine source. Hence there is no room for any kind of discrimination in it on any score."

Every part of Gandhi's life–even his clothing–expressed his Jupiterian moral ideals. With the *first house* Venus-Mars in opposition to Jupiter-Pluto, he used his *appearance* as part of his challenge to the inequities that he abhorred. As a young man, he enjoyed wearing expensive European clothes, but he soon adopted traditional middle class Indian garb, and ended up in the simple loincloth of the very poor. For Gandhi, the Jupiterian urge to expand beyond limits was paradoxically allied with the Plutonian drive for stripping down to essentials, for destroying narrow identities. Manmohan Choudhuri describes this well:

> *Throughout his life, in the small changes he made in his lifestyle and his way of doing things, one can discern his constant endeavour to divest himself of identities, attitudes and complexes that put limits on one's inner growth, that deflect one from one's central mission and dissipate one's energies. He sought to cast off all images of himself that stood in the way of his consciousness of unity with the human family and even with all creation.*

This "stripping" took an overtly political form when Gandhi began asking Indians to boycott foreign-made clothing. Gerald Gold notes: "He would call at rallies for everyone to strip off clothing made abroad and throw it into a pile to which he then set a match. He called on everyone to spin and weave their own clothing." Always participating personally in the reforms he promoted, Gandhi set aside time daily for handspinning.

Gandhi's enthusiasm for spinning was one facet of the extremely simplified lifestyle he adopted. Jupiter in Taurus is traditionally associated with material expansion and enjoyment of sensual pleasures. Gandhi's Pluto-Jupiter conjunction in Taurus (plus the influence of the oppositions to Scorpio planets) promoted instead a kind of *purging* of material accouterments: "He shrugged off worldly possessions, ate and drank abstemiously, wore few pieces of clothing, and lived with as few creature comforts as possible." (quoted from Howard Gardner) For Gandhi, the Taurus function was turned inside out: Gardner quotes Gandhi as declaring, "'I own no property and yet I feel that I am perhaps the richest man in the world.'" (Saturn in *Sagittarius* in the second house also echoes this theme of Gandhi's ideologically-based voluntary poverty.) Of course, while Gandhi owned virtually nothing, he relied at times on the generosity of financial benefactors to maintain his various *ashrams*. This irony did not escape notice by some observers in Gandhi's orbit. Howard Gardner quotes one of them as saying, "'It cost a great deal of money to keep Gandhi living in poverty.'" But Gandhi understood the potency and symbolic value of his choice to live personally as the poorest individuals in his country did.

With a tenth house Leo Moon at the apex of the T-Square, in very close aspect to the Jupiter-Pluto conjunction, Gandhi was adept at promoting his causes through dramatic gestures that had great emotional impact. One of these, which combines both *lunar* symbolism and the Plutonian drive for purification, was the use of *fasting* to exert pressure on his opponents, and even at times to curtail Hindu-Muslim violence. Gandhi would vow to "fast unto death." Soon his foes would agree to at least a compromise, since no one wanted to be responsible for the demise of the Mahatma. The tenth house Leo Moon (part of a fire sign grand trine) conferred enormous popularity on Gandhi, especially among the poorer Indian population who revered him as a saint. And, of course, Gandhi had the great charisma of the Jupiter-Pluto conjunction. Howard Gardner writes, "Virtually unique was Gandhi's hold on the Indian masses. Something, perhaps everything, about the way in which Gandhi held himself and conducted his life resonated with *his* people."

An example of Gandhi's masterful use of drama was his famous Salt March in 1930. At the age of sixty-one, Gandhi walked 241 miles to the coast, gathering an enormous following along the way. On April 6th, he defied the British law prohibiting Indians from producing their own salt by stooping to take salt from the sea's edge. The role of the tenth house Leo Moon as a focal point in the T-Square is evoked by Louis Fischer's comments on the Salt March (quoted by Howard Gardner): "To pick up a pinch of salt in defiance of the mighty government and thus become a criminal...required imagination, dignity, and the sense of showmanship of a great artist. It appealed to the illiterate peasant and it appealed to a sophisticated critic." The Salt March was a major turning point in the Indian independence struggle. As Gardner writes, "The moral hold Britain had exerted over India had been shattered."

Gandhi planned his Salt March in February 1930, the month when the planet Pluto was discovered. He started to walk to the coast on March 12, 1930, one day prior to scientists' announcement to the world of Pluto's existence. (Significantly, March 12, 1930 was also the publishing date of Gandhi's unorthodox translation of the Hindu text the *Bhagavad Gita*, which concerns the cosmic battle between good and evil.) At the time of the planet's discovery, transiting Pluto was at seventeen degrees of Cancer—*exactly* sextile Gandhi's natal Pluto and forming a trine to Venus-Mars in Scorpio. Immediately after the Salt March, when its earthquake-like impact rippled across India and Great Britain, Pluto made a station at seventeen Cancer. Clearly, Gandhi was a Jupiterian exemplar—showing ways of relating *constructively* to Plutonian forces, which represent the most profound challenges known to humans. Pluto can manifest destructively at times through violent change; Gandhi expressed it instead through an unrelenting quest for *reform*—of values and of obsolete structures in society. During a time that saw the rise of Plutonian dictators (Hitler, Mussolini, etc.), Gandhi turned enormous power into a positive force for the betterment of humanity.

The discovery of the planet Pluto also coincided with developments that led to the creation of the atomic bomb. Einstein, who was, of course, intimately aware of the evolution of the bomb, made some fascinating observations that confirm Gandhi's synchronistic connection with Pluto and with the moral issues associated with it. The following quote is from Howard Gardner in *Creating Minds*:

> In 1949, the year following Gandhi's assassination, Prime Minister Jawaharlal Nehru visited Albert Einstein at the Institute of Advanced Study in Princeton. Einstein took out a pad of paper and wrote down a number of dates on one side and a number of events on the other. Decade by decade he showed a parallel evolution of the nuclear bomb, on the one side, and of Gandhi's satyagraha methods and accomplishments on the other. The quite amazing parallels served as a list of human options available in the nuclear age. One might say Gandhi had achieved through his manipulation of relevant variables the kind of insight into human beings that Einstein had achieved about the natural order through his abstract conceptual experiments.

The birth charts of both Gandhi and Einstein contain a prominent aspect between Jupiter and a transpersonal planet. (In Einstein's case, it is the Jupiter-Uranus opposition—symbolic of his radical scientific breakthroughs. See Chapter 6 for Einstein's biography.) Interestingly, Einstein and Gandhi made contact via letter, and had hoped to meet, but the 1948 assassination of Gandhi cut off that possibility. A final quote from Einstein sums up Gandhi's expression of his highly challenging and dynamic birth chart:

> *Gandhi, the greatest political genius of our time, indicated the path to be taken. He gave proof of what sacrifice man is capable once he has discovered the right path. His work in behalf of India's liberation is living testimony to the fact that man's will, sustained by an indomitable conviction, is more powerful than material forces that seem insurmountable.*
>
> —B.McE.

♃ / Asc Jupiter-Ascendant Interchanges

Expansive, confident, and broad-minded qualities need to be expressed outwardly

Faith and optimism are integral to one's mode of self-expression and color one's entire approach to life

Any planet closely aspecting the Ascendant adds its quality to one's consciousness and generally provides a push to express one's rising sign energy. However, the *sign* that Jupiter is in (for any aspect besides a conjunction *in* the rising sign) invariably must be blended with the rising sign's quality to develop a complete picture of the individual's personality and attitude toward life. If Jupiter is in a close aspect to the Ascendant (which of course can be determined only if the birth time is quite reliable), one feels its optimism and buoyancy within oneself, usually at one's disposal quite easily, although–especially in the case of the less harmonious aspects–one might have to learn to acknowledge or integrate it within one's habitual mode of self-expression. Jupiter in such a relationship can provide a major source of energy and talent once one learns to develop and utilize it. Franklin D. Roosevelt, President of the U.S. longer than any other man, had Jupiter closely trine his Ascendant; and he was invariably described as jaunty, optimistic, and buoyant–even during the darkest days of World War II and the Great Depression.

As the author of *No Ordinary Time*, Doris Kearns Goodwin, wrote about Franklin Roosevelt's presidency, "Roosevelt's ebullience permeated every aspect of his leadership." This is a concise description of a Jupiter/Ascendant personality, although admittedly FDR was an exceptional case and more charismatic than most. She goes on to describe how Churchill once remarked that, to encounter Franklin Roosevelt, with all his buoyant sparkle, was like opening your first bottle of champagne. Curiously enough, Goodwin even resorts to an equestrian image when trying to describe Roosevelt's *modus operandi*:

> *Roosevelt never felt that he or his leadership was threatened by multiplicity and confusion. He could try everything; he could move in different directions at the same time; he could let the horses run, never doubting his ability to rein them in should they threaten to become uncontrollable.*

Roosevelt had the remarkable ability to inspire and instill confidence in others, even when the prospects looked bleakest. He never lost sight of the big picture. As his closest associate, Harry Hopkins, said just after FDR died:

> [In] *the little things, the unimportant things,....he knew exactly how little and how unimportant they really were. But in the big things–all the things that were of real, permanent importance–he never let the people down.*

This type of interchange makes the Jupiter *sign* more important and more prominent in the overall psychological make-up of the individual; and this is especially true in the conjunction, trine, and sextile. The flamboyance of Jupiter may be lacking, depending on its sign, but there will usually be a characteristic Jupiterian broadmindedness and desire to express one's better, more noble qualities in everyday life. Jupiter/Ascendant examples discussed in this book include Emerson, Cousteau, Thatcher, Mead, and Conan Doyle.

One who has such an aspect should never sell oneself short, for growth of this confidence can build momentum as the individual takes risks to develop and express this potential. The main negative expression of this interchange may be a tendency toward excessive display of self, an inordinate desire to be important to the world, or– on the other hand–sometimes an excessive urge to give to others and to society more than one really should–of self, time, or wealth.

♃/MC Jupiter-Midheaven Interchanges

*An expansive ambition to achieve something signifi-
cant in the world*

*Feels a calling to improve life, and thus needs a career
that incorporates idealism*

Those with close aspects between the Midheaven and Jupiter
are often "successful" in the eyes of the world, or at least usually have
a positive public reputation. The individual with this attunement, in
fact, values high-minded social ideals and wants his or her public
self-expression to be constructive and to be seen as broadminded and
ethical. At best, there may be a nobility of purpose in one's life work,
although—as always with Jupiter—one must be careful not to allow
hypocrisy to develop. Franklin D. Roosevelt was a good example of
this interchange; he had an exact semi-sextile of Jupiter and the
M.C. Astronaut and Senator John Glenn has Jupiter conjunct his
M.C., and he is renowned for his conscientiousness and ethical
propriety.

Ebertin states that this combination indicates a "consciousness
of aim or objective in life," as well as optimism. Often, at an early age,
these people begin to develop an interest in far-off, high-minded
dreams; and, although they may change their goals numerous times
over the years, they never seem to lack a sense of current purpose.
Many of these individuals need to promote their ideals in public,
which may entail speaking, writing, publishing, or demonstrating
on a large scale what they believe in. (Witness Jacques Cousteau,
whose Jupiter squares his M.C.) Jupiter's *sign* will take on more
importance with such interchanges, and that sign's energy may well
be used in the person's career or various vocational endeavors; and
this insight can be useful in career counseling. But once again, it
must be emphasized that the birth time must be reliable for these
aspects to be utilized in any chart interpretation.

CHAPTER 11
Transits Involving Jupiter

*Transits are not isolated events over which you have
no control but instead are part of an integral psychological process that you are participating in.*
—Donna Cunningham
(from *An Astrological Guide to Self-Awareness*)

This chapter bears the above title because I want to discuss not
only the transit *of* Jupiter to various natal planets and angles, but
also the transits of the other planets *to* natal Jupiter, which can be
equally important. I want to focus in this chapter mainly on some
specific guidelines and also on some new observations that have
become evident to me since I wrote about Jupiter transits some years
ago in previous books. Since I will emphasize these *new* ideas and
also want briefly to illustrate some Jupiterian transit experiences
with specific examples, it seems unnecessary as well as redundant
to repeat all the ideas that I have already published in some detail.
Hence, I refer the reader to my book *Relationships & Life Cycles* for
a lengthy section on transiting Jupiter through the houses, as well
as quite a bit of other commentary on specific Jupiter transits; and
I would like to remind the reader that my *Astrology, Karma &
Transformation* contains some practical and concise observations
about Jupiter transits on pages 196 to 198. Both books also now have
complete indexes in their new editions.

Many things already explored in detail in this book regarding
the essence of Jupiterian experience naturally apply directly to
Jupiterian transits. For example, some of the guidelines itemized
in Chapter 8 could be used beneficially and accurately to explore
the meaning of Jupiter's transit through any specific house of a
birth chart. The important thing for anyone trying to understand
oneself or others through such transits is to be sure to see such a
symbolic indication as only one part of a vast picture, of a panorama
of cosmic energies always changing and interweaving throughout
the cosmos and one's entire being. And, especially with Jupiter and
its tendency to go to excess, to expect too much, or to become overly

optimistic, one has to be careful to keep Jupiter transits in perspective and to relate them to all other transits, in some cases to reliable progressions, and certainly to the entire individual attunement reflected in the birth chart.

I have stated in previous books that, whenever I witnessed truly significant and profound changes in a person's life, there was generally present an entire pattern of transits (and sometimes–but by no means always–progressions) which reflected how pervasive this period of life change was for that person. In other words, one should not look only to Jupiter transits when trying to understand promising new developments, but also to all other significant alignments. Jupiter's more positive, constructive side may in fact have a better chance of being realized in practical life if certain other factors are also present to energize action, as well as to provide discipline and organization. Transits show *how* the energy is released rather than specifically *what* will manifest. Certainly, one might correctly guess that a *specific* event or development may occur during a Jupiter transit, but one will be wrong (and thus misleading) more often than right. However, one can certainly know that, during many Jupiter transits, energy will be released expansively, confidently, and possibly extravagantly or in an exaggerated fashion. And one may be able to reliably determine that the individual's state of mind and emotions would change to a more upbeat tendency during a Jupiterian period, even manifesting as one feeling "high," inspired, or (as Paul Wright put it) in a state of "dizzy, giddy elation." One's physical energy also may be expanded, especially under certain Jupiterian transits involving conjunctions or squares to personal planets or the Ascendant.

It is also worth noting that a transiting planet making a "station" (i.e., turning direct or retrograde) in close aspect to natal Jupiter, or transiting Jupiter making a station while in close aspect to a natal planet, will (depending on the other planets involved) usually be experienced as a profound time of personal change. Tracy Marks has observed that a transiting planet making its station within a degree of conjuncting one of our natal planets is one of the most important and powerful astrological "influences" we can experience. [In addition to the conjunction, I would also include a transiting station in a close square, opposition, or even sometimes other angular relationships.] Tracy Marks estimates that a transiting planet making a station is five times *more powerful* than the same planet moving at its normal speed. My experience leads me to agree with her completely. In fact, planetary stations are one of the most neglected factors in the interpretive art–far more important, I feel, than retrograde planets, for example. And any planet that was moving very slowly (i.e., close to the time of its precise station) at one's birth should always be regarded as providing, as it were, a cosmic herald of an extraordinarily powerful attunement in that individual. The use of "stationary" planets as a significant interpretive aid in astrology is yet another factor that can fall by the wayside if one looks only at computer-generated charts rather than studying the ephemeris to determine how fast a planet was actually traveling *in relation to its usual speed.*

I generally advise people to use all the "aspects" which are multiples of 30° when studying transits, although I completely acknowledge that the conjunction is the most powerful, followed by the square, opposition, and trine, with the sextile, quincunx, and semi-sextile of less dynamic intensity in most cases. However, if a transiting planet is stationary while forming even one of the more minor aspects, the chances are much greater that it will be noticeably felt as making a significant impact on the person's energy field. While speaking of aspects, it should be pointed out that oppositions formed by transiting Jupiter can sometimes be experienced as more frustrating than other aspects of transiting Jupiter; even if there is an urge to expand in whatever way is shown, sometimes it is difficult to effectively act upon that urge for improvement. There can be a sense of *blockage*, with no energy being released–no channel for the expansive energy one feels may be available. By no means will this always be the case, but the student of astrology should be aware of it.

As mentioned early in this book, Jupiter–like the sign Sagittarius–often promises more than it can deliver. Or, as Paul Wright wrote, "the great benefic...often enough calls without leaving a present." However, perhaps our occasional disappointments with Jupiter are due in part to our poor understanding of how Jupiter really operates; we so often have unrealistic expectations about what Jupiter will mean in our natal chart or by transit that we act like children throwing a tantrum when we do not get what we want from Santa Claus! I have discussed at length in this book how important the balance of Saturn and Jupiter is, and this is another instance where we should cultivate patience, to give Jupiter the time to mature and unfold. It is imperative that the individual studying Jupiter transits have faith in his or her potential and actively use such opportunities to improve one's life, but it is also absolutely necessary to realize that Jupiter transits are often *seeding* periods and that time must be allowed for the new seeds to germinate and bear fruit according to natural cosmic rhythms.

To put it another way, just because one has a vision of future possibilities and potentials during a Jupiterian period, it does not mean that they will materialize immediately. In fact, Paul Wright has written that Jupiter transits may coincide with "wishful thinking." As Edison is often quoted as saying, genius is a small percent inspiration but over 90% perspiration. Likewise, in financial investing, one must have the faith to risk capital and to walk through the door of opportunity when it presents itself, but one must also have the constancy and persistence to maintain that commitment through a period of time, without running away at the slightest fearful rumor. A full cycle of Jupiter takes almost exactly twelve years, and this rhythm gives us a framework for understanding how Jupiterian visions may unfold. And every three years, as Jupiter squares or opposes the place where any particular Jupiter cycle began, one must make some adjustments to one's vision or to how one is seeking to manifest it.

We have discussed Jupiter as a way of learning through exploration, and its transits definitely provide an opportunity for broadening our perspective on whatever is symbolized by the house it is transiting through or the planet it is aspecting. However, the more comprehensive *understanding* that Jupiter can enable us to develop does not come all at once! It unfolds through extensive experience, especially involved with extroverted action and/or risk-taking, interspersed with periods of reflection, practical thought, inquiry, and even doubt. In other words, more profound understanding—one of the greatest gifts of Jupiter—*comes later*, after one has interacted with the world, after one has made an effort to improve one's life, after taking a chance at expanding into new realms of experience. Without such faith-motivated initiatives, one would never have the opportunity for progress on any level, nor for the cultivation of one's character and deeper growing wisdom. Jupiter favors active risk-takers, but life favors those who also have patience, persistence, and moderation. Maintaining a positive attitude and faith in the future, even in spite of slow results or outright failure, is a Jupiterian lesson that some are born with but which most of us have to learn through experience. Maintaining the openness and truthfulness of Jupiter is a far more productive way of traveling Jupiter's road of learning than is resorting to negativity or defensiveness. As an anonymous proverb states,

More people would learn from their mistakes
if they were not so busy denying that they made them.

Jupiter's essential nature incorporates such an attunement to the future that enthusiasm and impatience are natural accompaniments of Jupiterian transits. In fact, with such transits, there can be an *anticipation* of significant developments as much as four to six months before a transit is exact, especially in cases where an upcoming *conjunction* of transiting Jupiter to a natal planet or point is preceded by Jupiter being in the same sign where that conjunction will take place. But I have found it more common that specific experiences coincide with almost exact aspects of transiting Jupiter to natal planets or points, especially if within one-half a degree from exactitude. I have seen numerous occasions when important experiences occurred as transiting Jupiter aligned with a natal planet exactly to the minute! In such cases, it is as if one of Zeus's lightning bolts has been hurled into one's life, often bringing startling surprises, new ideas, vast visions, or inspiring insights that sometimes remind me of Uranus transits–which are also known for being significantly *awakening*, enabling us to venture forth into completely new experiences and paths of awareness.

Guidelines for Interpreting
Jupiter Transits

By transit, Jupiter opens doors for new plans and tunes one in to future possibilities. It can inspire and provide a new aspiration toward which one travels or a goal toward which one strives. It usually gives an urge to improve whatever area or dimension of life it is "influencing." Jupiter urges one to expand into new areas of experience, which usually requires more extroverted activity and/or more social involvement than perhaps one has been used to.

Jupiter by transit often provides greater confidence to do what you have been wanting to do–consciously or subconsciously–and it may encourage far more freedom of expression and give you "room to operate" with a sense of liberation that seems a bit intoxicating and certainly energizing. It may quite suddenly be easier to "do what comes naturally" and to move beyond inhibiting influences. For example, during some Jupiterian transits, one may feel more free to express dimensions of one's self that were not allowed full expression in one's early environment or which are constrained by one's current personal or professional environment.

Jupiter's transits do provide opportunity, but often one must act quickly or, evidently, the window of opportunity closes. Jupiter is not particularly patient with fearful people. Jupiter's transits in fact seem more often conducive to excess risk-taking than to cautious moderation. Sometimes, during Jupiter transits, things come to fruition, whereas at other times, the *initial vision* of future possibilities is experienced, which may only bear fruit years later. But in any case, the individual must be willing to act upon the promptings toward a greater potential.

During some Jupiter transits, one may have an intuitive perception that various possibilities may be reachable, if only one has the ability to take a "leap of faith" toward that direction. Fortunately, one is often given a certain amount of extra confidence and optimism during many Jupiter transits, which enable the individual to give this new vision of life a try. And, realistically, if one won't pursue a big dream during a Jupiter transit, when will be a better time?

There is usually an urge to move bey*ond current limits* when transiting Jupiter is active; and this motivation from within applies both to possibilities for material progress and prosperity, and to maximizing one's potential for personal growth and satisfying self-expression. Jupiter transits signal that it is time to *expand* some aspect of one's life. One can never know what benefits and positive developments Jupiter transits can bring unless one unlocks its potential by rising above fear, habit, self-doubt, and worry. Employing (sometimes painful) honesty is often the extra source of strength that one can find at such times to confront the promising–but still frightening–unknown possibilities of one's future. However, one must have faith in the Biblical axiom: "The truth shall make you free." Of course, we should remember at such times that we have to be just as ruthlessly truthful with ourselves as we want to be with others.

A few other common manifestations during Jupiter transits are:

- promotion or successful outcome of an on-going enterprise

- worldly success or honors
- religious experiences, whether or not related to various worldly involvements
- travel, both literal (especially long journeys–these days, usually foreign trips) and mental, in exploring new vistas of understanding and perspective
- publication, publicity, or a satisfying experience of release from on-going pressure
- trying to take on too much new experience, thus scattering one's energies and often wasting one's resources

Jupiter Transits to the Ascendant

These transits often give a boost to one's physical energy and self-confidence, enabling the individual to project his or her personality more dynamically out into the world. There is sometimes a strong attunement toward future goals, visions, or plans for self-improvement. The conjunction is especially important, since it begins an entirely new twelve-year cycle of personal expression and development; and one should be alert to what visions and dreams appear in the mind's eye while the conjunction is exact, since this often gives a reliable clue to future possibilities.

Doors suddenly opening, enabling one to expand into larger realms of learning, social experience, or religious understanding, are very common. One person, while Jupiter transited opposite the Ascendant (i.e., conjunct the Descendant), had a personal religious experience that changed his life. A young woman who had to interrupt her college work because of lack of funds found her situation radically improved when transiting Jupiter trined her Ascendant and sextiled her natal Jupiter simultaneously. A scholarship covering all of her expenses for which she had not even applied was given to her by the managers of a private trust fund who had heard about her situation.

A number of people, I have observed, move to a new location as Jupiter crosses the Ascendant, one which they usually feel is more spacious and which gives them room to breathe. Sometimes there is a permanent or temporary move abroad. Jupiter conjoining the Ascendant was among many transits that John Lennon had when he traveled to the USA for the first time to appear on the national TV program, "The Ed Sullivan Show." This experience opened new international horizons for the Beatles and vastly amplified their fame.

Jupiter crossing the Ascendant, as mentioned above, gives one a focus on the future and begins a new cycle. Therefore, many activities started at this time grow to become larger than the person realized when beginning them. In other cases, there is a prophetic insight into what potential is inherent in that moment, such as in the case of an entrepreneur who envisioned an entire company, its nature and design, as well as its name at this time. And the entire vision came true over the next twelve years.

When Jupiter crossed the Ascendant for Maria Montessori, she received her medical degree, the first ever awarded a woman in Italy. During the same transit for Annie Lennox, the Eurythmics musical group was formed. Another young woman found herself exuberantly involved in new relationships, multiple educational options, and two opportunities for foreign travel as this identical transit occurred.

Jupiter Transits to the Midheaven

In contrast to the transits to the Ascendant, these transits are not usually quite as dramatic; neither do they seem to manifest so quickly and obviously, nor do they usually augment the physical vitality. Improvements, promotion, or recognition may come immediately; but in other cases there is a stronger urge from within to improve the scope of one's professional life or status in society, and the initial steps are taken toward that end. Confidence in one's self usually increases, and that is sometimes reflected in an enhanced reputation or opportunities for advancement—even if it is not dramatically apparent right away.

In some cases, this is a time of receiving the fruits of earlier work or experiencing successful outcome of an ongoing process or an earlier initiative. One promoter ventured his entire life savings on an international event, which wound up being remarkably successful and profitable just after Jupiter passed his MC. Author Norman Mailer published *The Naked and the Dead* as Jupiter conjoined the MC; it went on to sell 3 million copies and to make his reputation for life. One respected British priest felt the initial urge to be ordained during a major religious experience that he had at the time of this transit.

In short, as Jupiter aspects the MC by transit, one should expect an expanded–and often clarified–sense of what one's vocation is, or at least a more developed picture of what one's vocational direction should be.

Jupiter Transits to the Sun

These important transits often boost the physical vitality, as well as expanding one's creative energy. Confidence and optimism tend to be enhanced during these periods, and these times also occasionally coincide with prophetic dreams, hunches, or visions. On an even more essential level, it is quite common for people to have their entire sense of identity and scope of awareness expanded at these times. Religious experiences sometimes occur, encounters with spiritual teachers, or travel to ashrams or retreat centers.

In general, travel in order to expand one's scope of experience and creative possibilities is common during these periods. John Lennon had Jupiter's transit in opposition to his Sun (as well as conjoining his Ascendant) on his first hugely successful trip to the USA. Annie Lennox moved to London to start studying at the Royal Academy of Music as Jupiter conjoined her Sun. (When the same aspect repeated twelve years later, international stardom occurred with the Eurythmics.) Another singer, although less well known than the two musicians mentioned above, had her public career take off into more varied and challenging vistas when she went abroad repeatedly for five tours with an international group which included members from five nations! This period coincided with the year in which Jupiter conjuncted her Sun three times.

Author Arthur Schlesinger, Jr. was awarded his first Pulitzer Prize during a time of multiple transits, one of which was Jupiter conjunct his Sun. Sir Alexander Fleming, Nobel Prize winning discoverer of penicillin, appeared on the cover of *Time* magazine and was also knighted, as Jupiter transited over his Sun. During an identical transit, Indira Gandhi was elected President of the Congress Party.

One should always have faith in the creative inspirations that come about as Jupiter activates one's natal Sun. During such a time, whatever creative potential one has will be amplified, and the confidence needed to express those creative impulses will be maximized, allowing even somewhat shy people the chance of taking a creative risk and making real what may have long been felt inwardly as potential creative talent. Maria Montessori wrote *The Montessori Method* as Jupiter conjoined her Sun, and Mary Shelley published *Frankenstein* while Jupiter trined her Sun. As Jupiter made the conjunction with her Sun, Mary Shelley eloped with poet Percy Shelley!

Jupiter Transits to the Moon

Although not so indicative of creative achievement as the transits to the Sun, these transits also commonly coincide with increased confidence, a sense of well-being, worldly success, honors, and generally a feeling that things are flowing more effortlessly than usual. Most people have a greater urge at these times to express their feelings and personal intuitive understanding about life, and this usually comes with more ease and sensitivity while these transits are close—except, in some cases, when the more challenging angles give the same urge but may be accompanied by more inner tension. But all in all, it is a time to express one's natural emotional impulses, and other people's response may be surprisingly positive.

There is often an urge to improve one's living situation, home, family life, or relations with parents, as well as an expanded need to feel comfortable about oneself in a deeper way. All kinds of security factors related to the private spheres of life come to the fore in some cases, whereas in other cases there is increased interaction with the public. Whether one feels comfortable with a relatively public life or not may even be an important personal issue that is brought to prominence at this time.

Margaret Thatcher first got a seat in the "Shadow Cabinet" (bringing her much closer to assuming the powers of Prime Minister) as Jupiter crossed her Moon by conjunction. Various other public figures have been elected to office under the same transit. While Jupiter opposed his Moon, John Charles Reith became General Manager of the BBC (the British Broadcasting Corporation), an eminent and internationally influential position.

Numerous people win prizes, attain their goals, or otherwise gain a feeling of satisfaction as Jupiter activates the Moon. Diana Ross experienced Jupiter conjoining her Moon when the Supremes had their first #1 song. Renowned soccer coach (even mentioned in a Beatle song!) Matt Busby's UK soccer team finally won the European Cup as Jupiter formed the conjunction to his natal moon.

Jupiter Transits to
the Other Personal Planets

JUPITER TRANSITS TO MERCURY: These almost invariably expand the individual's curiosity, as well as prompting new plans and ideas. If the person is intellectually inclined, he or she may begin to pursue new interests by studying new subjects or reading widely in new areas. Sometimes new ideas are abundant, and the person may feel an expanded need to express those thoughts to a wider audience. Other people may begin to learn new skills or to make new social connections. At best, the conscious mind becomes more noble, more optimistic; and the person's thought processes become more comprehensive and inclusive. In other words, the very way that one thinks is being inspired toward improvement and exploring wider horizons.

JUPITER TRANSITS TO VENUS: These transits expand whatever social, romantic/erotic, artistic, or financial orientation each person has by nature. Relationship issues especially come to the fore for many people, and any problems with loneliness or a feeling of lacking satisfying closeness with others will likely to be brought to one's awareness rather strongly. There is often an urge to improve one's situation in any or all of the above areas; but of course one needs to be alert to Jupiter's tendency toward excess or greed. Experiences of interpersonal magnetism may be intensified–repulsion as well as attraction.

JUPITER TRANSITS TO MARS: The physical vitality is enhanced during most of these transits, as is any tendency toward impatience and temperamental displays. At best, while Jupiter is expanding the Mars energy, one is enlivened by greater energy and inspired by a heightened feeling of courage to tackle new challenges or to undertake new initiatives. The sex drive is often amped up to a more intense level, and all methods of self-assertion are enhanced, allowing people to feel a sense of mastery and confidence during such times. Many people feel stronger and more ambitious during these transits, and the scope of their personal leadership can be substantially enlarged. Risk-taking and cravings for adventurous activity are felt as strong urges during many of these transits, and the capacity and energy exists at these times to bring about a major impact toward achieving any goal so long as the overall picture is determined to be realistic.

Jupiter Transits to Jupiter

Since I have written extensively about the Jupiter cycle in *Relationships & Life Cycles*, here I only want to mention that Jupiter's return to its natal place, as well as when it squares or opposes that degree, should *always* be regarded as potentially key developmental phases. Especially the conjunction, which liberates vast new energies for self-improvement, should *never* be overlooked; for it *is* a time of *committing oneself to a new vision of the future*, whether that entails a major change from the past or merely a relatively subtle adjustment of one's previous attitudes and expectations about the meaning of life. The conjunction of Jupiter to Jupiter (and–to a lesser extent–the square and opposition also) is a key period of reorientation based on one's ideals and visions of the future. A renewal of faith (in life, self, God, truth, or one's ideals), and a clearer perception of one's life direction based on that faith, is perhaps the best outcome of a Jupiter transit to Jupiter.

Jupiter Transits to Saturn

These are quite important transits for most individuals. Since Saturn has so much to do with one's profession, vocation, priorities, long-term ambitions, and indeed overall life structure, when Jupiter activates Saturn, many of those concerns come alive through a strongly-felt inclination to improve exactly these areas of life. One's need to work especially hard is often exaggerated at this time, and the fruits of these labors are not always evident immediately. Remember, Saturn takes his time! For example, Sir Arthur Fleming discovered penicillin while Jupiter was conjoining his Saturn, which led *eventually* to his receiving the Nobel Prize.

These transits can have a dynamic impact on one's entire life structure and long-term goals and ambitions, which are often expanded enthusiastically during these times. Hence, there are often improvements in one's vocational situation at the times of such transits. At the least, a broader understanding can develop of how those parts of one's life *can be improved*–perhaps through initiatives, education, taking chances, or other methods.

Since Saturn in the birth chart is so often a point of restriction, tension, negative attitudes, or various other constrictive energy blockages, when Jupiter *expands those tendencies*, there can be quite serious problems, both psychologically and physically (especially when the aspect is a square or opposition) and one should be prepared to work on de-stressing during the entire period when the transit is in effect. At worst, one can experience a major amplification of his or her most constrictive tendencies; and hence, regular practice of meditation, Tai Chi, Yoga, or other methods of releasing stress is at this time especially advisable. Nevertheless, one should not lose sight of the fact that one can be making significant progress through concentrated effort at the time of these transits, even if it is accompanied by stress and physical tension.

Jupiter Transits
to the Outer Planets

JUPITER TRANSITS TO URANUS: These are some of the most dynamic combinations, as are the transits of Uranus to natal Jupiter. The periods when transiting Jupiter activates natal Uranus are known for an increased desire for change and excitement, strong urges toward greater freedom of lifestyle or personal expression, and often the energizing of one's most original and creative capacities. Sometimes inventiveness is strong, as is increased interest in political or social activism. Whenever these two planets are combined, there is the possibility of radical change or achieving significant breakthroughs in any field of endeavor. For example, Jacques Cousteau co-invented the aqua-lung (i.e., the "scuba") while transiting Jupiter was opposite natal Uranus, at the same time that transiting Uranus was trine natal Jupiter. And, as we shall see later in this chapter, significant experiences of personal liberation or radically new and clear perceptions can coincide with either Jupiter's transits to Uranus or Uranus' transits to natal Jupiter. They are exciting combinations—mentally and physically as well–for the nervous system is speeded up at this time.

JUPITER TRANSITS TO NEPTUNE: These transits often heighten psychic sensitivity as well as energize the individual's spiritual yearnings. This is a potent combination of planets for otherworldly and idealistic aspirations, and therefore these transit periods can increase spiritual, religious, imaginative, or merely escapist tendencies. In other words, subtle but profound changes in one's level of consciousness may be noticeable at these times, but there can also be a "spaced-out," unrealistic state of mind. It is a time when one can improve and broaden one's ideas, as well as amplify any artistic expression with which one is involved.

JUPITER TRANSITS TO PLUTO: Due to Pluto's unfathomable depth, it is difficult to say much that will predictably manifest when an individual's Plutonian nature is so amplified and energized. These transits can mark the end to an entire chapter of life, but that is more common when Saturn, Neptune, or Uranus activates Pluto. The use of one's inner powers and resources may come to the fore, and it is an excellent time for concentrated effort toward self-improvement. Psychic experiences and intuition may be heightened, but so may tendencies toward compulsive or obsessive behavior or thoughts. It is a perfect period to bring to the surface (of consciousness) and truthfully face some of the hidden or darker dimensions of one's nature. It is also a time when one can elevate and improve one's "darker dimensions" and lower tendencies.

Guidelines for Interpreting Transits to Jupiter

Jupiter's placement in any birth chart signifies a vast potential for positive change; and therefore, when it is activated–especially by transiting Jupiter, Saturn, Uranus, Neptune or Pluto, which coincide with the longer-lasting, more profound phases of personal change–it can be as if a storehouse of energy and potential is unlocked. A release of power and a greater sense of personal capability and confidence often accompany these transits. One's efforts at self-improvement are activated and energized, and a transformation often occurs in one's beliefs, aspirations, and plans for the future. In fact, these transits to natal Jupiter are crucial for taking advantage of the opportunities for growth and progress that I have referred to so often in this book. A great deal of effort may go into planning for the future when one's Jupiter is activated.

To present a more complete picture, I should also point out that even a New Moon aspecting natal Jupiter may create a period of such opportunity, although it may last for only a month, unless a series of New Moons repeatedly form close aspects to one's natal Jupiter, thus prolonging a Jupiterian rhythm in one's life that weaves through a period of several months. I should mention, in addition, that transiting Mars activating Jupiter can also provide a brief burst of optimistic energy. This effect will be prolonged considerably if Mars forms a station in the sky while closely aspecting natal Jupiter. Then the chances of significant Jupiterian ventures or improvements coinciding with such a Mars transit would greatly increase.

One dimension of Jupiter I should especially emphasize here is the connection of this planet to religious experience and, following from that, how often a personal experience that can broadly be characterized as having a "religious" quality coincides with various transits to natal Jupiter. (As mentioned earlier in this chapter, such experiences are also relatively common when *transiting Jupiter* is activating any number of factors in one's birth chart.)

There is in fact good reason to correlate the Jupiter principle with what Jung called the "religious instinct" in the human psyche, for this planet urges us to enlarge our consciousness and to connect to a greater wholeness. And, as mentioned above, this "instinct" can be strongly activated when natal Jupiter is energized by various transits. I have seen cases of religious experience coinciding with Neptune transiting opposite natal Jupiter, transiting Pluto semisextile natal Jupiter, and many other alignments; but I would like to focus here in particular on Uranus transits to Jupiter, which strikingly correlate with unusual experiences of all sorts, including personal religious awakenings.

In his book about Uranus, *Prometheus, the Awakener*, Professor Richard Tarnas presents extensive research regarding the interactions of Uranus and Jupiter. Many pages of fascinating correlations with major historical occurrences are presented in that book, but the essence of his findings about this pair of planets may be summarized in the following quotation:

> *Jupiter-Uranus transits seem to coincide consistently with sudden awakenings, the feeling of unexpected good fortune in one's life, the euphoria of liberation..., the happy discovery of childlike joy in the universe, the moment of rebirth. It is the moment of the quantum leap of consciousness....Jupiter-Uranus transits often coincide with what the psychologist Abraham Maslow called "peak experiences"....In their most exalted form, Jupiter-Uranus transits may coincide with the experience of ecstatic spiritual liberation: Prometheus Unbound.* (Page 98)

There is so much well-researched material in Dr. Tarnas's book that illustrates this metaphysical manifestation of those two planets' interaction that consulting astrologers would be overlooking a primary possibility during such a transit if they are not alert to it. Similarly, whenever natal Jupiter is being activated, there is a wide range of possibilities that could take place: from a religious awakening, to a peak experience, to an only-vaguely-conscious sense that one needs to find more meaning in life. A conscientious astrologer, therefore, may want to inquire about this area of life and explore it with the client.

On a more down-to-earth level, many other types of Jupiterian benefits or insights coincide with Uranus transits to natal Jupiter. Jacques Cousteau acquired his ship *Calypso* through the financial beneficence of a philanthropist as transiting Uranus squared Jupiter. While Uranus transited in trine to natal Jupiter during his boyhood, Albert Einstein experienced a powerful sense of independent thinking and, rejecting authoritarian presentation of ideas, dedicated himself to his own unique path of truth-seeking. Some years later, as Uranus transited in conjunction to his Jupiter in the ninth house, Einstein was suddenly hit by tremendous world fame, as a result of his theoretical breakthroughs in physics.

When transiting Uranus opposed her natal Jupiter-Mars conjunction, Amelia Earhart received her pilot's license—an unconventional and liberating achievement for a woman in that era. Historian Arthur Schlesinger, Jr. was awarded his first Pulitzer Prize in 1945, as Uranus transited in conjunction to his tenth house Jupiter (and transiting Jupiter was also in his Sun sign). Then, in 1965, he published his second Pulitzer Prize winner, *A Thousand Days: John F. Kennedy in the White House*, as transiting Uranus again activated his tenth house Jupiter, this time by a square aspect.

Such examples illuminate why Jupiter has for so long been regarded as the "great benefic." Its manifestations are not always dramatic, but sometimes they are indeed quite sizable. However, at a more significant level, Jupiter always gives us a chance to become better, to elevate ourselves, and to improve our lives for our own inner benefit and for the good of others. Happiness requires a certain faith in life and a broad-minded acceptance of what life gives us. If we can extract from Jupiter's teachings an essential optimism about life and a willing adjustment to the infinite varieties of human beings and life experiences, we should be able to go through this uncharted journey with a greater cheerfulness—yes, even with gratitude toward the greater power that supports us from within as we walk upon life's path with faith in the future.

Bibliography

Arroyo, Stephen, *Astrology, Karma and Transformation*, CRCS
   Publications, Sebastopol, California, 1978, 1992

Arroyo, Stephen, *Chart Interpretation Handbook*, CRCS Publications,
   Sebastopol, California, 1989

Arroyo, Stephen, *The Practice and Profession of Astrology*, CRCS
   Publications, Sebastopol, California, 1984

Arroyo, Stephen, *Relationships and Life Cycles*, CRCS Publications,
   Sebastopol, California, 1979, 1993

Aveni, Anthony, *Conversing with the Planets*, Times Books,
   New York, 1992

Carter, C.E.O., *The Astrological Aspects*, N. Fowler & Co., London,
   1930, 1967

Carter, C.E.O., *An Encyclopaedia of Psychological Astrology*, The
   Theosophical Publishing House, London, 1972

Carter, C.E.O., *Essays on the Foundations of Astrology*, The
   Theosophical Publishing House, London, 1978

Carter, C.E.O., *The Principles of Astrology*, The Theosophical
   Publishing House, London, 1963

Carter, C.E.O., *Some Principles of Horoscopic Delineation*, Dorothy
   B. Hughes, Seattle, Washington, (orig. pub. 1934)

Carter, C.E.O., *The Zodiac and the Soul*, The Theosophical
   Publishing House, London, 1972

Cunningham, Donna, *An Astrological Guide to Self-Awareness*,
   CRCS Publications, Sebastopol, California, 1978, 1994

Davison, Ronald, *Synastry*, Aurora Publishing, Santa Fe,
   New Mexico, 1980

Eberton, Reinhold, *The Combination of Stellar Influences*, American
   Federation of Astrologers, Tempe, Arizona, 1992

Gammon, Margaret H., *Astrology and the Edgar Cayce Readings*,
   A.R.E. Press, Virginia Beach, Virginia, 1967

Goodwin, Doris Kearns, *No Ordinary Time*, Simon & Schuster,
   New York, 1994.

Green, Landis Knight, *The Astologer's Manual*, CRCS Publications,
   Sebastopol, California, 1975

Hickey, Isabel M., *Astrology, A Cosmic Science*, CRCS Publications,
   Sebastopol, California, 1992

Hone, Margaret E., *The Modern Text Book of Astrology*, L.N. Fowler
   & Co., London, 1964

Jenkins, Palden, *Living in Time*, Gateway Books, UK, 1987

Leinbach, Esther V., *Sun-Ascendant Rulerships: Their Influence in
   the Horoscope*, Vulcan Books, Seattle, Washington, 1972

Lewi, Grant, *Your Greatest Strength*, Samuel Weiser, Portland,
   Maine, 1986

Matthews, E.C., *The Ascending Sign*, Motivation Development
   Centre, Albuquerque, New Mexico, 1970

Mayo, Jeff, *The Planets and Human Behavior*, CRCS Publications, Sebastopol, California, 1985

Mayo, Jeff, *Teach Yourself Astrology*, Hoder & Staughton, London, 1964

MaCaffery, Ellen, *Graphic Astrology*, Macoy Publishing, USA (out-of-print)

Moore, Marcia and Douglas, Mark, *Astrology the Divine Science*, Arcane Books, York, Maine, 1971 (out-of-print)

Pagan, Isabelle M., *Signs of the Zodiac Analysed*, The Theosophical Publishing House, London, 1978

Roszak, Theodore, *Why Astrology Endures*, Robert Briggs Assoc., San Francisco, 1980

Rudhyar, Dane, *An Astrological Study of Psychological Complexes and Emotional Problems*, Servire, The Netherlands, 1969

Sargent, Lois Haines, *How to Handle Your Human Relations*, American Federation of Astrologers, Tempe, Arizona, 1970

Sasportas, Howard, *The Twelve Houses*, Aquarian Press, London, 1985

Smith, Page, *Killing the Spirit: Higher Education in America*, Viking, Penguin, New York, 1990

Tarnas, Richard, *Prometheus the Awakener*, Spring Publications, Woodstock, Connecticut, 1995

Vaughan, Richard, *Astrology in Modern Language*, CRCS Publications, Sebastopol, California, 1985, 1992

Wright, Paul, *Astrology in Action*, CRCS Publications, Sebastopol, California, 1989

Wright, Paul, *The Literary Zodiac*, CRCS Publications, Sebastopol, California, 1987

Wright, Paul, *The A-to-Z of Jupiter*, unpublished talk given in England, 1994

Sources of Birth Data & Charts Used

Erlewine, Stephen, *The Circle Book of Charts*, Circle Books, Ann Arbor, Michigan, 1972

Gauquelin, Michael and Francoise, *The Gauquelin Book of American Charts*, Astro Computing Services, San Diego, California, 1982

Rodden, Lois M., *Astro-Data II*, American Federation of Astrologers, Inc., Tempe, Arizona, 1993

Rodden, Lois M., *Astro-Data IV*, American Federation of Astrologers, Inc., Tempe, Arizona, 1990

Rodden, Lois M., *Profiles of Women: A Collection of Astrological Biographies*, American Federation of Astrologers, Tempe, AZ, 1979

Wright, Paul, *Astrology in Action*, CRCS Publications, Sebastopol, California, 1989

& also files of the author

OTHER CRCS BEST-SELLERS

STEPHEN ARROYO'S CHART INTERPRETATION HANDBOOK: Guidelines for Understanding the Essentials of the Birth Chart. ISBN: 0-916360-49-0, $10.95, 184 pages. Shows how to combine keywords, central concepts, and interpretive phrases in a way that illuminates the meanings of the planets, signs, houses, and aspects emphasized in any chart.

YOUR SECRET SELF: Illuminating the Mysteries of the Twelfth House by Tracy Marks, ISBN: 0-916360-43-1, $15.95, 280 pages. Demonstrates in a unique and fascinating way how themes of a birth chart emerge in one's dreams and how to liberate oneself from destructive patterns.

ASTROLOGY: The Classic Guide to Understanding Your Horoscope by Ronald C. Davison, ISBN: 0-916360-37-7, $10.95, 204 pages. This classic work includes the author's remarkable keyword system.

A SPIRITUAL APPROACH TO ASTROLOGY: A Complete Textbook of Astrology by Myrna Lofthus, ISBN: 0-916360-10-5, $15.95, 444 pages. A complete astrology textbook from a karmic viewpoint.

THE ART OF CHART INTERPRETATION: A Step-by-Step Method of Analyzing, Synthesizing, and Understanding the Birth Chart by Tracy Marks, ISBN: 0-916360-29-6, $9.95, 180 pages. A guide to determining the most important features of a birth chart. A must for students!

THE ASTROLOGY OF SELF-DISCOVERY: An In-Depth Exploration of the Potentials Revealed in Your Birth Chart by Tracy Marks, ISBN: 0-916360-20-2, $13.95, 288 pages. A guide for utilizing astrology to aid self-development, resolve inner conflicts, and discover and fulfill one's life purpose.

THE ASTROLOGER'S HANDBOOK by Julia Parker, ISBN: 0-916360-59-8, $12.00, 256 pages. This book, designed in handbook format for easy reference, offers far more astrological information and detail than most astrology books meant for the general public.

ASTROLOGY: A Cosmic Science by Isabel M. Hickey, ISBN: 0-916360-52-0, $14.95, 351 pages. This comprehensive textbook of spiritual astrology is the definitive work on the interplay of astrology, karma, and reincarnation.

ASTROLOGY, KARMA, & TRANSFORMATION: The Inner Dimensions of the Birth Chart by Stephen Arroyo, ISBN: 0-916360-54-7, $14.95, 264 pages. An insightful book on the use of astrology as a tool for spiritual and psychological growth, based on the theory of karma and self-transformation.

AN ASTROLOGICAL GUIDE TO SELF-AWARENESS by Donna Cunningham, M.S.W., ISBN: 0-916360-09-1, $12.00, 210 pages. Written in a lively style by a social worker who uses astrology in counseling, this book includes chapters on transits, houses, interpreting aspects, etc.